Intercultural Memories

Critical
Intercultural
Communication
Studies

Thomas K. Nakayama and Bernadette Marie Calafell
General Editors

Vol. 25

The Critical Intercultural Communication Studies series
is part of the Peter Lang Media and Communication list.
Every volume is peer reviewed and meets
the highest quality standards for content and production.

PETER LANG
New York • Bern • Berlin
Brussels • Vienna • Oxford • Warsaw

Intercultural Memories

Contesting Places, Spaces, and Stories

Edited by Ahmet Atay, Yea-Wen Chen,
and Alberto González

PETER LANG
New York • Bern • Berlin
Brussels • Vienna • Oxford • Warsaw

Library of Congress Cataloging-in-Publication Control Number: 2020040866

Bibliographic information published by **Die Deutsche Nationalbibliothek**.
Die Deutsche Nationalbibliothek lists this publication in the "Deutsche
Nationalbibliografie"; detailed bibliographic data are available
on the Internet at http://dnb.d-nb.de/.

ISSN 1528-6118
ISBN 978-1-4331-4784-5 (hardcover)
ISBN 978-1-4331-4785-2 (paperback)
ISBN978-1-4331-4786-9 (ebook pdf)
ISBN 978-1-4331-4787-6 (epub)
ISBN 978-1-4331-4788-3 (mobi)
DOI 10.3726/b17575

© 2021 Peter Lang Publishing, Inc., New York
80 Broad Street, 5th floor, New York, NY 10004
www.peterlang.com

Table of Contents

Introduction: Intercultural Communication, Memory, and Stories   1
AHMET ATAY, YEA-WEN CHEN, AND ALBERTO GONZÁLEZ

Cultural Memories of Places and Spaces

1. *Communities of Memory, Coalition, and Race Trauma: The Moore's*
   Ford Lynching Reenactment   13
   PETER EHRENHAUS AND A. SUSAN OWEN

2. *(Be)Coming Home: Transformative Places and Koreamerican Identity*
   in Itaewon, South Korea   33
   EUN YOUNG LEE AND ALBERTO GONZÁLEZ

3. *When "Chiang Kai-shek Memorial Square" Became*
   "Liberty Square": A Case of Contested Public Memories in Taiwan   53
   YEA-WEN CHEN AND CHUNYU ZHANG

4. *Remembering Communism: The Site of Witness and Memory and the*
   House of Leaves Museums in Albania   69
   NINA GJOCI

Cultural Memory, Identity Politics, and Intersectionality

5. *(Mis)Remembering Stonewall: Narrative Authority and the American*
   Monomyth in Queer Public Memory   95
   KATHRYN HOBSON, BERNADETTE MARIE CALAFELL, AND SPENCER
   B. MARGULIES

6. *Queer Fantasy: A Memory of Michael Sam's Big Gay Kiss*   115
   SHINSUKE EGUCHI

7. *Photographs as Diasporic Memories: Turkish Cypriots, Home, and Memory*   135
AHMET ATAY

8. *Displaced Memorials: Commemorating the "Comfort Women" in the United States*   149
MARIKO IZUMI

9. *"Funk Isn't a Trend; It's a Necessity": Favela Funk's Vernacular Discourse and the Struggle for Cultural Legitimation*   163
RAQUEL MOREIRA

Contributors   183

Index   187

Introduction: Intercultural Communication, Memory, and Stories

AHMET ATAY, YEA-WEN CHEN, AND ALBERTO GONZÁLEZ

This Volume's Origin Story

We begin our introduction with a story. After all, our stories that we narrate and share are based on our memories. We story our memories to keep people, places, and events alive and sometimes relevant. We remember details that might have been forgotten as we narrate our stories both verbally and visually.

The idea behind this project dates back to 2015 when Alberto González conceptualized a panel on public memory and intercultural conflict for the annual Central States Communication Association (CSCA) conference. In 2016 in Grand Rapids, Michigan, the three of us along with other members of the panel presented our own work. The panel attracted a large audience, and the presentations were received enthusiastically. We carried out more conversation on intercultural communication and the concept of memory throughout the conference. Soon after the conference, we decided to reformat our panel and explore the role of memory in cultural communication and feature pieces that theorize the notions of "memory and remembering." Moreover, we were interested in presenting case studies that employ some of these theorizations but also discuss the links between culture and memory and illuminate different aspects of public and personal memory. Hence, this book was born out of our curiosity about the past and how we remember it as well as the cultural politics surrounding what we remember and what we forget. It also shows our commitment to further stretch the scholarly reach of critical intercultural communication to include memory studies.

Ahmet

I have been studying different aspects of intercultural communication for about 20 years now. Primarily, I have been examining issues pertaining to culture and transnationality in various settings, including media, classroom, or everyday interactions. However, a big portion of my research is focused on diaspora studies in general, and queer diasporic experiences in particular. My first book engaged with diasporic queer bodies in queer social networks sites and the ways in which they use these sides to make sense of their identities, to perform queerness, and cultivate communities to belong to. Along with this research, I have been interested in thinking and writing about the meanings of home, belonging, and memory for diasporic communities. Within that, I have been curious about the role of visual texts and new media technologies in remembering the past and also documenting a diasporic archive to capture in-between and hybrid experiences. More particularly, I have been invested in theorizing digital memory from critical intercultural communication perspective and within diasporic contexts.

Yea-Wen

I have been formally studying intercultural communication since fall 2004 when I entered U.S. academia as an international graduate student and instructor. Primarily, my research trajectory focuses on understanding and unpacking the cultural, relational, and material impacts of how we experience and communicate cultural identities (or not) across contexts (e.g., intercultural relating, identity-based nonprofit organizing, and higher education). Though cultural identities and memories are often not explicitly linked, memories, whether personal, public, or cultural, inform, shape, and/or affect the constructions and contestations of cultural identities. I am grateful to Alberto González for inviting me to participate in the 2015 CSCA panel, which became an opportunity for me as a Taiwan-born and U.S.-based scholar to (re)engage with personal and cultural memories about Taiwan that often feel both intimate and distant. Later, I had another opportunity to unpack memories and memorable moments of weathering institutionalized whiteness vis-a-vis oral history as an immigrant woman-scholar and faculty of color at a historically white institution for six years (Chen, 2018). Given the commitment of critical intercultural communication scholarship to the power, authority, and impact of histories and historical conditions on intercultural communication (e.g., Halualani & Nakayama, 2010), cultural memory offers a rich and exciting direction for such endeavors.

Al

My early and more recent writing on Ohio Mexican Americans concerns how they enter and navigate the public sphere as a marginalized community. I have focused on *Latinidad* and arts activism (2014), poetic expressions of otherness by migrant workers (1990), and strategic uses of media by Mexican Americans in Northwest Ohio (1989). As I recall those articles and the residents of Mexican heritage (both "settled out" and temporary) I am struck by how they expressed their goals, how they crafted their identities, and how these were strongly tied to memory.

In private conversations and in public discourse, residents would tell stories about Mexico or South Texas. Some of the stories were their own and some were stories told by their elders. The stories often involved cooking methods like learning how to make the best tamales, celebrations like *quinceaneras*, or stories of mythical creatures like the *chupacabra*. Whether told out of nostalgia, ethnic pride, or social defensiveness, the stories were connections to an idealized time, the time before migration.

The chapter in this book is co-authored with Eun Young Lee. It emerges from my opportunity to teach in Seoul over the course of several summers and Eun Young's summer visits to her hometown of Cheongyang. The first restaurant I went to in Seoul was *Hiraku*, a tiny Japanese place near where I lived. The second restaurant was a Tex-Mex place in Itaewon. (I began to wonder when I was going to eat at a Korean food restaurant!) In my view, *Vatos* Urban Tacos was better than many Mexican food restaurants in the U.S. In our chapter, we attempt to unpack the layers of diasporic remembering in the origin stories and the material elements of two well-known Korean restaurants.

Intercultural Communication Research and Memory

Cultural memory as an area of study has been widely examined in cultural studies, memory studies, peace studies and even to a degree in rhetorical, media and film studies; it has yet to occupy a large role in intercultural communication. Even though rhetorical and performance studies scholars, such as Aden, 2014; Dickinson, Blair, & Ott, 2010; Hasian & Wood, 2010; Phillips & Reyes, 2011; Demo & Vivian 2012, have examined cultural memory as an idea in relation to political discourse(s), as an area it is under-examined in intercultural communication. Considering that critical intercultural communication scholars often focus on social and cultural ideas, such as marginalized voices and experiences and issues of power in social and cultural structures and practices (e.g., Collier et al., 2002; Halualani & Nakayama, 2010; Willink, Gutierrez-Perez, Shukri, & Stein, 2014) and deal with displacement, immigration, diasporic experiences, and cultural identity/ies (e.g., Atay, 2015; Cheng, 2008; Flores, 2003; Yep, 2013), it is rather surprising that (inter)cultural memory as an area of inquiry is not widely present in the field. Drzewiecka (2010) echoes this when she states: "While intercultural communication scholars are beginning to account for the formative function of history, fewer yet have turned their attention to the twists and turns of memory" (p. 292). Moreover, a branch of intercultural communication research examines cultural conflicts and their aftermaths. For example, the ongoing Syrian crisis generated research by intercultural communication scholars who study not only the different dimensions of the cultural conflict but also migration that has been taking place as the direct outcome of the ongoing war in the area (Wilmott, 2017). As these examples illustrate, intercultural encounters and representations regardless of their contexts and domains are often linked to the past. Hence, memory studies is highly relevant to (critical) intercultural communication research.

This edited volume aims to fill this void. The authors in this book use different critical intercultural communication and cultural studies frameworks to approach cultural memory. By utilizing various critical and cultural studies and ethnographic and narrative-based methods, they examine the notion of cultural memory in intercultural encounters, everyday experiences, and identity performances that evoke memories of colonial pasts, immigration processes and in some cases, memories of places and spaces that suggest or represent a cultural past that is shaped by power structures and different ideologies. Hence, they focus upon the link between space/place and cultural memory, memories of nationally, places constituted by markers of ethnicity, race, and sexuality, spaces and cultural experiences and identity performances and presentations that represent or embody intercultural conflicts, oppressions, struggles and memories that help to make sense of, deal with or reconcile with the past.

Storytelling emerges from the present relationship with representations of a particular past. Our publicly performed relationship with the past and the ways in which we tell stories of the past is negotiable and contestable. Who remembers what, and why? In juxtaposition, who or what is forgotten, and why? When and how is a consensual meaning achieved and maintained over time? When and how are meanings challenged and renegotiated?

Borrowing from different critical intercultural frameworks, such as intercultural and transnational identity formations, feminist and queer theories, accommodation and acculturation theories and postcolonial theory, the authors of this collection collectively argue that as intercultural or transnational bodies, we remember cultural events and upbringing, performances, and conflicts, wars and peace negotiations in particular ways. Our cultural, ethnic, racial, and national backgrounds and ideological perspectives guide us to remember the past in a particular way. Hence, stories that we grow up with and stories that we tell about our past, influence how we remember the past, how we try to preserve it, or in some cases how we try to erase it. Furthermore, the ways in which we experience and make sense of politically, culturally, and emotionally charged spaces and places that either represent the past or narrate the past in particular ways are infused with and influenced by our intercultural experiences and ideological standpoints in relation to these cultural spaces and places. Hence, the way in which we remember the past, and narrate the past is an intercultural performance, act, encounter and representation.

Cultural Memory and Sensemaking

This book examines different ways of remembering the past through commemorative sites and events as locations for the negotiation and contestation of shared individual and collective narratives. We argue that cultural memory is preserved and represented through commemorative and commercial sites, visual and oral stories, and performances. Hence, how we remember is always a cultural negotiation between individuals and between individuals and society. Therefore, storytelling and cultural representations of the past through use of space and places play a paramount role in remembering the past. Stories and visual representations (built environments, film and media representations, and performances) play an important role as we construct a sense of reality, make sense of our everyday lives, and remember the past. As human beings, we use oral, written, and visual stories to communicate, express our ideas, narrate our experiences, and present our identities. Walter Fisher (1989) argues that we use stories to make sense of our lives and lived experiences.

While some of the chapters employ ethnographic research and rhetorical analysis, some of them feature personal stories to examine memorial sites, film and visual texts, or lived experiences to understand how the commemorations, memory and storytelling work as inter/cultural performance and function as cultural memory. The commemorative sites and events, cultural, political and personal stories analyzed in this book emphasize how the meaning making process of historical events and the ways in which they are represented in media are not always consensual but instead are often contested and potentially reproduces the original struggle. When put in the regional, global, and intercultural contexts, the performance of cultural memory reveals the conflicted nature of personal and collective narratives.

Chapter Summaries

The book is divided into two sections: Cultural Memories of Places and Spaces, and Cultural Memory, Identity Politics and Intersectionality. In the first section, the authors examine different spaces and places that evoke memory of the cultural past, how the past is articulated or how it is performed or enacted. In the second section, authors use visual texts or everyday practices to analyze the links between intersectional aspects of cultural identity and memory.

Peter Ehrenhaus and A. Susan Owen's chapter, titled "Constructing Coalition at the Moore's Ford Lynching Reenactment: Fractures and Alliances between Communities of Memory" reflects on the past and the memory of the race relationships in the U.S. by focusing on Ford lynching reenactment. This chapter reminds us that the memory of the past is always present, especially now when as a society we are trying to grapple with issues pertaining to race and discrimination. Ehrenhaus and Owen are also concerned with the constant cultural tensions between remembering and forgetting and how to negotiate some of these frictions.

"(Be)Coming Home: Transformative Places and Koreamerican Identity in Itaewon, South Korea" (Eun Young Lee and Alberto González) explores how place and memory intersect as Koreamericans work to gain cultural citizenship in Seoul, South Korea. The chapter focuses on two Tex-Mex-themed restaurants founded by Koreamericans who have returned to the Itaewon district of Seoul, *Coreanos* and *Vatos*. The restaurants are constructed as intercultural places where the memories of the Korean homeland are invoked alongside the memories of the U.S. Southwest. The authors argue that Koreamericans uniquely valorize and disrupt the ontology of *Han minjok* (one Korean identity) through the transformative discursive and material rhetorics performed in Tex-Mex food restaurants.

In their chapter, "When 'Chiang Kai-Shek Memorial Square' (un)became 'Liberty Square': A Case of Contested Public Memories in Taiwan," Yea-Wen Chen and Chunyu Zhang examine divided public memories about Taiwan's first president, Chiang Kai-shek (1887–1975). In particular, they focus on shifting, evolving, and contested public discourses surrounding Chiang Kai-shek Memorial Hall (CKSMH) over time. They conclude by arguing for a need to put the public back in "public" memory in that consensus building and honoring peoples' lived stories are key in the healing process of (re)writing public memory about controversial public figures.

"Remembering Communism: The Site of Witness and Memory and the House of Leaves Museums in Albania" (Nina Gjoci) investigates the role that places of memory play in the rhetorical constructions of the communist past in Albania. The analysis focuses on two museums: The Site of Witness and Memory museum in Shkoder and the House of Leaves museum in Tirana, capital of Albania. Gjoci argues that the different constructions of the communist past at these museums demonstrate the difficulty of staging public representations of oppressive regimes and they reveal the ambiguity of Albania's reconciliation with its communist past.

In "(Mis)Remembering Stonewall: Narrative Authority and the American Monomyth in Queer Public Memory," Kathryn Hobson, Bernadette Marie Calafell, and Spencer B. Margulies take an intersectional approach to examine Ronald Emmerich's film *Stonewall* (2015). While the film tries to spotlight the LGBTQA+ struggles during the late 1960s by focusing on the Stonewall riots, how the film decided to remember the past is geared towards white mainstream U.S.-American audiences. In their chapter, Hobson, Calafell, and Margulies focus on the absence of "radical queer and trans people of color" from the Emmerich's film. Hence, they argue that the film ignores and also erases certain individuals and their complex queer identities from the historical event. In a way, the way it is remembered, erases the present of certain bodies and their significance from our collective queer cultural memory.

Shinsuke Eguchi's chapter, "Queer Fantasy: A Memory of Michael Sam's *Big Gay Kiss*," critiques "the performative rhetoric of queerness" by focusing on Michael Sam's kiss. As Eguchi reflects on the mediated memory of this significant event, because it was the first publicly televised kiss by an openly queer NLF football player, he examines racism, sexism and homophobia surrounding the discourse of this significant queer moment. Hence, he offers culturally significant alternative readings of the memory of this kiss to challenge and resist cisheteronormativity.

In "Diasporic Memories: Place, Space and Home," Ahmet Atay uses autoethnographic writing to articulate how the notion of memory and home works for diasporic individuals. In his chapter, Atay focuses on the role of photographs as a visual memory in diasporic experiences. He uses three interrelated stories from three different time periods to embody and represent diasporic memory. In doing so, he also theorizes how visual representations, such as photographs or stories that diasporic individuals share create as a sense of belonging. Thus, he theorizes diasporic memory through storytelling.

Mariko Izumi's chapter, "Displaced Memorials: Commemorating the 'Comfort Women' in the United States," examines transnational memorials across U.S. cities and towns for former "comfort women" who were and are victims and survivors of the Japanese Imperial Military's institutionalized sexual servitude and atrocities between 1930 and 1945. In particular, Izumi asks and analyzes if memorials could "work" beyond national borders to generate political potential and vibrancy. Guiding by conceptualization of memory-in-action for political organization and mobilization, Izumi concludes that, when the transnational "comfort women" statues serve as partial and displaced objects, the invitation to empathize with global Others is nothing but elusive and salutary.

In "'Funk Isn't a Trend, It's a Necessity': Favela Funk's Vernacular Discourse and The Struggle for Cultural Legitimation," Raquel Moreira argues that favela funk is modeled after samba's cultural memory and analyzes discourses surrounding favela funk as a musical and cultural movement born in the outskirts of Rio de Janeiro, Brazil that has gained popularity locally since the 1990s and has enjoyed global consumption in the mid-2000s. Specifically, Moreira unpacks three distinct yet interrelated vernacular discourses in favela funk's quest for legitimization: (a) a political and self-affirming 2008 manifesto published by APAFunk (Association of Professionals and Friends of Funk); (b) the favela funk circles; and (c) the vernacular discourse of an Afro-Brazilian MC, Carol Bandida. Moreira concludes that artists and supporters of favela funk utilize both self-affirming and oppositional rhetorical strategies to legitimize and keep reinventing favela funk outside of mainstream media.

References

Aden, R. C. (2014). *Upon the ruins of liberty: Slavery, the President's House at Independence National Historical Park, and public memory.* Philadelphia, PA: Temple University Press.

Atay, A. (2015). *Globalization's impact on cultural identity formation: Queer diasporic males on cyberspace.* Lanham, MD: Lexington Books.

Chen, Y.-W. (2018). "Why don't you speak (up), Asian/immigrant/woman?": Rethink silence and voice through family oral history. *Departures in Critical Qualitative Research, 7*(2), 29–48. doi:10.1525/dcqr.2018.7.2.29.

Cheng, H.-I. (2008). *Culturing interface: Identity, communication, and Chinese transnationalism.* New York, NY: Peter Lang.

Collier, M. J., Hegde, R. S., Lee, W., Nakayama, T., & Yep, G. A. (2002). Dialogue on the edges: Ferment in communication and culture. In M. J. Collier (Ed.), *Transforming communication about culture: Critical new directions* (Vol. 24, pp. 219–280). Thousand Oaks, CA: Sage.

Dickinson, G., Blair, C., & Ott, B. L. (Eds.) (2010). *Places of public memory: The rhetoric of museums and memorials.* Tuscaloosa, AL: The University of Alabama Press.

Demo, A. T., & Vivian, B. (2012). *Rhetoric, remembrance, and visual form: Sighting memory.* New York, NY: Routledge.

Drzewiecka, J. A. (2010). Public memories in the shadow of the Other: Divided memories and national identity. In T. K. Nakayama & R. T. Halualani (Eds.), *The handbook of critical intercultural communication* (pp. 286–310). West Sussex, UK: Wiley-Blackwell.

Fisher, W. R. (1989). Clarifying the narrative paradigm. *Communication Monographs, 56,* 55–58.

Flores, L. A. (2003). Constructing rhetorical borders: Peons, illegal aliens, and competing narratives of immigration. *Critical Studies in Media Communication, 20*(4), 362–387. doi:10.1080/0739318032000142025.

González, A. (1989). "Participation" at WMEX-FM: Interventional rhetoric of Ohio Mexican Americans. *Western Journal of Speech Communication, 53*(4), 398–410.

González, A. (1990). Mexican "Otherness" in the discourse of Mexican Americans. *Southern Communication Journal, 55*(2), 276–291.

González, A., Chavez, J. M., & Englebrecht, C. M. (2014). *Latinidad* and vernacular discourse: Arts activism in Toledo's Old South End. *Journal of Poverty, 18*(1), 50–64.

Halualani, R. T., & Nakayama, T. K. (2010). Critical intercultural communication studies at a crossroads. In T. K. Nakayama & R. T. Halualani (Eds.), *The handbook of critical intercultural communication* (pp. 1–16). West Sussex, UK: Wiley-Blackwell.

Hasian, M., & Wood, R. (2010). Critical museology, (post)colonial communication, and the gradual mastering of traumatic pasts at the Royal Museum for Central Africa (RMCA). *Western Journal of Communication, 74*(2), pp. 128–149. doi:10.1080/10570311003614484.

Kendall, R. P., & Reyes, G. M. (Eds.) (2011). *Global memory spaces: Contesting remembrance in a transnational age.* Tuscaloosa, AL: University of Alabama Press.

Willink, K. G., Gutierrez-Perez, R., Shukri, S., & Stein, L. (2014). Navigating with the stars: Critical qualitative methodological constellations for critical intercultural communication research. *Journal of International and Intercultural Communication, 7*(4), 289–316. doi:10.1080/17513057.2014.964150.

Wilmott, A. C. (2017). The politics of photography: Visual depictions of Syrian refugees in U.K. online media. *Visual Communication Quarterly, 24*(2), 67–82. doi:10.1080/15551393.2017.1307113.

Yep, G. A. (2013). Queering/Quaring/Kauering/Crippin'/Transing "other bodies" in intercultural communication. *Journal of International and Intercultural Communication, 6,* 118–126. doi:10.1080/17513057.2013.777087.

Cultural Memories of Places and Spaces

1. Communities of Memory, Coalition, and Race Trauma: The Moore's Ford Lynching Reenactment[1]

PETER EHRENHAUS
Pacific Lutheran University

A. SUSAN OWEN
University of Puget Sound

In recent years American communities have been compelled to confront their histories of race violence and race lynching.[2] Situated within the tensions of remembrance and forgetting, the collective will to confront these pasts is fraught with challenge, and calls to confront the legacies of white-on-black race violence are often met with deep ambivalence. Some fear that commemoration will "produce nothing but anguish, grief, and a righteous, desperate rage that only risks fueling more violence." Others worry that instead of producing "a reconciled future, memories of victimization" will only exacerbate "social division and conflict" (Simon, Rosenberg & Eppert, 2000, p. 1).

In this chapter, we examine one call to remembrance through the annual reenactment of the 1946 lynching of four African Americans in Walton County, Georgia.[3] Our research at the Moore's Ford Lynching Reenactment concerns one iteration by a coalition formed from two communities of memory—one white, cosmopolitan, financially secure, feminist, and religiously and politically progressive, and one black, rural, of modest economic means, and grounded in the conservative social mores of the patriarchal Southern black church. Communities of memory coalesce around particular relationships to enduring cultural trauma—in this case, trauma produced by a legacy of race lynching. While each community "occupies a distinctive historical relationship" to those traumas, "points of intersection" may support coalitional efforts in pursuit of common commitments (Owen & Ehrenhaus, 2010, p. 132). In this coalition, both communities displayed their own rhetorical strategies for reading the past and its representation, and for managing their positional anxieties. Both exhibited distinct relationships to the traumas of race lynching and to their responsibilities *to* the past through reenactment. Consequently, despite a shared commitment to "justice and remembrance," the struggle to control the meanings of the reenactment fractured the coalition.

Managing the tensions between remembrance and forgetting is a "delicate enterprise, demanding astute judgment about what to keep and what to let go ... to memorialize or to anathematize" (Lowenthal, 1999, p. xi). But astute judgment is never neutral; the quandary of what, when, and how to remember is always problematic. Communities that bear the scars of race violence consist of historically entangled groups whose interests differ and may be antithetical. Even among those advocating remembrance and cooperation across cultural boundaries, competing interests emerge in struggles to shape and control commemorative practices.

Reenactment is distinctive among commemorative practices. It creates a liminal space for constructing memory through embodied, affective experiences. Liminality owes to the "temporal tangle" that reenactment creates (Schneider, 2011, p. 10). By folding time upon itself, reenactment opens a liminal space of "cross-temporal slippage" in which "something other than the discrete 'now' of everyday life" occurs, and this is manifested in the "explicit *twiceness* of reenactment" (Schneider, 2011, p. 14, italics in original).

Our research at the Moore's Ford Lynching Reenactment spanned three days. It encompassed rehearsals, the reenactment, and the denouement. The reenactment comprised three performance tableaux staged in their original locales, giving context and temporal order to the narrative. Performers and spectators traversed material space in an orderly caravan of cars and buses. The liminal space created by reenactment invited all to become witnesses.

We begin by discussing how the reenactment constructed memory of race trauma by reproducing the traumatizing social drama of the "lynching performance" (Fuoss, 1999). The Moore's Ford Lynching Reenactment is a redressive ritual performance, operating within both the local social drama of the 1946 lynching and the expansive national social drama of race violence and race lynching (Turner, 1980). We then recount the narrative of the lynching, noting the centrality of conspiracy in that narrative. We next share our field observations and analysis. Because we had access to the interior spaces of the performance—which we detail later in this chapter—we were privy to the dynamics that resulted in coalitional fracture. We read this fracture as resulting from the entanglement of intersections and contradictory interests of two communities of memory, each standing in distinctive relation to the legacies of race lynching.

Reenactment, Trauma, and Public Memory

Reenactment has "become the most widely consumed form of popular history" (McCalman & Pickering, 2010, p. 3); this genre of remembrance reveals "a yearning to experience history somatically and emotionally" (p. 6). The immersive experiential character of reenactment creates a liminal space in which participants and observers are invited to foster "sympathetic understanding" (p. 7) of what original participants might have experienced. Reenactment calls attention to "unfinished business" (p. 11), by enabling "the creation and contestation of public memory" (p. 12). Moreover, as a hallmark of unfinished business, "compulsive repetition," such as we find in annual commemorative reenactment, "is a response to trauma" (Sturken, 2007, p. 26). Telling a trauma story is "a kind of double telling, the oscillation between a *crisis of death* and the *crisis of life*: between the story of the unbearable nature of an event and the story of the unbearable nature of survival" (Caruth, 1996, p. 7, italics in original).

The iterative character of the Moore's Ford reenactment signals the enduring trauma of race lynching. We read this haunting of memory through Turner's theory of social drama (1980): (1) the initial breach; (2) the subsequent crisis; (3) communal effort to seek redress through ritual reenactment; and (4) communal reconciliation or acknowledging an "irreparable breach" (p. 151). The 1946 lynching precipitated the breach. Its unresolved status perpetuates the crisis. The ritual reenactments, begun in 2005, seek redress, particularly after failed investigations by a grand jury, efforts of the Federal and Georgia Bureaus of Investigation, and financial incentives to reveal the perpetrators. But reconciliation necessitates bringing perpetrators to justice; the inability to secure this outcome suggests an enduring "irreparable breach" across racial divides, inter-racial coalitions notwithstanding.

In response to a traumatizing social breach, redressive ritual divines "the hidden causes of misfortune" (Turner, 1986, p. 41). The struggle to control that "hidden cause" in the reenactment was the source of the coalition's fracture. One community approached the reenactment as a resource for ritually redressing the Moore's Ford lynching and fostering inter-racial cooperation through dramatized historical authenticity. The other appropriated it as a vehicle for metonymically redressing grievances based broadly in the nation's history of white supremacist race violence.

The Lynching Conspiracy Narrative

On July 25, 1946 four African Americans, Roger and Dorothy Dorsey Malcolm and George and Mae Dorsey, were lynched in rural Walton County, Georgia. Coined "the last mass lynching in the United States" (Wexler, 2003), these murders were perpetrated in broad daylight in a field adjoining the Moore's Ford Bridge, approximately 45 miles east of Atlanta. The lynching was carried out by twenty or more unmasked white perpetrators, none of whom were ever indicted.[4] Local lore claims that now-elderly perpetrators continue to reside in the area.

Events leading to these murders are well documented. On July 14, in the front yard of white farmer Barney Hester, Roger and Dorothy Malcolm argued loudly and drew Barney's attention. Hester interceded. Roger stabbed him and fled. Allegedly, Roger was intoxicated and suspected Barney was having an affair with his wife; this presumed infidelity was the basis of Roger's arguing with Dorothy. Roger was quickly tracked down and surrendered. Sheriff's deputies arrested and transported Roger to jail in Monroe, the county seat. Barney was taken to the hospital, where he lingered for eleven days. It was commonly understood that if he died, the white community would take matters into their own hands. On July 25, Barney Hester's fever broke; he recovered.

That same day a wealthy white farmer, Loy Harrison, posted Roger's bail. Harrison was accompanied to the jail by Dorothy Malcolm and George and Mae Dorsey. They had pleaded with Harrison to post bail, which Roger would reimburse with labor. Late that afternoon they headed for Dorothy's mother's home. Rather than taking the direct route, Harrison took back roads that led to the Moore's Ford Bridge. As Harrison approached the bridge, his route was blocked by three cars; a fourth was behind him, barring retreat.

A group of at least twenty unmasked white men with guns approached Harrison's car. They pulled Roger from the car and bound him. Then they took George. Dorothy Dorsey reportedly cursed at one of the perpetrators by name; the mob then pried both women from the car, breaking their arms to loosen their grip on the car doors. All four were dragged to the clearing by the river. Under verbal command, three volleys of gunfire followed. The lynch mob returned to Harrison and asked if he recognized any of them; Harrison said he did not. The perpetrators then drove off, leaving Harrison behind. Harrison drove to a store to telephone the sheriff's office and report the crime.

Conspiracy narratives share at least two generic features. First, they assert the "uneven distribution of resources and coercive power" (Fenster, 1999, p. xiv) and claim that "some individual or group . . . has secretly seized power by illicit means" (p. 110). Second, they invent the possibilities for moral agency, pitting "the actions of the perpetrators of evil conspiracy" against "the defender[s] of the moral order" (Fenster, 1999, p. 106). Moral agents discover, expose, and confront the web of secrets and illicit actions. Conspiracy narratives advance claims about "what really happened" (Fenster, 1999, p. 110) and expose what had been concealed.

As performed ritual redress, The Moore's Ford Lynching Reenactment responds to the social breach and crisis by revealing what was concealed through conspiracy and silence. Reenactors instantiate moral agents committed to social justice; an oft-repeated goal of the reenactment was to reveal the identities of the perpetrators, living or dead, and to hold them morally and legally accountable for the conspiracy to commit murder. The reenactment re-stages the conspiracy for the benefit of spectators, affirming that "this happened" and thwarting the original logic of disappearance lynching. The reenactment appropriates the structural logic of historical lynching performance complex[5] as it confronts and explores the horrors of race lynching (Fuoss, 1999). Importantly, the liminal space of reenactment invites spectators to witness, and to position themselves as moral agents, as well.

Participant Observations at Moore's Ford

Our work with the Moore's Ford Lynching Reenactment spanned three days of intensive participant-observations, guided by principles of naturalistic inquiry (Jorgensen, 1989; Lofland & Lofland, 1995). Our preparation began well in advance of our arrival, focusing upon the original lynching, the coalition between the Moore's Ford Memorial Committee (MFMC) and Georgia WAND, press coverage and opinion pieces, and YouTube videos of previous reenactments. We also contacted Bobbie Paul, director of Georgia WAND (Women's Action for New Directions) and of the reenactment.[6] This relationship gave us access to the interior spaces of the reenactment. Moreover, Bobbie's personal endorsement and our self-identification as educators established us as trustworthy to coalition members.

Two questions emerged during fieldwork: How does the reenactment's liminality open space for constructing affective memory? How do these communities of memory use reenactment to articulate their relationships to the traumas of race lynching?

Rehearsals

Rehearsals for the reenactment over two days were highly collaborative and supportive, suggesting a high degree of commitment to the coalition and its goals across the two communities of memory. Rehearsals for each of the three tableaux were steeped in theatrical logistics which included: a detailed script with stage instructions; a published list of names and cell phone numbers of cast and crew; a published list of transportation options and scheduled travel times for the day of the reenactment; travel to three geographic sites of performances; site preparation; blocking of each staged tableau; the coaching of five primary actors; telephone exchanges between actors and other participants; and testing props.

Bobbie Paul, director of the reenactment, kept in regular contact with performers and production assistants, community event planners, and the coalition's leadership team. Rehearsals were relatively brief, given the complex logistics of the reenactment, actors' availability for rehearsal due to employment obligations, distance from reenactment sites, and prior role experience. Approximately 20 actors participated in the reenactment, most as members of the lynch mob. Bobbie worked most closely with actors who played the historical figures of Barney Hester, George Dorsey, Mae Dorsey, Roger Malcolm, and Dorothy Malcolm. Ray Mikelthun, a retired Methodist minister and peace activist, played both Barney Hester and the leader of the lynch mob. Betty Maddox, a retired police officer and non-violence activist, played the pregnant Dorothy Malcolm. Jillian Wells, a college student and intern with WAND, played Mae Dorsey; she worked closely with Bobbie on logistics for the reenactment.

Bobbie envisioned tableaux performances which she described as "postcard" or "snapshot" moments. She coached actors to use precise, minimalist body movement and gestures to convey moments of terror and violence. She demonstrated slow-motion action and freezing to convey moments of intense violence. She stressed the importance of physical and emotional safety when enacting performances of violence. She discussed the emotional intensity of reenacting a race lynching. She coaxed the white actors toward the performance of racially motivated rage, and the black actors to perform helplessness, panic and terror. She facilitated conversations in which actors reassured each other as they practiced physical and emotional confrontation.

The first tableau was rehearsed at Monroe's First African Baptist Church. The scene, featured for the first time, was of the precipitating altercation between Barney Hester and Roger Malcom at the Hester farm. The Hester family disapproved of the reenactment, and razed the original homestead to remove a site of reenactor congregation. The Hesters also informed the Sheriff that reenactors were banned from their property. Bobbie coached actors on positioning themselves on the county road right-of-way in front of the farm, and instructed them to leave the site immediately if approached by members of the Hester family. As a precaution and in consultation with other coalition leaders, a law enforcement escort and presence was arranged for the entirety of the reenactment.

The second tableau was rehearsed outside the county courthouse and jail annex in the county seat of Monroe. Under Bobbie's direction, Walter Reeves, a white activist from Atlanta, rehearsed his race-baiting speech as Gov. Eugene Talmadge. Betty rehearsed as Dorothy Malcom plaintively calling up to her husband, Roger (Randy Ansley), on the second floor of the jail, urging him to be strong. Discussion then focused on moving quickly from the jail to the car that would carry the unwitting victims to their demise.

Rehearsal of the final tableau occurred at the site of the actual murders, an untended field adjacent to the two-lane bridge.[7] Activities included site preparation, prop selection, actor preparation, and marking spatial boundaries for the press corps and spectators. Safety hazards were noted and volunteers cleaned and prepared the site. In consultation with lead reenactors, Bobbie determined the spatial contours of the reenactment site with yellow caution tape, taking into consideration road access and parking for spectators and performers, actor access to the field, the safety and comfort of actors who would be lying on the ground for several minutes, and press and spectator viewing areas.

Bobbie's concern was apparent for her actors' physical and emotional safety while reenacting the violence of the original event. The two female victims would be dragged from the car. The perpetrators were to dramatize breaking the women's arms to loosen their grip on the car doors; they would then place ropes around the necks of the two black men and drag them to the killing field. Bobbie rehearsed with her actors how to perform the action; as in the church rehearsal, she reiterated the "snapshot" composition of the performance through precise body motion and freeze-action to convey the horror of the moment. She coached her actors on how to use their voices to convey victim panic or the vocal and verbal menace of the perpetrators. Bobbie and Betty reviewed the challenges of playing Dorothy Malcom as (allegedly) seven months pregnant. They worked on how Betty would support her belly prop with one hand as she is dragged from the car to the kill site. Bobbie reminded Betty of the coalition leaders' agreement that this year's reenactment *not* include a dramatization of the lynch mob cutting the fetus from Dorothy's abdomen. Bobbie insisted that the reenactment not venture toward cheap spectacle. Betty Maddox agreed.

Sound effects were tested to mimic the sound of gunfire. From the edge of the clearing, standing among trees, Bobbie struck a snare drum in a staccato beat. She relocated the drum repeatedly to gauge the sound effect's authenticity and its audibility. She compared the effect to using an overturned metal washtub. Bobbie and her lead role actors discussed firecrackers to stand in for gunfire: the grass was dry and could catch fire; timing firecrackers is hard to control. Discussion turned to the mechanics of applying ketchup blood prop to the "bodies" of the lynched victims after they have been shot.

As we observed the rehearsal and spoke with reenactors, we realized how seamlessly the components of the lynching performance complex were integrated with the conspiracy narrative that figures prominently in disappearance lynchings. Three interrelated strategies dominated the rehearsal activities: narrativizing the original conspiracy; creating community and connectedness within the liminal space of rehearsal; and fostering affective memory through attention to sensory experience.

For our benefit and their own, participants told stories about their connection to the 1946 lynching and their involvement in the reenactment. Their stories expressed a felt sense of the devastating effects of historical silence upon the local African American community. Foremost in the story is the lack of criminal accountability. Participants shared a belief that some now-elderly perpetrators were still alive and that their families and friends knew the truth about the lynching. Bobby Howard, local civil rights activist, recounted his efforts since 1968 to investigate the crime. He claimed to know the identities of some of the perpetrators and hoped that the reenactment would encourage those with information to come forward. He and other local participants viewed the reenactment as a way to expose perpetrators before they die, thereby enacting justice for the victims and providing closure for their surviving families. Participants expressed their hopes that the reenactment would draw a broad audience, and that justice would prevail—whether through attending the reenactment, consuming media coverage, or a renewed F.B.I. investigation. Several cited our interest in their stories as further evidence of the reenactment's import.

Deacon Ron Brown of Monroe's First African Baptist Church, a reenactment facilitator, shared his efforts to educate young African Americans about the history of racial violence in Georgia. "The children need to know the truth." Hattie Lawson, board member of the Moore's Ford Memorial Committee (MFMC), was another key facilitator; she spoke of her life-long commitment to educating young black people about their history. Both of them echoed the commitments of the MFMC: "telling the story, honoring the dead, promoting healing and social justice, and creating a living memorial to the victims of this horrible crime." Betty Maddox connected the original lynching to contemporary problems with violence among and against black youth, and shared the story of losing her 25-year-old son to gun violence; she had kept the shirt he was wearing when he was killed, and uses it as a visual aide when she gives motivational talks at schools and community meetings. For Ron, Hattie, and Betty, the reenactment is a pedagogical resource for motivating young African Americans to embrace educational opportunities, to eschew violence, and become involved in local civil rights activities. They viewed us as educators who could take their stories to a broader audience.

As the reenactment's director, Bobbie Paul advocated public theatre as an appropriate and productive space for truth telling and healing. "Peace," she said repeatedly, "is an action verb." She expressed two goals: to offer participants and spectators a way of knowing and discovering, and to build inter-racial trust and coalition through community activism. To us she expressed both satisfaction and concern about the reenactment's impact. She advocated the value of racial reconciliation among the reenactors who have done important emotional and political work across the years, yet wondered whether the reenactment deepens political and racial polarization in Walton County. She questioned whether some spectators attended the reenactment out of voyeuristic curiosity. She was deeply disturbed with past reenactments in which white perpetrators cut Dorothy Malcolm's unborn child from her body, calling it "lurid and sensationalistic." She expressed misgivings that the performance was being appropriated for pro-life (i.e., pro-birth) activism, which she opposes. She viewed us as sympathetic to her political commitments to racial and reproductive justice.

Reenactment Day

Reenactment Day was organized in three phases: a two-hour program at Monroe's First African Baptist Church, coordinated travel to three locations in Walton County for the reenactment, and a communal meal at the church after the reenactment.

The church overflowed with congregants, visitors, local citizens, visiting dignitaries, reenactors and facilitators, local politicians and religious leaders, and electronic and print media professionals. The three primary planners of the reenactment, several of the reenactors, and invited speakers took seats on the stage. State Representative Tyrone Brooks[8] offered opening remarks and introduced the reenactment planners: Hattie Lawson, Bobbie Paul, and Bobby Howard. Each spoke briefly. Hattie Lawson addressed the urgency that the children "know the legacy of their history." Bobbie Paul introduced the reenactors and described those playing perpetrators as "some of the most peaceful social activist folks in Atlanta." The audience replied with a standing ovation. Bobby Howard told the story of the Moore's Ford lynching and the ensuing efforts to secure justice.

The next four speakers connected themselves to the Moore's Ford lynching through kinship. Dorothy Malcolm Woods identified herself as a namesake of Dorothy Malcolm and a representative of the Malcolm family. Sarah Maddox self-identified as Mae Dorsey's cousin. Muriel Scott and Ariel Young Sullivan represented their fathers' roles in the lynching's aftermath. Each woman emphasized the reenactment's significance for achieving justice and closure. Each spoke of a life-long connection to the lynching.

In a spirited and provocative speech, Dorothy Malcolm Woods gave her version of what happened to Dorothy Malcolm:

> Dorothy Malcolm was pregnant with a precious baby. After she was so brutally massacred, and her baby excised from her body, the two of them, along with George and Mae Murray, were deprived of the most precious possession that even now some take for granted, and that is the right to be here. The baby that was denied -- he also had rights of being born, of bonding, of being nursed from a mother's breast.

Woods then employed parallel structure to emphasize what the unborn child was denied:

> the right to have playmates ... the right to grow up ... the right to march down an aisle as a graduate ... the right to become a productive American citizen ... the right to become a loving husband ... the right to be loved by his family.

In closing, she shared that "in a moment of revelation," and in consultation with Tyrone Brooks, she was moved to name Dorothy Malcolm's baby:

> He will no longer be denied a life or a name. For as this baby was conceived in a natural body and denied rights in the natural body, so he has been conceived in the spirit ... and now born in the spirit. And ladies and gentlemen, he will forever live in the spirit of each of us so long as we stand for justice [applause]. And *this* day ... we mark his name in history as "Justice" [applause].

The elderly, frail Sarah Maddox thanked the audience and reenactors repeatedly and profusely. She described her family's long relationship with the legacy of the lynching: "You don't know what it is for your nerves to be 'toh' [torn] down and wracked. And live so long in fear and injustice." She hoped that the reenactment would advance the pursuit of justice for the murdered four: "I just want to thank god for people like you all who try to stand up for us . . .. I just wanted to thank you together one and all for being here for the families of each of us and taking part in giving us justice."

The next two speakers introduced themselves as the daughters of men who resisted, investigated and publicized the original lynching. Ariel Young Sullivan, daughter of the late Dan Young, Monroe's funeral director for the African American community in 1946, related her father's trauma from witnessing the "terrible injuries" inflicted upon the bodies of the Dorseys and Malcolms. With the consent of both families, Dan Young arranged a public viewing of the bodies because he believed the local community should witness the brutality of the murders, anticipating Mamie Till-Mobley's decision in 1955 to publicize the image of her son's brutalized body. More devastating to Mr. Young than preparing the mutilated bodies was the absence of accountability. "Fifty-two years later, the killers still remain unpunished." Saying that "justice for the Malcolms and the Dorseys" was "my father's dream," Ms. Sullivan thanked the Committee and the reenactors for their efforts to keep attention focused on the crime.

Muriel Scott, daughter of publisher A. O. Scott who co-founded *Atlanta Daily World*, related the devastating effects of the lynching upon her father. He worked with Dan Young to investigate the crime, publicize the lynching in African American newspapers throughout the country, and protect African American witnesses called to testify before a grand jury. She urged the audience to "never give up" in their quest for accountability and justice. Projected above and behind her was an image of the family of Roger and Dorothy Malcolm looking on as two coffins were lowered into open graves.

As reenactors departed for their performances, Tyrone Brooks and others distributed a petition supporting federal adoption of the Emmett Till Unsolved Civil Rights Crime Act. For the next hour, audience members offered stories of local and national struggles for racial justice. They praised the efforts of the Moore's Ford coalition and their dedication to racial justice. Visitors from Nigeria and Ethiopia described race struggles in their own nations and marveled at the audacity of a public reenactment of historical race violence. The program concluded with recognition of the Georgia Association of Black Elected Officials, political candidates, religious leaders, newspaper editors, and activists in the audience. Audience members were given copies of the reenactment timeline with brief explanations of performances at various sites.

A caravan comprising a church bus (bearing the slogan "Bible Fed, Spiritually Led"), twenty-five cars, and one large van traveled to the three reenactment sites under law enforcement escort. We were assigned to ride the bus, the lead vehicle in the caravan. The ride featured Hattie Lawson narrating again the original incident. As she spoke, passengers talked about their relationship to the reenactment. Several lynch mob reenactors discussed how to handle the media, the intensity of past performances, and their motivation for participating in the reenactment. They spoke of African American friends and co-workers who had shared their family histories of race trauma. Many reflected on their previous experiences of feeling emotionally drained after the performance. They joked with us and others about their performances as white supremacist murderers, declaring, "We're just actors, you know!" Precisely whom they were reassuring was unclear.

At key intersections, Sheriff's cruisers stopped traffic to permit the caravan to proceed. Other law enforcement vehicles were already at the Hester farm to monitor traffic flow and reenactor safety. As rehearsed, the reenactors repeatedly performed the violent altercation between Barney Hester and Roger Malcolm along the right-of-way until the entire caravan had passed. Bobby Howard narrated the scene with a bullhorn; Tyrone Brooks held aloft a sign captioning the scene. Amateur videographer Judy Conder exited the bus to record the scene. We exited as well. As soon as the caravan passed, performers moved quickly to the second tableau site in downtown Monroe. When we rejoined the bus for the trip to the Moore's Ford Bridge, the reenactors teased us: "Never get off the bus at the Hester farm! Those people don't like us!"

At the Walton County Courthouse Annex building, spectators were directed to Walter Reeves's race-baiting speech as Gov. Eugene Talmadge. Walter constructed his script from excerpts of Talmadge's speeches. Some spectators appeared offended by the racist sentiments and language; others laugh openly.[9] As Walter concluded, facilitators directed the spectators to the nearby jail site where Loy Harrison (Bert Skellie) bailed out Roger Malcolm while Dorothy, Mae and George looked on. This scene unfolded quickly as reenactors scrambled to the third and final scene at Moore's Ford Bridge. The caravan reformed for the thirty minute drive to the lynching site. As we approached the Moore's Ford site, the mood of the reenactors shifted and chatter abated abruptly. "This is the longest ride, the last ride," said one reenactor, referencing both performance anxiety and the fates of the Malcolms and the Dorseys.

The scene at Moore's Ford Bridge was frenetic. Facilitators supervised parking, crowd management and spatial boundaries. Media professionals grumbled because they were not allowed inside the performance space marked by the yellow caution tape; some in the press section audibly mocked the sincerity of the reenactors and the production. As spectators milled about in hushed anticipation, lynch mob reenactors donned costumes, checked props and waited quietly in the woods lining the road. Using a bullhorn, Tyrone Brooks announced that the reenactment was starting, and the car driven slowly by Loy Harrison and carrying George, Mae, Roger and Dorothy arrived. Spectators ringed the scene on the road, as facilitators quieted them and moved them back from the performance space. The lynch party emerged from the woods; the crowd became hushed and solemn. Some spectators held hands as they watched. The elderly Sarah Maddox, cousin to murdered Mae Dorsey, sat in a lawn chair near the bridge, weeping and crying out softly, "lord have mercy, lord have mercy." Professional media workers appeared unmoved.

The perpetrators menaced the car's occupants with slurs and spitting. They pulled Roger and then George from the car. Then, Dorothy and Mae were dragged from the backseat, screaming and clinging to the car door handles. Roger and George pleaded for the women's lives. Spectators stood transfixed as the lynch party reenactors "broke" the women's arms; some moaned softly as they watched. Many spectators took photos throughout the performed scene. The reenactors moved from the road, down the steep embankment and into the field of execution. As the victim reenactors were dragged down the slope to the killing site, spectators from the road joined those already assembled in the designated viewing area. As rehearsed, on the count of three the lynch mob reenactors fired at the victims in concert with the staccato beat of the snare drum and the crackle of firecrackers. The victim reenactors slowly fell to the ground, freezing twice on their way down. After they collapsed, the command was given twice more to fire volleys into the victims' bodies. The echoing sounds of simulated gunfire filled the sultry late-afternoon air. The acrid aroma of gunpowder from the firecrackers lingered; clouds of smoke drifted upward. Silence dominated the scene as reenactors froze and spectators stood mute. The liminality of reenactment was palpable.

One perpetrator moved forward and squirted simulated blood on the fallen victims. Another pulled out a knife belt and performed the excision of a small, anatomically correct male black baby doll from Dorothy's body. He threw the doll down by Dorothy's head. At this moment an African American woman in a church choir robe stepped into the performance space and began to sings the hymn "Precious Lord." As she finished the first verse, Bobbie signaled the professional media to enter the space and photograph the reenactors holding their poses as murdered victims. Bobbie re-entered the space and helped the actors to their feet, hugging each in turn. The silence broke. In the moments after the performance several of the reenactors hugged and wept in anguish. Spectators talked animatedly and shared their affective experience with the reenactors, the press, and each other. On the ride back to the church, most of those who portrayed the perpetrators were deep in reflection. Most were beset with a sense of *aporia*, incapable of articulating their feelings and thoughts; several simply offered us their apologies.

Participants and spectators reconvened at the First African Baptist Church for a locally catered meal and conversation. The mood was upbeat and celebratory. There were widespread expressions of pride in having contributed to the day's significance. Several local residents asked us how we felt about the reenactment: "Are you glad you came? Was it worth it?" In part, the questions suggested that local citizens gauged the importance of the reenactment by the length of our journey. But they also underscored our status as outsiders perceived as having little or no experience with the culture and history of the Deep South. Word had spread that we exited the bus at the Hester farm; we were told "how things work in small rural towns." Some locals were nervous about the reenactment: "After you leave, we still live here. They hold the mortgages and they can make things very uncomfortable." Implicit in the utterance is the assumption that we knew who "they" were, without being told.

Concluding Observations

The performances we observed confirmed for us the manner in which the components of the lynching performance complex are integrated with conspiracy narration, attention to sensory experience, and liminal space. The formal orations at the church rally, on the bus, and at the three reenactment sites narrativized the original conspiracy. The Reenactment opened a liminal space of possibility for witnessing historical injustice then, and motivating activism now.

In this coalition we observed the impact of the traumas of race violence upon two communities of memory. Despite their mutual commitment to a progressive racial politics, struggles to shape and control the reenactment produced a rupture, centering upon the ritual excision of an unborn male child from Dorothy Malcolm's body.

We listened to WAND-affiliated reenactors as we returned to Atlanta. Many were dismayed by the ritual excision of the unborn child, now named

"Justice." Bobbie Paul was irate that the contractual promise with Tyrone Brooks and reenactor Betty Maddox was broken. For Bobbie, the naming of "Justice" was further evidence that a pro-life agenda was being imposed upon the reenactment, a political act of gender appropriation by patriarchal and socio-religious conservative interests. For her, this violation created a breach that could not be redressed. Since 2008, WAND has no longer been institutionally affiliated with Moore's Ford.

Our immersion in the Moore's Ford Lynching Reenactment enabled us to appreciate how reenactment provides the opportunity to experience the past viscerally, to occupy the moral position of witness, and to construct memory of the past affectively through the liminal space that performance opens. To illustrate this opportunity, we juxtapose Reginald Marsh's 1934 anti-lynching illustration, "This Is Her First Lynching," with a photograph highlighting of one of the young spectators at the 2008 reenactment.[10]

The visual homology we construct with these images inverts a relationship between past and present which reveals the possibility for witnessing historical injustice. Marsh's illustration comments on the disturbing practice of white families taking their children to lynching scenes. Positioned amidst black witnesses, the contemporary photo features the white daughter of the family that made their land available for the performance.

Figure 1.1: Reginald Marsh, 1934, "This is her first lynching."

Figure 1.2: 2008, "This is her first lynching, redux" (Photo by P. Ehrenhaus).

Despite opportunities for moral witnessing and reconciliation, the reenactment was infused with an array of tensions that mitigated some of its goals. We question whether any surviving perpetrators will be identified for financial reward or come forward, awakened by moral conscience. (In the subsequent years none has.) But we saw compelling evidence of how reenactors, facilitators and spectators drew their own restorative justice from the performance. We observed earnest dedication to social justice and activism, and to selfless cooperation by people whose life circumstances and experiences differ dramatically; yet we also saw how differing relationships to the traumas of race violence in two communities of memory was manifested in struggles over how best to give presence to the past.

At the center of the 2008 Moore's Ford reenactment was an entanglement of race and gender. On one hand was WAND's commitment to women's agency and activism, and to the reproductive politics entailed by that commitment. Alternatively, we saw the local black community's resolve to reveal the conspiracy of silence regarding publicly celebrated violence against black women and children. And in this entanglement, in agreements reached and then breached, and in public performance, we encountered the "performative constitution of race and gender" and the "rhetorical use of performance in disputes" (Fuoss, 1997, p. 5).

Both communities of memory are inheritors of a national legacy of race trauma, yet their historical trajectories place them in disparate relationships to memory of race violence and race lynching—and to the obligations and opportunities for creating memory through reenactment. One community willingly admits that they stand as beneficiaries of an economic and social system borne of white supremacy. Their pursuit of racial justice and racial reconciliation derives from acknowledging their privilege, and it motivates many from the white Atlanta activist community to reenact the roles of the morally corrupt Moore's Ford lynchers. Responsible *to* the past, these reenactors find expiation through performance. The rural black community bears no responsibility for the horrors of race lynching. Nor have they benefited from a white supremacist system against which they still struggle. Beyond the pragmatic goal of bringing surviving perpetrators to justice, this community finds restitution and reparation through public performance that reveals what had been concealed. And as a vehicle to affectively constitute meanings of the past in the present, this community claims its right to expand the reenactment metonymically to proclaim that all black lives—potential and actual—is sacred.[11]

For the local black community, the liminal space of the reenactment produces and reproduces affective memory of racial subordination and victimization, and of moral agency and resistance. The voice of agency and resistance declares the legitimacy and importance of *black life* as cultural experience and as individual human sanctity. This voice names the unborn child "Justice" and cuts him from Dorothy Malcolm's womb, alluding to the 1918 lynching of Mary Turner and the documented excision of her unborn child.[12] This voice proclaims we must remember that such things did happen.

Performance, as Bobbie Paul observed, is a productive space for truth telling and healing. Yet as the 2008 Moore's Ford Lynching Reenactment coalition demonstrated by its fracture at the intersections of race, gender, and religious faith, productive spaces can also be highly contested sites for negotiating and constructing public memory.

Notes

1 Some materials in this chapter appear in Owen, A. S. & Ehrenhaus, P. (2014). The Moore's Ford Lynching Reenactment: Affective memory and race trauma. *Text and Performance Quarterly*, 34, 72–90.
2 Among these are Abbeville, SC, Atlanta, GA, Chattanooga, TN, Duluth, MN, Greensboro, NC, Tulsa, OK, Waco, TX, and Wilmington, NC. Atlanta (1906), Tulsa (1921), and Wilmington (1898) were sites of mass violence against African Americans.
3 The reenactment began in 2005. Our work pertains to the 2008 performance.

4 Reports on the number of perpetrators vary. A grand jury hearing in 1946 developed a list of 55 names.
5 Fuoss (1999) characterizes lynchings as "performance-saturated events" (p. 5) and identifies five strands of the performance complex; his focus in this essay is upon two of those strands.
6 WAND was founded by Dr. Helen Caldicott as Women Against Nuclear Destruction in 1982. WAND later became Women's Action for New Directions. Bobbie Paul was asked to direct the reenactment by the Moore's Ford Memorial Committee because of her formal education in drama.
7 The current owners of the property gave their permission and support for the reenactment.
8 Brooks is founding member of GABEO, Georgia Association of Black Elected Officials. As the most prominent public face of the Reenactment, Brooks made the agreement with Bobbie Paul to delete the excision of the fetus from the performance.
9 Reeves's Talmadge speech offers insight into the liminal experiential space created by reenactment and its role in creating affective memory. Spectators' laughter suggests that some experienced the "then" of "1946 white racists" while others were in the temporal "now," and disparaged Talmadge's racism.
10 Marsh's illustration was first published in *The New Yorker*, September 8, 1934, and reprinted in *The Crisis* in January 1935.
11 We intentionally use the phrase "all black life" rather than "all black lives," precisely because this 2008 reenactment preceded the emergence of the Black Lives Matter movement in 2013 and 2014. Nonetheless, the connections and continuities of historic and contemporary race violence, are indisputable.
12 Mary Turner's lynching on May 16, 1918, in Valdosta, GA, is among the most horrific on record. Mary and her husband, Haynes, worked for a wealthy white farmer, Hampton Smith, who was murdered by an unknown assailant. Smith's wife accused a local black man, who fled. A white lynch mob selected ten black men, including Haynes Turner, in retaliation. Because Mary sought redress from local law enforcement, she, too, was lynched—hung by her ankles, doused with gasoline, and burned alive. Her eight-month-old fetus was cut from her abdomen and crushed (See Armstrong, 2011; Dray, 2002; Zangrando, 1980).

References

Armstrong, J. B. (2011). Mary Turner, hidden memory, and narrative possibility. In E. M. Simien (Ed.), *Gender and lynching: The politics of memory* (pp. 15–35). New York, NY: Palgrave Macmillan.

Caruth, C. (1996). *Unclaimed experience: Trauma, narrative, and history*. Baltimore, MD: Johns Hopkins University Press.

Dray, P. (2002). *At the hands of persons unknown: The lynching of Black America*. New York, NY: Random House.

Ehrenhaus, P., & Owen, A. S. (2004). Race lynching and Christian evangelicalism: Performances of faith. *Text and Performance Quarterly, 24*, 276–301.

Fenster, M. (1999). *Conspiracy theories: Secrecy and power in American culture.* Minneapolis, MN: University of Minnesota Press.

Fuoss, K. W. (1997). *Striking performances/performing strikes.* Jackson, MS: University Press of Mississippi.

Fuoss, K. W. (1999). Lynching performances, theatres of violence. *Text and Performance Quarterly, 19,* 1–37.

Jorgensen, D. J. (1989). *Participant observation: A methodology for human studies.* Newbury Park, CA: Sage.

Lofland, J., & Lofland, L. H. (1995). *Analyzing social settings: A guide to qualitative observation and analysis* (3rd ed.). Belmont, CA: Wadsworth.

Lowenthal, D. (1999). Preface. In A. Forty & S. Kuchler (Eds.), *The art of forgetting* (pp. xi–xiii). Oxford, UK: Berg.

McCalman, I., & Pickering, P. A. (2010). From realism to the affective turn: An agenda. In I. McCalman & P. A. Pickering (Eds.), *Historical reenactment: From realism to the affective turn* (pp. 1–17). New York, NY: Palgrave Macmillan.

Owen, A. S., & Ehrenhaus, P. (2010). Communities of memory, entanglements, and claims of the past on the present: Reading race trauma through *The Green Mile.* *Critical Studies in Media Communication, 27,* 131–154.

Schneider, R. (2011). *Performing remains: Art and war in times of theatrical reenactment.* London, UK: Routledge.

Simon, R. I., Rosenberg, S., & Eppert, C. (2000). The pedagogical encounter of historical remembrance. In R. I. Simon, S. Rosenberg, & C. Eppert (Eds.), *Between hope and despair: Pedagogy and the remembrance of historical trauma* (pp. 1–8). Lanham, MD: Rowman & Littlefield.

Sturken, M. (2007). *Tourists of history: Memory, kitsch, and consumerism from Oklahoma City to Ground Zero.* Durham, NC: Duke University Press.

Turner, V. (1980). Social dramas and stories about them. *Critical Inquiry, 7,* 141–168.

Turner, V. (1986). Dewey, Dilthey, and drama: An essay in the anthropology of experience. In V. W. Turner & E. M. Bruner (Eds.), *The anthropology of experience* (pp. 33–44). Urbana, IL: University of Illinois Press.

Wexler, L. (2003). *Fire in a canebrake: The last mass lynching in America.* New York, NY: Scribner.

"Who We Are." *Georgia WAND.* Retrieved from https://gawand.org/who-is-georgia-wand/.

Zangrando, R. (1980). *The NAACP crusade against lynching, 1909–1950.* Philadelphia, PA: Temple University Press.

2. (Be)Coming Home: Transformative Places and Koreamerican Identity in Itaewon, South Korea

Eun Young Lee
Central Washington University

Alberto González
Bowling Green State University

The transnational movements of people, information, and economy that have affected South Korean culture on various levels reveal a new transformative space in which Korean identity discourse is increasingly complicated. In communication studies, scholarship on space and place has flourished for the last two decades. Many studies explore how identities are constructed through spatial means of communication (Clark, 2004; Dickinson, 1997; Enck-Wanzwer, 2011; Ewalt, 2011; Gallagher & LaWare, 2010). The symbolic and material elements of spatial rhetoric are articulated in examinations of memorials, museums, and monuments (Halloran & Clark, 2006; Zagacki & Gallagher, 2009). The purview of these rhetorical studies extends to urban sites and landscapes (Clark, 2004; Dickinson, 2015; Fleming 2008; Lee, 2015). Our goal in this study is to reveal urban spaces as socially constructed environments within which intercultural encounters circulate (Lee, 2015). Particularly in an effort to comprehend the changing identity discourses in South Korean culture, we direct our attention to the intercultural urban environment in which a range of identities are performed and interact. We argue that Koreamericans (people born in the U.S. who are of Korean heritage) uniquely valorize and disrupt the notion of *Han minjok* (one Korean identity) through the transformative spatial and material rhetorics performed in Mexican food restaurants in Seoul. Our focus is *Itaewon*, the distinctive multicultural district in Seoul, South Korea, known for its global openness and its distance from Korean cultural conservatism.

According to the Korean census, there have been drastic changes to the demographic makeup of the country due primarily to steady immigration from Asian countries. Additionally, the number of international students has continuously increased throughout the last decade (Korean Statistical Information Service, 2016). In the meantime, an increasing number of Koreans are of mixed heritage, such as Koreamerican and Korean Chinese (Korean Statistical Information Service, 2016). Rather than being resistant to change, Koreans are adapting to a new demographic environment. As Shin (2019) notes, "Korean society has emphasized the necessity of Koreans living together with mixed-race or foreign people on the peninsula" (Shin, p 62). Population changes are becoming more and more visible in Korea and especially in the city of Seoul. In this context, this essay seeks to illustrate how Itaewon operates for Koreamericans, sojourners who aspire to contribute to the homeland of their cultural heritage, as a space to enact their identities. In doing so, we explore and critique how Itaewon facilitates a unique intercultural space for Koreamericans in South Korea.

Along with examining Itaewon as the intercultural urban space containing possibilities for transformations, where identity transformation is welcomed and even celebrated, we strive to initiate discussion about a more diversified and complicated understanding of Korean identity that, we argue, has become possible partly through Koreamericans in Itaewon as rhetorical agents who perform evolving identities while crossing geophysical, cultural, and discursive borders. The identities of Koreamericans have evolved by crossing not only nation-states but also by crossing discursive borders within the Westernized hybrid cultures of Itaewon and Korean indigenous culture. Further, the material presence of Koreamericans in Itaewon allows the urban environment to play a role in constituting a more complex Korean identity.

Endres and Senda-Cook (2011) argue that "places, imbued with meaning and consequences, are rhetorical performances" (p. 260). With that in mind, we approach the restaurants founded and operated by Koreamericans in Itaewon as intercultural rhetorical sites within which cultural identities and memories are constituted and mediated. We focus on two restaurants, *Coreanos* and *Vatos*, which gain rhetorical significance in part due to their location in the city and also through the complex interplays of physical, political, historical, and cultural resources. Following the idea that "the urban built environment is communicative: It contributes to transforming and reproducing major ideological and structural conditions that, quite literally, mediate the everyday lives of individuals and communities" (Dickinson & Aiello, 2016, p. 1295), this study explores how Koreamericans and their material rhetoric in Itaewon are influencing (re)negotiations of Korean identity in the nation's capital city. Also, given that food can be a rhetorical means of human agency to signify cultural associations and thus (cultural) identities (Shugart, 2008), this study, then, approaches food, restaurant layout, and menu items as material elements that rhetorically advance a new cultural being or sensibility.

These restaurants have been well received by people in/of Korea, which is evidenced by their expansions to other areas in Seoul throughout the last couple of years. Having been introduced in the early 2010s, as of 2017, they have three to four locations beyond Itaewon. As "materiality and symbolicity are entwined and enmeshed" (Dickinson, 2015, p. 12), throughout this analysis, we seek to demonstrate how those restaurants' material and symbolic performances make present the cultural identities and experiences of Koreamericans. Especially as food becomes more and more "necessary for lifestyle" and "available for signification" (Cooks, 2009, p. 95), we argue that food items serve to highlight the cultural experiences and memories of Koreamericans, making those valuable and visible. Therefore, a part of the primary intention of this study is to address the following question: "How do we perform *through* food to constitute, resist, and critique the politics of power and identity?" (Cooks, 2009, p. 96, emphasis in original). By attending to the restaurants as cultural spaces, we argue that there is a shift in the social nexus of Korea due to the dismantling of the traditional binary of Korean identity, namely Korean or non-Korean (Shin, 2006). Then we examine how this shift alters identity politics in Korea.

As Mountford (2001) illuminates that "rhetorical spaces carry the residue of history upon them, but also, perhaps something else: a physical representation of relationships and ideas" (p. 42), such an examination of the dynamic between Koreamericans and Koreans in terms of their negotiations of identities helps us deepen our understanding of a complex nexus of the (re) creation of identity in the era of increasing transnational movements. In the following section, we briefly illuminate the rhetorical landscape of Itaewon in terms of the ways in which it works to (re)negotiate Korean identities. We also introduce the two restaurants under our examination, *Coreanos Kitchen* and *Vatos: Urban Tacos*. First, we contextualize this case study in concepts of diasporic citizenship and cultural belonging.

Diaspora and (a Sense of) Home

The notion of a fixed sense of national identity that is primarily based on race and birthplace has been critiqued (Buisseret, 2000; Gilroy, 1993; Siu, 2005). Siu (2005) notes, "citizenship has become widely accepted as a set of cultural and social processes rather than simply a political status or juridical contract" (p. 7). Adopting this view, our approach to Koreamerican identity deploys the idea of "cultural citizenship" as a framework. Cultural citizenship allows us to keep our flexibility in understanding Koreamerican identity in terms of subject formation. We want to understand their "diasporic subject formation" (Siu, 2005, p. 13) by paying attention to how Koreamericans mediate their marginality in Korea with the "practices of belonging" (p. 6) that Koreamericans engage to affirm their heritage. Gilroy (1993) urges cultural critics to challenge "the ontological essentialist view" (p. 31) by adopting a view that takes an identity of people who traverse as something "routed" (p. 28). His emphasis on the routes instead of roots helps us to shift our focus to the processual nature of transnational living. Such a framework unveils in the Korean context, "the tragic popularity of ideas about the integrity and purity of cultures" (Gilroy, 1993, p. 7). Particularly in terms of foodways, "a relational approach gives dynamism to what could otherwise be a very static analysis of how a group's foodways are rooted in timeless tradition" (Wilk, 2012, p. 30).

The return of Koreamericans occurs at a time of a hyper-charged political economy driven by what Lie (2015) calls the South Korean "export imperative" (p. 114). K-pop, electronics, home appliances, and cars are targeted primarily to overseas markets, not domestic markets. Through globalization, Koreamericans (in Texas or elsewhere) are never removed from the material reminders of their homeland. Siu (2005) contends that, "our increasingly interconnected world is changing the way we think, feel, act, and imagine ourselves in relation to home and community" (p. 207). For Koreamericans, the material and quotidian reminders of South Korea are dynamic and provide an avenue toward belonging. Siu emphasizes the contingency of belonging and highlights the complexity of affiliations that diasporic persons enact, affiliations that may be continuous or ruptured in the process of "diasporic subject formation" (p. 13). Those continuities and ruptures, an inevitable consequence of border crossings, are sources of cultural syncretism (Rath, 2000).

Koreamericans in Itaewon

> Where people live, work, and play – the geographies they negotiate, the situations they find themselves in, the physical and human environments in which they think, act, and interact – these influence, directly and indirectly, subtly and forcefully, the experience they have, the people they know, the skills and habits they develop, the values they acquire (Fleming, City of Rhetoric, 2008, p. 185)

Itaewon, located at the center of the capital city of South Korea, is a very distinctive urbanscape that is primarily a result of its closeness to a longstanding U.S. military base. Organically starting to function as a comfort town for U.S. military personnel since the Korean War, Itaewon has become distinctively internationalized throughout the rest of the 20th century (Choi, 2002; Lee, 2015). Endres and Senda-Cook (2011) clearly point out that "Places exist in the interrelationship with spaces . . . influenced by and influences spatial structures . . . that links localities into broader social structures and practices" (p. 260). Around the beginning of the 21st century, the dominant Western character of Itaewon has given way to a multicultural urban space with a greater variety of diasporic identities flowing into the district, taking advantage of the openness Itaewon provides in an arguably conservative and purist cultural atmosphere of South Korea (Hur, 2013; Lee, 2015).

Amid the sojourners, expats, and tourists in Itaewon, there are Koreamericans. Korean immigration to the U.S. began in the early 1900s when the small number of Koreans went to Hawai'i as farm laborers (Kim, 2008). Since then, however, the major wave of Korean immigrants to the U.S. occurred around the mid-1960s with the U.S. immigration policy reform (Kang, 2013; Kim, 2008; Yuh, 2005). In the modern history of South Korean emigration, until 2003, the U.S. was the most common destination, followed by China (Korean Statistical Information Service, 2016). The trend makes sense in that the U.S. has been one of the most influential Western countries in South Korea ever since the Korean War of the 1950s as a flow of migration tends to be "molded by the history of prior relationships between the country of origins and those of potential destination" (Portes & Stepick, 2003, p. 308). However, given the relatively shorter span of Korean immigrants to the U.S., the discussion has been scarce concerning Koreamericans sojourning to Korea with their U.S. citizenship. No significant number of Koreamericans back to Korea has been recorded until 2010. Since 2010 (and coinciding with the explosive growth of Korean exports), the number of Koreamericans visiting and staying in Korea has steadily increased (Korean Statistical Information Service, 2016). From 2015 to 2016, for example, the number of Koreamericans who came to Korea with an F-4 visa, which allows Koreamericans to stay in South Korea, increased by 12.9% (Korean Statistical Information Service, 2016).

Within this context, Koreamericans seem to be flowing into Itaewon. It is not rare to find American-themed bars and restaurants, and several are operated by Koreamericans. Especially in the last several years, the new fusion cuisine, Korean-Mexican food (more accurately Korean-Tex-Mex), has been gaining popularity in South Korea. Two restaurants in Itaewon, *Coreanos* and *Vatos*, have become the spearhead of the scene for cultural transformation in the Korean cultural landscape. Both restaurants are founded and run by Koreamericans. *Coreanos* means Korean in Spanish (*Coreanos*'s Facebook page). A food truck with the same name that was operated by the founders in Austin, Texas, since 2010, is the inspiration for this restaurant. They opened their place, *Coreanos Kitchen*, in Itaewon in 2014. Two founders of *Coreanos*, Gene Cho and James Kwon, lived in California and Texas until they moved to South Korea.

Vatos is a "Mexican slang meaning men or dudes" (*Vatos* Website). Co-founders and owners of *Vatos* are three men, Kenny Park, Juweon Jonathan Kim, and Sid Kim. On their website, they explain who they are as follows:

> Vatos Urban Tacos sprang from the minds (and bellies) of three Korean-Americans who wanted to offer a new type of dining experience in Korea. Kenny and Sid hail from Southern California, and Juweon planted his roots in Texas; hence, all three spent the majority of their lives growing up on authentic Mexican food. Simultaneously, all three were fed a steady diet of home-made Korean food lovingly prepared by their first generation mothers. Inevitably, such an environment led to the natural progression towards Korean-Mexican fusion cuisine. (*Vatos* Website)

The restaurant initially planned by Kenny Park was originally named "Seoul Taco" in 2011. He created a video to get funding from *Kickstarter* and started the campaign called "Seoul Taco: Tacos for the Seoul!" It is also important to remember that one of the motivations for Kenny to come up with the idea for the restaurant was that he was missing foods he used to have in California and found his friends from the U.S. also had the same struggles in South Korea. Therefore, *Vatos* caters not only to Koreans who are introduced to Tex-Mex food but also to Koreamericans who miss "a taste of home" (Olozia, *T Magazine*, 2013). When opening the restaurant in Itaewon in November that year, Seoul Taco became *Vatos Urban Tacos*. In 2015, John Kerry, then the U.S. Secretary of State, visited *Vatos* during his visit to South Korea. His visit boosted the restaurant's profile and authenticity among Korean customers. In their eyes, it was now certified even by the Americans as well.

Postcolonial critic Raka Shome (2003) contends that, "[Space] functions as a technology – a means and medium – of power that is socially constituted through material relations that enable the communication of specific politics" (p. 40); hence, the materiality of Itaewon as an urban environment, which has emerged as the Americanized space, makes it accessible and porous for various cultures. The flexibility and permeability, which characterize the district on symbolic and material levels, drive its spatial rhetoricity within which borders are embodied and embraced. The urbanscape of Itaewon is a manifestation of cultural border-livings that originate from the shared border with the U.S. military base adjacent to it. On such a multicultural landscape that has been designed to mediate cultures and to translate them into commerce, *Coreanos* and *Vatos* are located. The liminality of Itaewon is ideally suited for the Koreamericans. The enactments of "Korean Americanness" by Koreamerican sojourners transform Korean culture internally, in the heart of Seoul, since "Spaces have heuristic power over their inhabitants and spectators by forcing them to change both their behavior (walls cause us to turn right or left; skyscrapers draw the eye up) and, sometimes, their view of themselves" (Mountford, 2001, p. 50). For example, from the balcony of *Coreanos*, patrons can see the U.S. military base that borders Itaewon-ro, the main street of Itaewon. People dining at *Coreanos* get to visually consume the suburban look of the military base with its trees and lawns and American-style houses. That is as American as it can get. Both restaurants thread the fabric of the urbanscape as critical nodes that continue to stimulate the Korean disposition toward globalism. As Dickinson and Aiello (2016) argue, "the bricks and mortar of cities and their contribution to both enabling and impeding particular actions, identities, and practices" (p. 1295), offers Koreamericans the possibility of imagining and enacting cultural citizenship. In doing so, Koreamericans (re)create Itaewon as a transnational and transcultural place in South Korea. In attempting to understand the spatial practices contextualized within intercultural communicative acts in the era of transnationalism, we note what Asante and Miike (2013) suggest as a caveat:

> It is not so meaningful for intercultural communication critics to merely demonstrate that cultures are internally complex and historically hybrid. What they ought to do is to assess the trajectories and directions of cultural hybridity in postmodern spaces toward the healthy and balanced centering of cultural heritage. (Asante & Miike, 2013, p. 9)

In addition, with the premise that rhetorical space entails a cultural dimension as well as a material dimension (Lefebvre, 1984; Mountford, 2001), our analysis attends to the materiality of Itaewon's cultural landscape and its relations to the restaurants that are the focus of our study. In what follows, we begin with describing the restaurants and then interpret how these Koreamerican spaces provide ways to understand belonging and identity in South Korea.

The Restaurants

Koreamerican owned restaurants, especially *Vatos* and *Coreanos*, are important anchors in the urban landscape of Itaewon. Their visibility comes from their popularity and elevated spots along the main street, Itaewon-ro.

Coreanos is located on the hill close to the west entry of Itaewon. This particular hillside has been rapidly developed in the last few years and *Coreanos* has been largely responsible. *Vatos* is also plainly visible from most of the western portion of the main street. In addition to their now well-known signboard and logo, crowds lining up especially during dinnertime and over weekends make the restaurant hard to ignore. To accommodate the increasing number of customers, the restaurant was expanded in 2015. The placement of the restaurants works with discursive aspects of the places as well. Their names are quite clearly situate them among Koreans (*Coreanos*), Americans (written in English), and cosmopolitan (*Urban tacos*) sensibilities.

Shome (2003) argues, "The materiality … of spatial relations and how one is distributed within those relations raises issues about access and mobility that are usually not addressed" (p. 44). Urban space, for example, can be a site that provides us a way to understand how such spatial practices as "representations of space" and "representational spaces" (Lefebvre, 1983) come to create the identity of an urban site especially in terms of being "intertwined with the individual lives of the people living through the site" (Simpson, 1999, p. 313). It is important to note that urban space is being produced by a complex dialectic between what it is and how it is taken up, which constitute its identity.

In the nexus of various parts of the district, these restaurants em*place* themselves into the cultural grid and in doing so they invite new subject relations as "Spaces are *productive* of meaning as well as endowed with meaning" (Mountford, 2001, p. 58). The physical, therefore material, emplacement of the restaurants and their success as businesses, demarcate their value on the cultural and mental map of Seoul. In turn, the spatialization of the restaurants directs customer attention to the intercultural aspects of their dining experiences and to their own participation in the transnational and transcultural era of globalization. The space of these restaurants as a "material and cultural communicative form" (Dickinson & Aiello, 2016, p. 1297) invites people to experience the biculturalism of Koreamericans. Diners experience the culture within the space because of the particular way that space is structured. The restaurants manifest American ways of using space beyond cultural artifacts and references on their walls. Bars and balconies, for example, reproduce American preferences for a casual and social atmosphere. "People watching" is inescapable due to the large open indoor and outdoor seating spaces. Figuring out how to move your body is to know how to properly engage with the world. The movement of bodies within the sites is conscious and preconscious (Dickinson and Aiello, 2016), therefore being in the restaurants structured by different spatial norms and being conscious about how to move your body (what to do and where to go, for instance) reformulate diners' awareness, which is a part of the (re)culturing transformation. Navigating themselves in the restaurants that are assembled in American ways, people experience the culture, the way of living.

The way the two restaurants are designed—with a bar section and dining areas (dining tables)—also recreates American ways (or, surely non-Korean ways) of structuring the space that distinguishes them from prototypal Korean diners. The restaurants facilitate socializing across tables and accommodate individualism by offering "combo" or mixed-item platters as well as a variety of side dishes. In traditional *banchan* (side dishes that accompany a Korean meal), the diner does not choose the side dishes, they are provided with the meal. A full bar with a tip jar on it (tipping is not a part of Korean custom) and spacious outdoor balcony/patio distinguish these restaurants from typical dining places in Korea as those are the features that appeal to people with desires for the Western (read: American) and international experiences. In this way, the restaurants become an "aspirational place" (Simon, 2009, p. 332) in which diners can imagine themselves in South Texas or Southern California.

Bars with the variety of draft beers on tap, which have become one of the newest culinary and cultural trends in Korea nowadays, and tall bar stools are the American look of restaurants and taverns, or at least nominally so. The option of choosing to dine or drink either at the bar or table is the American custom, that is, American habitus to which these Koreamericans are accustomed. Although there are few visible signs that indicate that these are American-themed restaurants, there are unexpected norms, for example, people need to "wait to be seated" (not a typical custom that would be experienced in most Korean restaurants). An open-kitchen concept also adds a contemporary appeal to the space. Even baby booster seats—rarely found in typical Korean restaurants—are stacked in a corner ready for use. As little as those seats are, they create a discernible mood of American flexibility and inclusion that most Koreans would notice and many tourists would expect.

Furthermore, for the experience of being "worldly," the urban aesthetic of the restaurants speaks to the lifestyles of global nomads. For that purpose, the very spacious (given the density of the city generally and Itaewon in particular, the spaces these restaurants occupy are impressively big) balcony that looks out over Itaewon-ro, where flows of all kinds (people, vehicles of all sorts, and the occasional K-pop video shoot) are constant and eye-catching. Balconies and terraces are appealing for their rarity in the city of Seoul (Jeong, 2014) and thus their spatial significance is maximized. Instead of sitting inside of a cramped eatery where toilet tissue dispensers are used for napkins, people can sit outside where the border between inside and out-side becomes blurred. Those spaces such as terrace and balcony, which are legally allowed only in a few districts in the entire city, propel an affective (and sensual) intensity in the process of consumption. At the same time, enunciating the Western and American cultural space, the balcony and ter-race, both of which are also designed to be viewed by pedestrians from the streets below, are quite literally construed as a stage where people can per-form a cosmopolitan identity. Therefore, the "agentic materiality" of those distinctively spatialized sections of the restaurants, "directs attention to the ways in which material things ... co-produce the culture of which they are a part" (Dickinson & Aiello, 2016, p. 1297). Korean diners especially, are free to encounter the bicultural experience of Koreamericans and view it posi-tively. Through these ways of moving, diners "produce their own texts which become part of the identity of the place" (Simpson, 1999, p. 313).

On the other hand, the rhetorics of the restaurants can also be understood by what is not present. Adopting a modern quasi-brutalist design, the places do not use color; instead, color palates feature monotones such as black, gray, and brick colors. The ceiling and floor are dark gray, which is close to cement color. Pipes and air ducts are exposed. The brick walls are exposed. Tables and chairs are very minimalistic with few decorations on them. Chidester (2008) argues that texts can reveal "treatment of the racial Other as a form of visual and discursive absence" (p. 161). While the restaurant décor reveals a U.S.- informed sensibility, the connection to Mexico and Tex-Mex relations is hidden. *Coreanos* features an image of a mustachioed Mexican wearing a sombrero but any connections to Mexican culture or the origins of the dishes served are absent. Mexico, as a nation-state and as a cultural presence in the U.S. is without direct representation. Tex-Mex is already a hybrid cuisine that has emerged from the appropriation and commodification of Mexican and North American indigenous cultures. The restaurants successfully render invisible the Mexican presence in the U.S. and they elide the very cultural influences and histories that the Koreamerican founders experienced as resi-dents in Latinx dominated regions of the U.S.

Rather than designing a space with significations of a particular ethnic locality, these restaurants open up the space through which people can be offered opportunities to practice and/or enact their urban and worldly iden-tities. As these restaurants aspire to look like they could be in any metropol-itan city in the world (but probably imagined as to be in the U.S.), diners are invited to enact their urban and worldly selves. The restaurants, through their symbolic and material modes, exemplify, "a productive form of cultural citizenship" (Enck-Wanzer, 2011, p. 346) even as they ignore the historical immigration dynamics between the U.S. and Mexico. Similarly, the restaurants visually re-territorize the cultural scene of the city to create a new vision for Korean identity. The restaurants rhetorically repurpose the space so that it can be filled with new Western ways for Koreans to imagine themselves and the Koreamericans who make this experience possible. In doing so, the restaurants open up a space where new identities are created, transformed, and performed.

The Food

Shugart (2008) contends that "food functions as a form of communication" and highlights the "rhetorical function of food as a means to construct and negotiate cultural identity" (p. 70). Food and acts of creating and consuming food within designed spaces, then, can be understood as political performances of identity (Cooks, 2009). Also, the power and importance of such acts lie in their normality or everydayness (de Certeau et al., 1998). Organizing cultural politics on the daily-experienced urbanscape, the rhetorics of space in these restaurants are fueled by their foods when they intersect with nomadic-consumer bodies. Within this rhetoric, Koreamericans offer their foods as the imaginations of their being, which allow diners to identify with their transcultural and intercultural experiences and accept Koreamericans as cultural citizens.

> Food takes on even broader functions for negotiating our relationship to the world and to others. Whether thinking about food within the context of the environment and sustainability, health and obesity, globalization and localization, food has become a nexus of crucial conversations about our most intimate and embodied selves and our most social and abstract identities (Dickinson, 2015, *Suburban dreams*, p.101)

Food and food practices such as cooking and dining are performances that are informed by and reflect cultural identity. Dickinson (2015) suggests that they are "powerfully embodied topoi for thinking and performing contemporary culture" (p. 104). He continues to argue, "Connected to region and geography, food can help people imagine their place in the world . . . Food and food practices offer fully embodied and performative rhetorics of locality" (104).

Foods invented by Koreamericans, particularly those Korean-Mexican restaurants, are "a compellingly embodied rhetoric of locality" (Dickinson, 2015, p. 100). Pilcher (2014) points out how Mexican cuisine, particularly the taco, has been picked up by Koreamericans by fusing tacos with Korean home cooking. In other words, their food is at once their sense of their place of origin *and* their experience of moving across geographical and cultural places. The Koreamericans offer their food as a reminder of and as a testimony to those movements that connect them to a different time and place. Their foods invoke both a sense of pride in the Korean heritage and recognition of U.S. allegiance, that is, an intercultural hybridity that provides themselves and eaters with "particularly resonant ways of locating the body in reference to an idea of home and also in the context of globalization" (Dickinson, 2015, p. 100). At the same time, food fusion acknowledges the *local* understanding of the international reach and significance of Seoul as the center of the South Korean economy.

At *Coreanos*, food reifies, "being *Coreanos*." For example, *Three Wise Fries* is one of the most popular dishes on the menu. On their website, they introduce it as follows: "Voted best fries in America by Yahoo, *Travel*, and *US News*. Our fries are loaded with three meats (*galbi* beef, chicken, and al pastor pork), three different sauces, all topped with onions and cilantro. The fries have been our number one selling item since opening!" (*Coreanos* Website). *Galbi* (Korean for rib) beef is a staple of Korean barbeque. This is their signature menu that brought *Coreanos* to fame as is seen in news articles framed on the wall in the downstairs section of the restaurant. The articles tell customers that *Coreanos* was voted one of the best food trucks in the U.S. due to the Wise Fries. They also have *Pork Kimcheese Fries*, which has pork meat, kimchi, and cheese toppings. Their taco menu includes *Galbi* beef and pork belly tacos. Those two types of meats and the ways they are prepared (marinated or braised) are popular in the Korean restaurants. In the burritos section, the menu offers *Kimchi BKB burrito*, which is a kimchi and fried rice burrito. Kimchi is arguably the most known Korean food. The main components of this menu are *galbi* and kimchi. Those Korean cuisine-inspired ingredients are wrapped in a tortilla. Hence, the diner can "be Korean" and experience the Americanness of the Koreamericans.

A post on the *Coreanos* Facebook page states, "Our *Carne Asada Fries* are available across all four of our locations! A favorite from LA, it's perfect for some daydrinking" (July, 29, 2016). The Korean language version of this announcement says, "... The taste you used to enjoy in LA, enjoy it here in Seoul too!" (Translated from Korean by the first author.) The statement announces two things. First, it makes a clear connection to popularity in the U.S. Second, it appeals to people who are craving a certain taste enjoyed only back in LA. While *Coreanos Kitchen* serves anyone who likes or wants to try Mexican (fusion) food in Korea, it also specifically meets a demand from a certain demographic, arguably the many affluent-class Koreamericans who share the nostalgia of the U.S. We pointed out earlier that the increasing number of Koreamericans sojourning back to Korea is a relatively recent phenomenon. It is the relative scarcity of fusion-style restaurants like *Coreanos* that allows it to uniquely tap into the cultural memories of a slice of American culture and allows *Coreanos Kitchen*, in a dual sense, to provide returned Koreamericans with home.

Similarly, the *Vatos* brochure explains that their food is a "Korean-Mexican fusion that incorporates the *ssam* culture in the Korean cuisine into tacos from the Mexican cuisine" (translated from Korean by the first author). *Ssam* is a way Koreans enjoy barbecued meats such as marinated beef and grilled pork belly with vegetables such as lettuce. One puts pieces of grilled meats (typically grilled on a tabletop gas or electric stove) on a leaf of lettuce and adds more toppings and sauces according to preference. That is similar to how tacos are assembled. For the creators of the Korean-Mexican fusion, the founders/owners of *Vatos*, such similarities between two different cuisines became clear only because they have directly experienced the two. The hybrid cuisine reflects their hybrid identity. In other words, these foods reflect the way the creators of the food grew up in Southern California and Texas as Koreamericans. The path of their lives, memories, and experiences along the way is evoked in the recipes for Korean-Mexican cuisine.

In addition to the fusion dishes that embrace cultural hybridity, the burgers section, which is very American, reveals more directly their cultural influences. *Vatos* features three types of burgers including *SID Burger*, *Cali Burger*, and *Longhorn Burger*. Each burger represents one of the three co-founders of *Vatos*: Sid, Kenny who is from California, and Juweon who lived in Texas and is an alumnus of the University of Texas (whose mascot is *Bevo*, a Texas Longhorn). These are not a fusion of any kind but they are examples of how they represent their route from the U.S.

These food items are not simply about being global or being cosmopolitan but about the "route" to the U.S. of the first-generation emigrants and the return to Korea of the second generation. In the same vein, the hybridity of a good number of Korean-Mexican dishes couched in other non-fusion ones on the menus strengthens their rhetoric of belonging precisely for the paradoxical tension brought between something familiar and something not quite familiar at once. The familiar aspects of the foods assure comfort while the less-familiar dimensions invite an exciting global experience. Finnis (2012) contends that "the foods associated with inclusion, exclusion, taste, and distaste may change over time, which in turn may reshape social boundaries" (p. 5). In the same vein, the rhetorical function of the restaurant menus is to produce a particular vision of how to understand and place oneself in the global flow and reconsider the boundaries of belonging. The food locates and materializes ideas of border-living as "the gastronomic memory of diaspora" (Finnis, 2012, p. 9), which leads us to "understanding the ways we experience the everyday, practical reordering and mixing of food tradition with new ideas" (p. 10). The food practices reimagined by Koreamericans shift the aesthetics of taste and the criteria for belonging. In this sense, food is situated in the nexus of what Koreans and tourists desire and value. Consuming particular foods announces and directs our values and desires. Also, since food can be a less intimidating way to have an intercultural experience, the experience of eating could be pleasurable as well as instrumental to encountering a variety of cultural identities. These foods provide diners with ways to "an embodied experience of multiculturalism" (Dickinson, 2015, p. 106). That is, consuming food centers their (consumers/eaters) bodily experiences and constitutes their multicultural/cosmopolitan identities. In addition, the act of eating includes a range of activities from picking out a place to eat, deciding what to eat from the menu, which requires us to read through the menu, and figuring it out how to (properly) eat. These varying activities, especially reading and navigating through the menu, can be intercultural encounters. In these restaurants, customers are learning the cultural interactions as well as transformative processes in performing Koreamerican identity.

Conclusion

Shome (2003) argues, "Mobility in and of itself is neither good nor bad ... What matters are the material relations of empowerment and disempowerment that are enabled through the production of mobility" (p. 52). How do we understand the places of Koreamericans? Does their transnational and transcultural mobility produce an emancipatory potential for Koreans? Mannur (2007) observes that "Culinary discourse bears witness to the complicated historical processes that have occasioned international migration and diasporic dislocation" (p. 28). Throughout this analysis, our effort was to map how Koreamerican identities are constructed and shared by examining the elements of Koreamerican-operated Tex-Mex restaurants *Coreanos* and *Vatos*, in *Itaewon*. We examined the spatial rhetoric of Koreamerican identity as performed by Koreamericans in Korea and explored its possibilities for social transformation. By approaching the restaurants as rhetorical practices that mediate their hybrid identity with the dominant *Han* identity, we investigated the ways in which the physical appearance and locations of their stores, menus, and references challenged the ontology of *Han minjok* (one people) to transform traditional Korean understandings of Korean identity.

The particular memories shared among the co-founders of the restaurants are aspects of their identities which are reflected in their menu creations. Restaurants such as *Vatos* and *Coreanos* provide a physical place where layered memories are performed and where diners can enjoy the food they have missed from both homelands. Therefore, to a degree, their rhetoric is invitational; they create an environment that accepts Koreans who identify themselves in ways that would not necessarily line up with the nationalistic discourse of Korean identity. Those restaurants, therefore, ultimately serve to bridge a nationalistic distance between Koreans and Koreamericans. Pilcher (2014) argues that "the physical experiences of taste may well help to encourage the acceptance and naturalization of people" (p. 459) which allows Koreamericans to claim cultural citizenship in South Korea and make acceptable a new geocultural identity. As Pilcher further notes, "outsiders offer fresh perspectives on our society and help to reinterpret what it means to be Old Stock" (2014, p. 460).

Along with such possibility, the articulation of Koreamerican identity entails a potential to dismantle the essentialism undergirding Korean identity. This essentialism is sutured in Korean identity in terms of its ethnic specificity and results in cultivating the very particular way in which a notion of "foreign" is socially and culturally perceived, defined, and understood in identity discourses in South Korea. Pollock (1994) points out that, "Identity is so often a matter of origins" (p. 83), making a degree of connection between identity and nativity, the location of origin. This (un)conscious link is political to and has been "languaged" (Hall, 1986, cited in Grossberg) in Korean nationalist discourse. The predominant idea of the Korean identity, perpetuated by ethnic nationalism, has resulted in the conflation of national identity and cultural identity for Koreans. The distinction between those two different ways of defining identity becomes impossible to separate. Such a conflation in Korean identity discourse has brought about a very exclusionary identity politics in Korean culture and society. Thus, the construction of a delimited sense of Korean identity has benefited certain groups at the expense of others. Those whose identity would be defined with hyphens have been excluded from the mainstream discourse of identity and belonging in Korean. The articulation of a hybrid identity complicates the assumptions embedded in Korean identity discourse, assumptions which restrict the ways in which Koreans can imagine and define themselves. Within this circumstance, the presence and influence of Koreamericans attests to a gradual liberation from Korean essentialism. A fuller acknowledgement of the notion of Korean cultural identity and its variations disrupts the bedrock of the national identity discourse. Such disruptions possess the potential to facilitate constructive changes in identity politics of Korea.

Koreamericans enrich the meaning of what it means to be Korean through the newly constructed and acknowledged differences they project at the very heart of Korean society. Their acceptance as cultural citizens enriches the composite threads of the Korean people. Their visibility shifts not only the physical landscape of the urban space but also the cultural landscape of Korea. Those places, *Vatos* and *Coreanos*, invite people to enjoy the transnational exchange and difference and in so doing ultimately celebrate them. As such, the rhetorical practices in those places reveal the arbitrary set of divisions woven into identity politics in Korean culture. The dichotomy between Korean and foreign becomes obsolete for grasping their (Korean) identity.

Furthermore, debunking essentialism in the construction of Korean identity, the participation of Koreamericans leads us to reconsider the undoubtedly accepted and shared idea of home and the sense of ethnic and cultural purity. On one hand, the idea of home connotes a certain degree of purity and absolutism. In this sense, the idea of home is delimited, clear-cut either/ or, and exclusive. However, as this essay has shown, for many, hybridized culture itself *is* home. In this sense, "home" is a product of movement animated by memory. The cultural and social meaning of home is refined in understanding Koreamericans' rhetoric expressing their cultural identities through their own spaces. As Calafell (2004) states, "home was no longer a physical space but the feeling or affect created through the community" (p. 183). Koreamericans dislocated from their physical home not only expand but also complicate its meaning—home—as it is where you make yourself at home; where you *feel* home.

The restaurants, the spaces of enactments of a transnational hybrid being, invite people walking in the city to vicariously experience transformations through border-living. Their material rhetoric, then, opens opportunities to reflect on the extent to which essentialism is seeded in Koreans' perceptions of identities. Through the process of place-making, those restaurants as the embodied rhetoric of sojourners who are back in the land of their cultural heritage facilitate spaces for intercultural dialogue. Mediating their (re)territorializing of identities, those places are both the reflections of their identities as well as the sites of identity negotiations. In other words, *Vatos* and *Coreanos* are more or less the reflection of the consciousness of hybrid cultural identities. The restaurants act as "performative transgressions and potential transformations" (Cooks, 2009, p. 96). Therefore, these restaurants located on the cultural urbanscape of Itaewon function as "constitutive elements in the identity" (Dickinson, 1997, p. 19) for Koreamericans as well as Koreans in relation to Koreamericans. Those sites continue to (re)construct a community (of Koreamericans and their allies) through an ongoing public performance of identities, and promisingly, in a long term, establish ways in which memories of those identities are remembered in more culturally inclusive terms.

References

Asante, M., & Miike, Y. (2013). Paradigmatic issues in Intercultural Communication Studies: An Afrocentric-Asiacentric dialogue. *China Media Research, 9*(3), 1–19.

Buisseret, D., & Reinhardt, S. G. (2000). *Creolization in the Americas.* College Station, TX: Texas A&M University Press.

Calafell, B. (2004). Disrupting the dichotomy: "Yo Soy Chicana/o?" in the New Latina/o South. *The Communication Review, 7,* 175–204.

Calafell, B. (2007). *Latina/o Communication Studies: Theorizing performance.* New York, NY: Peter Lang.

Chidester, P. (2008). May the circle stay unbroken: Friends, the presence of absence, and the rhetorical reinforcement of Whiteness. *Critical Studies in Media Communication, 25*(2), 157–174.

Choi, J. I. (2002). *A study on 'Americanization' expressed in Itaewon space.* Seoul: Seoul National University, Master's Thesis.

Clark, G. (2004). *Rhetorical landscapes in America: Variations on a theme from Kenneth Burke.* Columbia, SC: University of South Carolina Press.

Cooks, L. (2009). You are not what you (don't) eat? Food, identity, and resistance. *Text and Performance Quarterly, 29*(1), 94–110.

de Certeau, M., Giard, L., Mayol, P., & Tomasik, T. I. (1998). *The practice of everyday life: Living and cooking (Vol.2).* Minneapolis, MN: University of Minnesota Press.

Dickinson, G. (1997). Memories for sale: Nostalgia and the construction of identity in Old Pasadena. *Quarterly Journal of Speech, 83*(1), 1–27.

Dickinson, G. (2015). *Suburban dreams: Imagining and building the good life.* Tuscaloosa, AL: The University of Alabama Press.

Dickinson, G., & Aiello, G. (2016). Being through there matters: Materiality, bodies, and movement in Urban Communication Research. *International Journal of Communication, 10,* 1294–1308.

Drzewiecka, J., & Nakayama, T. K. (1998). City sites: Postmodern urban space and the communication of identity. *Southern Communication Journal, 64*(1), 20–31.

Enck-Wanzer, D. (2011). Tropicalizing East Harlem: Rhetorical agency, cultural citizenship, and Nuyorican cultural production. *Communication Theory, 21,* 344–367.

Endres, D., & Senda-Cook, S. (2011). Location matters: The rhetoric of place in protest. *Quarterly Journal of Speech, 97*(3), 257–282.

Finnis, E. (2012). Introduction. In E. Finnis (Ed.), *Reimagining marginalized foods: Global processes, local places* (pp. 1–14). Tucson, AZ: The University of Arizona Press.

Fleming, D. (2008). *City of rhetoric: Revitalizing the public sphere in metropolitan America*. Albany, NY: SUNY Press.

Gallagher, V. J., & LaWare, M. R. (2010). Sparring with public memory: The rhetorical embodiment of race, power, and conflict in the Monument to Joe Louis. In G. Dickinson, C. Blair, & B. Ott (Eds.), *Places of public memory: The rhetoric of museums and memorials* (pp. 87–112). Tuscaloosa, AL: The University of Alabama Press.

Gilroy, P. (1993). *The Black Atlantic: Modernity and double consciousness*. Cambridge, MA: Harvard University Press.

Grossberg, L. (1986). On postmodernism and articulation: An interview with Stuart Hall. *Journal of Communication Inquiry*, 10 (2), 45–60.

Halloran, S. M., & Clark, G. (2006). National park landscapes and the rhetorical display of civic religion. In L. J. Prelli (Ed.), *Rhetorics of display* (pp. 141–156). Columbia, SC: University of South Carolina Press.

Hur, J. (2013). *A study on multicultural space: The case of Itaewon World Cuisine Street*. Seoul: Yonsei University, Master's Thesis.

Kang, H. S. (2013). Korean American college students' language practices and identity positioning: "Not Korean, but not American". *Journal of Language, Identity, and Education*, *12*, 248–261.

Kim, L. M. (2008). Doing Korean American history in the twenty-first century. *Journal of Asian American Studies*, *11*(2), 199–209.

Korean Statistical Information Service. *2016 Korean Demography Statistics*. Retrieved in August 2017.

Lee, E. Y. (2015). *Rhetorical landscape of Itaewon: Negotiating new transcultural identities in South Korea*. Bowling Green State U, PhD dissertation.

Lefebvre, H. (1983). *The production of space*. Cambridge: Blackwell.

Mannur, A. (2007). Culinary nostalgia: Authenticity, nationalism, and diaspora. *MELUS*, *32*(4), 11–31.

Mountoford, R. (2001). On gender and rhetorical space. *Rhetorical Society Quarterly*, *31*(1), 41–71.

Pilcher, J. M. (2014). "Old Stock" tamales and migrant tacos: Taste, authenticity, and the naturalization of Mexican food. *Social Research: An International Quarterly*, *81*(2), 441–462.

Pollock, G. (1994). Territories of desire: Reconsiderations of an African childhood. In G. Robertson, M. Mash, L. Tickner, J. Bird, B. Curtis, & T. Putman (Eds.), *Travellers' tales: Narratives of home and displacement* (pp. 63–89). New York, NY: Routledge.

Portes, A., & Stepick, A. (2003). The transformation of Miami. In J. Stone & R. Dennis (Eds.), *Race and ethnicity: Comparative and theoretical approaches* (pp. 306–319). Malden, MA: Blackwell Publishing.

Rath, R. C. (2000). Drums and power: Ways of Creolizing music in Coastal South Carolina and Georgia, 1730–90. In D. Buisseret & S. G. Reinhardt (Eds.), *Creolization in the Americas* (pp. 99–130). College Station, TX: Texas A&M University Press.

Shin, G. W. (2006). *Ethnic nationalism in Korea: Genealogy, politics, and legacy.* Stanford, CA: Stanford University Press.

Shin, J. (2019). The vortex of multiculturalism in South Korea: A critical discourse analysis of the characterization of "multicultural children" in three newspapers. *Communication and Critical/Cultural Studies, 16*(1), pp. 61–81.

Shome, R. (2003). Space matters: The power and practice of space. *Communication Theory, 13*(1), 39–56.

Shugart, H. A. (2008). Sumptuous texts: Consuming "Otherness" in the food film genre. *Critical Studies in Media Communication, 25*(1), 68–90.

Simon, B. (2009). The not-so-flat world: Exploring the meaning of buying at the intersection of the global and the local at a Starbucks in Singapore. *Comparative American Studies, 7* (4), 319–337.

Simpson, T. A. (1999). Recycling urban spaces. *Western Journal of Communication, 63*(3), 310–328.

Siu, L. C. D. (2005). *Memories of a future home: Diasporic citizenship of Chinese in Panama.* Stanford, CA: Stanford University Press.

Wilk, R. (2012). Loving people, hating what they eat: Marginal foods and social boundaries. In E. Finnis (Ed.), *Reimagining marginalized foods: Global processes, local places* (pp. 15–33). Tucson, AZ: The University of Arizona Press.

Yuh, J. Y. (2005). Moved by war: Migration, diaspora, and the Korean War. *Journal of Asian American Studies, 8*(3), 277–291.

Zagacki, K. S., & Gallagher, V. J. (2009). Rhetoric and materiality in the museum park at the North Carolina Museum of Art. *Quarterly Journal of Speech, 95*(2), 171–191.

Magazine and Newspapers Articles

Jeong, C. (2014). "It's okay for Itaewon but no for other places," *SBSCNBC,* 2014, http://sbscnbc.sbs.co.kr/new_mobile/interface_mobile_end.jsp?article_id=10000657540

Olozia, J. (2013). "The Hot Table: Vatos Urban Tacos," Travel Essentials in *T Magazine,* March 22, 2013.

Websites

Coreanos Kitchen Facebook page. https://www.facebook.com/CoreanosKitchen/
Coreanos Kitchen Main website. http://coreanoskitchen.com/en/
Vatos: Urban Tacos Main website http://vatoskorea.com/en/about/our-story/

3. When "Chiang Kai-shek Memorial Square" Became "Liberty Square": A Case of Contested Public Memories in Taiwan

YEA-WEN CHEN
San Diego State University

CHUNYU ZHANG
Wuhan University

On September 7, 2017, the National Chengchi University (NCCU) in Taiwan announced its intent to remove one of their two Chiang Kai-shek (蔣介石) bronze statues. As the founder of NCCU, the removal of the Chiang Kai-shek statue signals the further "de-Chiang[-]ification" (去蔣化) in contemporary Taiwan (Matten, 2011, p. 83). As a political and military leader, Chiang Kai-shek (1887–1975) is a historically significant yet controversial figure in Taiwan. He is remembered simultaneously as a hero who led the Kuomintang Party (KMT) to liberate Taiwan from Japanese colonization during World War II, and also as a dictator who orchestrated the February 28th massacre (also referred to as 228 Incident) in 1947 and enforced martial law for almost four decades on the island. Nonetheless, many people, especially KMT party members and supporters, still refer to Chiang as the father and the guardian of Taiwan, which has resulted in a personality cult of Chiang. A year after his death in 1975, a 25 hectares memorial park, including the Chiang Kai-shek Memorial Hall (CKSMH), a surrounding square, and a traditional Chinese style garden, was built to commemorate his legacy. Because of its feudal-temple-like design and Chiang's dictatorship, the CKSMH has been likened to "Marquis Chiang's Temple" (Hatfield, 2008). In this essay, we focus on competing public memories about Chiang Kai-shek and controversies over his legacy by analyzing public discourses of the CKSMH as a site of contestations, a site that includes Chiang Kai-shek Memorial Park and Memorial Square.

The CKSMH has become an important site of public and cultural memory that not only conserves the collective memory of Chiang Kai-shek but also provides a public avenue for political activities as Taiwan embarks on a journey toward democratization (e.g., Matten, 2011). With the lifting of martial law after four decades of "White Terror" in 1987, a reflection and criticism of Chiang's culpability during the White Terror period emerged, resulting in an official apology from the Chairman of KMT and President Lee Teng-hui (李登輝) in 1995. Also, the National 228 Memorial Museum was established in 1998, a place just two miles away from the CKSMH. Meanwhile, supported by President Lee Teng-hui, a Taiwanese localization movement took place, advocating for democracy and Taiwanese independence from Mainland China, which not just departed from but betrayed Chiang's China-centered vision. Due to its political significance and large-sized space, the square in Chiang Kai-shek Memorial Park (CKSMP) has witnessed, if not facilitated, several political protests and key movements, including the Wild Lily Student movement of 1990, the Wild Strawberries Movement of 2008, the Sunflower Student Movement of 2014, and others. As an increasingly powerful political opposition, the Democratic Progressive Party (DPP) had sponsored some of the protests and movements that took place at the square in the CKSMP. The criticism of Chiang's authoritarian regime culminated when the DPP took power and ended KMT's one-party rule in Taiwan in 2008 with the successful election of President Chen Shui-bian (陳水扁) from the DPP.

The renaming and later name restoration of the CKSMH reflect changing political powers and conditions in Taiwan. To further de-Chiang-ification and promote Taiwanese localization and democracy, on May 19, 2007, the DPP under the leadership of then President Chen Shui-bian renamed the CKSMH to "National Taiwan Democracy Memorial Hall (國立臺灣民主紀念館)" and changed the surrounding square to "Liberty Square" (Matten, 2011). As the leader of the DPP party, President Chen Shui-bian announced in the name changing ceremony that "since the Democratic Progressive Party (DPP) came to power in 2000, his administration had made every effort to remove relics of authoritarianism" (Ko, 2008). As soon as the KMT Party and its candidate, Ma Ying-jeou (馬英九), won the presidential election in May 2008, the conversation of restoring the CKSMH to its original name began. Symbolically, the name restoration of the CKSMH communicated the need that the KMT saw to conserve its historical and political root while avoiding associations with efforts to restore an authoritarian power. Secured with barricades and barbed wires, the reinstatement of the Chiang Kai-shek plaque to the CKSMH took place on July 19, 2009 (Matten, 2011). The two-year (re) naming process not only has transformed the meaning(s) of the CKSMH and the surrounding square and park, but also represents a rewriting of public memory about the first and late President Chiang Kai-shek.

The controversy over the CKSMH ties together contestations over Chiang's legacies, Taiwan's local histories, political powers, and public memories. Thus, in this chapter, we—as a native of Taiwan (first author) and a native of Mainland China (second author)—investigate both historical and contemporary as well as archival and popular discourses about the CKSMH, including the material and symbolic functions of site, the official guidebook of CKSMH, government news releases, news articles, relevant research, etc. We will trace evolving discourses of/about the CKSMH over time in relation to Taiwan's democratizing achievements, unpack the particular ways in which memories of Chiang become (de)politicized, and conclude with implications for public memory as a contested cultural site.

Public Memory, Disputed Sovereignty, and Conflicting Histories

The name changes to the CKSMH becomes a rich site—symbolically, culturally, and politically—to delve into the intricate relationship between public memory about Chiang Kai-shek and disputes over Taiwan's national identity and political sovereignty. Following Morris III (2004), we approach public memory in this essay as "a purposeful engagement of the past, forged symbolically, profoundly constitutive of identity, community, and moral vision, inherently consequential in its ideological implications, and very often the fodder of political conflagration" (p. 90). This understanding of public memory fits the goal of our essay to unpack the evolving and contested collective understandings of Chiang Kai-shek as they intersect and reflect ideological, political, and social changes in Taiwan. Our choice of focusing on the CKSMH as a rhetorical site is supported by Dickinson, Ott, and Aoki's (2006) remark that "As official and institutionalized cultural expressions, public museums, memorials, and other historical sites play a crucial role in the construction and maintenance of national mythologies, histories, and identities" (p. 29).

As Matten (2011) has stated, the CKSMH as a place of political/social/ethnic memories "will shed light on how visions of the collective identity of people on Taiwan developed and changed since the collapse of the ideological hegemony of the KMT in the 1980s" (p. 51). The evolving public memories about Chiang Kai-shek parallel Taiwan's ongoing struggles and searches for a "national" identity that are rooted in conflicting politics, histories, and ethnic cultures (e.g., Brown, 2004). Simply put, is Taiwan an independent country or is Taiwan a part of People's Republic of China (PRC)? According to Taiwan's Ministry of Foreign Affairs (Diplomatic Allies, 2018), currently, there are 20 countries that maintain diplomatic relations with Taiwan, excluding the United States and all European countries except for the Holy See. To help contextualize controversies over Chiang Kai-shek's legacy, we briefly review Taiwan's historical backgrounds.

Is Taiwan Chinese?

Whether Taiwan is rendered part of "China" remains contested. There are two distinct political entities who would like to claim ownership of Taiwan: (a) the Republic of China (ROC) that retreated to Taiwan after losing to the Chinese Communists and has remained there since 1949; and (b) the Communist-led PRC who took control of the mainland in 1949. Prior to 1971, the ROC in Taiwan was the representation of "China" in international affairs. When the PRC won the Chinese seat in the United Nations in 1971, the ROC delegates left. Since then, Taiwan has been diplomatically isolated as a result of the PRC's efforts to undermine the ROC sovereignty (Cooper, 2003). For instance, in December 2016, Donald Trump as the President-Elect of the United States caused great controversy when he initiated a phone conversation with Taiwanese President Tasi Ing-wen (蔡英文). In a way, the ongoing disputes over Taiwan's political identity and sovereignty have (re)shaped how Chiang Kai-shek and his legacy is (re)framed over time.

From Dutch Invasion to Japanese Colonial Occupation. Taiwan's 400 years of modern history can be characterized by a constant shift of political powers if not foreign invasions. Around 1590, the Portuguese gave Taiwan its unofficial name: *Ilha Formosa* (a beautiful island), marking the beginning of the island's modern colonial history. The Dutch came in 1624. In 1662, a loyalist of the old Ming Dynasty and a privateer, Cheng Cheng-kung (鄭成功), defeated the Dutch. Two decades later, the Manchu troops of the Ching Dynasty took over Taiwan. In 1887, worry about competition from the Japanese motivated the Manchu Imperial authorities to officially declare Taiwan one of its provinces. Eight years later, the sovereignty of Taiwan changed hands again. Military defeat forced the Manchu authorities to sign the Treaty of Shimonoseki and ceded Taiwan to Japan in 1895. Taiwan was under Japanese colonial occupation for half a century until 1945. Essentially, different ethnic groups (i.e., indigenous peoples, the Hoklo, the

Hakka, and Chinese mainlanders) in Taiwan have varying historical relationships with the changes in political powers. Some groups have lived through the Japanese occupation and others came after the occupation.

From Chiang Kai-shek to Chen Shui-bian. The ending of WWII changed Taiwan's status again. At the Cairo Conference of 1943, Chiang Kai-shek, leader of the ROC, requested the return of Taiwan to China. Shortly afterwards, the Chinese Civil War broke out between the Communists and the KMT. When the KMT lost the war, two million Chinese mainlanders led by Chiang Kai-shek fled to Taiwan in 1949. From 1949 until 1987, the people in Taiwan lived under martial law. On March 23, 1996, the first popular presidential election took place in Taiwan, which marks an important political moment in Taiwan's journey toward democratization. For the first time, the people in Taiwan were given the choice to elect their own president. Four years later in 2000, Taiwan-born Chen Shui-bian, presidential candidate of the DPP, won the second direct presidential election in Taiwan's history. The successful election of Taiwan-born Chen Shui-bian marks a historic milestone in Taiwan's political development in which political power was transferred from the leading KMT to the opposing DPP for the first time. In 2016, Tsai Ing-wen became the first woman and second DPP candidate (after Chen Shui-bian) to be elected as the President of Taiwan.

Divergent Voices within Taiwan. Stratified along ethnic lines, groups in Taiwan also struggle over how they perceive their and others' identities in relation to Taiwan. Primarily, Taiwan's population is composed of at least four major ethnic groups: (a) different indigenous peoples (原住民), the natives who have lived in Taiwan for approximately 6,000 years; (b) the Chinese mainlanders (外省人) who came to Taiwan between 1945 and 1949; and two groups of Taiwanese (Chinese): (c) the Hoklo (閩南人) and (d) the Hakka (客家人), whose ancestors moved to Taiwan prior to the Japanese colonial period (Brown, 2004). As the newly-arrived Chinese mainlanders established a minority-run KMT government in Taiwan, there was soon friction between the native Taiwanese (Chinese) and the accelerating influx of Chinese mainlanders (Long, 1991). On February 28, 1947, simmering resentment against the Chinese mainlanders boiled over into a near-revolution. During the February 28th Incident of 1947, the KMT troops raped and pillaged people in Taiwan. Initially, the KMT government attempted to erase the 228 Incident from the collective national conscience, but it later came to formally apologize to the people of Taiwan in 1992 (Rawnsley, 2003). Thus, Taiwan's identity contestations are contingent on and complicated not only by political identifications but also the socio-historical situated-ness of the different groups in Taiwan, which in turn inform, shape, and affect disputes over public memories about Chiang Kai-shek and his contribution to Taiwan (e.g., Heylen, 2011).

Commemorating Chiang Kai-shek vis-à-vis the CKSMH

Groundbreaking on October 31, 1976—a year after Chiang's death, the Chiang Kai-shek Memorial Park (CKSMP) was built as both a material and discursive site to commemorate Chiang's legacies. Designed by Yang Cho-cheng, an architect known for his incorporation of the traditional Chinese palace, the park was intended to demonstrate Chinese ethical and political philosophies that Chiang embodied and the aesthetics of Chinese architecture.

Entering the memorial park, visitors will first cross a majestic ceremonial archway gate named "Liberty Square (自由廣場)," which was originally inscribed as "Da Zhong Zhi Zheng (大中至正)" as to echo Chiang's style name—"Zhong Zheng (中正, meaning impartial and uprightness)." Walking further into the park, visitors encounter the Liberty Square flanked by the National Theater Hall on the north and the National Concert Hall on the south, both of which were modeled after a traditional Chinese palace, and a traditional Chinese garden in the back (see Figure 3.1). The square was used as a ceremonial place to welcome foreign guests but later became a public and political venue for social movements and political protests in 1990s. Passing through the Liberty Square and along the Democracy Boulevard, visitors arrive at Chiang's memorial hall (a.k.a. the CKSMH) with an octagonal sapphire-blue glazed tile roof in the shape of the Chinese character "人" (meaning human being) that points directly into the sky, symbolizing the unification of heaven and human ("Introduction," 2017). Each side of the roof represents one eight Confucian principles: loyalty (忠), piety (孝), humanity (仁), love (愛), trust (信), righteousness (義), harmony (和), and peace (平) (Matten, 2011). Consistent with the design of the roof, two side gates surrounding the hall were named: "Gate of Great Loyalty (大忠門)" and "Gate of Great Piety (大孝門)." In this way, the design of CKSMH entails a rhetorical intention that "used [the Neo-Confucian spirit of] piety and loyalty to inspire respect," and imaged Chiang as the "paterfamilias" of the Chinese nation (Fenby, 2003, p. 225).

In its entirety, the CKSMP not only represents and constructs Chiang as a moral leader, but also as a savior of Chinese traditional culture in Taiwan. The architectural gestures, including three archway gates, the Theater Hall and Concert Hall, paved squares, two water ponds located in the front of hall along with the hall itself, and the Chinese style garden, corridoes and pavilions surrounding the hall, all serve to highlight Chiang's role in a Chinese Cultural Renaissance to contrast with the Communist Party's cultural deconstructions during the Cultural Revolution period (1966–1976). Although the meanings of the architectures have largely been reduced to cultural heritage nowadays, the political implication of Chiang's hope to "restore China" remained as the name of a water pond indicates: "Guanghua" (光華, meaning restore China). The political ideology of restoring China and Chinese cultural traditions penetrates and guides the design, architecture, and symbols throughout the CKSMH.

The hall was completed and opened to the public on April 5, 1980, a traditional Chinese holiday when people practice the ritual of visiting ancestral tombs, expressing gratitude, and paying respect. The whole building, made up of blue and white colors, symbolizes Chiang and his party's political ideals of liberty and equality. Before entering the hall, visitors need to climb 89 white granite steps, which represent the 89 years of Chiang's life. At the end, visitors see a large bronze statue of Chiang facing to west, indicating his hope to recover (Mainland) China. Behind the statue, the wall is inscribed with three key characters of Chiang's political beliefs and ideals: Ethics (倫理), Democracy (民主), and Science (科學), which visually link to Sun Yat-sen (孫中山)—the founder of KMT—and his "Three Principles of the People." Alongside the statue of Chiang, the CKSMH also presents to the public with different historical relics and exhibits of Chiang, ranging from his family life, ascending to power, wartime leadership, his retreat from mainland to Taiwan, presidency in Taiwan, and the gallery of his office. Safeguarded by a daily military honor-guard performance that is intended to cultivate deep respect in visitors, the CKSMH has legitimized an exaltation of Chiang's ethical values and political merits while neglecting Chiang's controversies over his authoritarian governance. Meanwhile, the park was originally enclosed by walls that prevented the public using the place for non-commemorative purposes, which also served to uphold the ruling status of Chiang.

Over time, changes—both material and discursive—to the CKSMH have taken place, representing ongoing (re)constructions of and struggles over memories of Chiang. Different from the symbolic construction of Chiang as a moral political leader that is advanced by the memorial hall, his culpability in 228 Incident and White Terror, all which actually betrayed his political principles of democracy, liberty, and equality. When visiting the hall, visitors may simultaneously be called to honor and exalt Chiang and cultivate a fear of his dictatorship by recalling his brutality. As Blair, Dickinson, and Ott (2010) suggest, many memory materials all "encode power and possibility … no matter how overtly a place may exert power through its incorporation, enablement, direction, and constraints on bodies, it has its own power dimension that becomes part of the experience" (p. 29). Due to its oppositional and contesting possibilities, the transformation of CKSMH seems inevitable as Taiwan moves toward democratization.

Due to its central locale right in the heart of Taipei City, the square of the CKSMP has not only served as a commemorative site conserving a collective memory of Chiang, but also as a public avenue for political activities as Taiwan embarks on a journey toward democratization (Nora, 1989). Since the 1990s, the square has witnessed serval political protests and movements such as the Wild Lily Student movement in 1990 featuring six-day student demonstrations for democracy and other demonstrations that have been sponsored by the DPP, an increasingly powerful political opposition. Coincidentally, the CKSMH as a gathering place has unintendedly "participated" in promoting a rising local Taiwanese identity that gradually questions the coherence of memories about Chiang as a moral and loyal father enacting his principles and ideals of ethics, democracy, and science.

Renaming and Later Restoring the CKSMH

Led by the ruling DPP party, the public debates over whether or not to rename CKSMH occurred in mid-February of 2007 and coincided with the 60th anniversary of the February 28th Incident. In December 2007, the CKSMH was briefly renamed the "National Taiwan Democracy Memorial Hall" and the archway gate changed to "Liberty Square" accordingly. In doing so, the DPP intended to remind Taiwanese people of Chiang's authoritarian governance and to promote a localization of Taiwanese identity and politics. With the change of political power, the renaming of the CKSMH was abandoned after President Ma Ying-jeou and his KMT party won the presidency in May 2008. Overall, the brief renaming of the CKSMH resulted in more public outcries, debates, and controversies than material changes to the structure and displays within the CKSMH itself. Matten (2011) described the renaming process as "politically motivated" by both the DPP and the KMT to serve their own political agendas (p. 75).

The genesis of the name change started with the Taiwan Thinktank (臺灣智庫) (Matten, 2011). In October 2006, the Taiwan Thinktank held a transitional forum to discuss the possibility of renaming the CKSMH. Forum speakers suggested the name "National Taiwan Democracy Memorial Hall" as a way to reflect a history of Chiang's dictatorship and represent Taiwan's transition to democracy. They declared that changing the name was not "a form of revenge," but rather a way of attaining justice (Taiwan Thinktank,

2016). In addition to renaming the hall, a possible relocation of the Chiang's exhibits and relics housed at the hall was also discussed but was not carried out. Moreover, the renaming process fueled by partisan conflicts involved changing jurisdictions over the CKSMH. Symbolically, the question of who *ought to* have jurisdiction over the CKSMH and thus the public memory of Chiang was critical but rarely considered.

In May 2007, this name change proposal was approved by President Chen Shui-bian and the DPP party. In 2008, DPP President Chen remarked that the (re)opening of the hall symbolized the " 'opening of the door of democracy' and that it transformed 'a temple' worshipping a dictator to a venue where all people can freely reflect and learn the true meaning of democracy and human rights" (Ko, 2008, para. 10). In addition to renaming the hall as "National Taiwan Democracy Memorial Hall," Ko (2008) reported that the statue of Chiang Kai-shek remained in the lobby but was "decorated with kites to reflect the theme of 'a democratic wind,' " which symbolized achieving freedom (para. 1). Also, the main hall was decorated with larger posters featuring Taiwan's democratic movement. The inscription on the gateway to the square was changed from "Da Zhong Zhi Zheng (referring to Chiang's uprightness and morality)" to "Liberty Square." President Chen concluded the reopening ceremony by stating, "We believe history will speak for itself and people will learn from history . . . That is the true meaning of the reopening" (Ko, 2008, para. 11).

Under the KMT President Ma and his administration, the CKSMH's original name was restored in 2009 and the Chiang Kai-shek plaque was reinstated on July 19, 2009 (Matten, 2011). Lu Mu-lin (呂木琳), Vice Minister of Education at the time said in a press conference that the DPP-led move to rename the CKSMH "was controversial in part because the changes were made without legislative approval" (Wang, 2009, para. 6). Despite a lack of legislative approval, the "Liberty Square" inscription at the gateway to the memorial hall remained because "the square plays an important role in Taiwan's democratic and cultural development," Lu explained (Wang, 2009, para. 12). Also, the inscription remained unchanged "so that [the public] can keep a shared memory of the development," Lu said (Wang, 2009, para. 13). When asked if the Ministry of Education considered arranging a public forum, Lu responded that he did not "because the majority of experts invited to a separate forum on educational issues felt that a forum gauging public opinion on the plaque change could increase tensions between supporters of different political parties" (Wang, 2009, para. 10). Despite of heated debates over the name changes (e.g., what was restored and what remained changed), the majority of the structure and displays in the CKSMH remained unchanged.

Even though politically motivated controversies over Chiang's legacy prevented the renaming of the memorial hall, the efforts resulted in changing the gateway plaque to "Liberty Square," which has remained to this day. However, the move felt like an after-thought as both political parties were more invested in their own political gains than in elevating the voices of the people of Taiwan. Ironically, when Chiang's legacy was challenged in the name of democracy, the processes used were undemocratic and lacked public involvement and participation. As Blair aptly argues, "struggle for power in social groups often are waged under the sign of memory—what the group will choose to remember, how it will be valued, and what will be forgotten, neglected, or devalued in the process" (p. 57). Nonetheless, few details can be learned about the name changing debate from the official website of CKSMH. In the next section, we examine efforts to depoliticize, decontextualize, and neutralize the CKSMH as a site of public memory.

Depoliticizing and Neutralizing the CKSMH

> Come to the Chiang Kai-Shek Memorial Hall,
> linger in this place of art and culture,
> wander at leisure through the wide elegant spaces,
> appreciate the beauty of the architecture and gardens, and
> experience the joy of growing and learning.

Today the landing page of the CKSMH website welcomes visitors with the particular words above (Introduction, 2018). Even though the CKSMH remains a site "established to commemorate Chiang Kai-Shek," its purpose has been as depoliticized as much as possible with greater emphasis on driving "culture promotion activities." The controversies surrounding Chiang's legacy has been neutralized and has left him simply as "(late) President Chiang" whose memories provide "a view of the history of the ROC"—an unspoken agreement across political divides.

The depoliticization of the public memory about Chiang is also evidenced in the Exhibition Yearbook of 2016. In it, the National Chiang Kai-shek Memorial Management Office defined the purpose of the CKSMH in the following four ways. The first purpose is to organize "international large-scale expositions or art exhibitions to promote cultural exchanges across different countries; enhance the humanistic cultivation of the general public." Second, it aims to integrate "resources from the private sector; extend help and show concern to minorities and disadvantaged groups so as to promote the welfare of society as a whole." Third, it strives to set "up a superior environment of quality and aesthetics to enrich the cultural and artistic sensibility of the general public." Fourth, it seeks to fully "utilize the resources of the Memorial Hall and establish it as a creative and diverse educational venue." The rhetorical depoliticization of the CKSMH has rebranded it as a civic, cultural, and artistic space for enjoyment, relaxation, and exercise in various forms and senses.

Discourses from the Ministry of Culture further reveals the continuing depoliticization of Chiang and the CKSMH (until consensus can be reached and address public expectations). As the Ministry promotes efforts toward "transitional justice" seeking to restore "historical truths, clarifying responsibilities, advocating political rehabilitation, and implementing human rights education" (Ministry of Culture, 2017), the exhibit rooms, gallery, and concert hall become transformed to artistic and cultural uses. In February 2017, to commemorate the 70th anniversary of 228 Massacre and the 30th anniversary of the lifting of the martial law, the Ministry of Culture announced its intent to transform the CKSMH into a place that "facing history, recognizing agony, and respecting human rights" (Ministry of Culture, 2017). At that time, visitors were no longer able to purchase any products associated with Chiang Kai-shek or hear any commemorative songs inside the CKSMH. Any promotional materials about Chiang were removed or replaced with more neutral artifacts. Specifically, the Cultural Minister Cheng Li-chiun carefully described Chiang as "an authoritarian ruler." Also, Minster Cheng promised to carry out transformation of the CKSMH on a legally defensible basis and organize "civic discussions regarding measures, purpose, and urban planning of the transformation." Until then, the paper-cut logo of late President Chiang has been replaced with an image of the memorial hall itself for neutrality.

Putting the Public Back in "Public" Memory?

As a country that has lived through martial law (1949–1987) and an authoritarian regime under late President Chiang Kai-shek, various ethnic groups in Taiwan struggle with and contest how to commemorate Chiang and what to remember and/or rewrite about his legacy in Taiwan. The controversies and name changes associated with the CKSHM and its surrounding space reflect a deep-seated uneasiness in grappling with memories about Chiang Kai-shek as it relates to both Taiwan's historical past(s) and future(s). As Heylen (2011) puts it, "In Taiwan, the project of recovering historical memory cannot be separated from the broader context of politics" (p. 17). Through analyzing archival and popular discourses about the CKSMH's name changes, we identify an evolution of: (a) the original design that commemorated Chiang as a moral and loyal father/leader/guidance who embodied the cores of Chinese aesthetics; (b) a contested period of politically motivated renaming and restoring the CKSMH that rarely involved public voices; and (c) the somewhat depoliticized and neutralized memories about Chiang today. Ultimately, rewriting memories about Chiang means having to confront painful histories and work through difficult memories (e.g., the 228 Incident and the White Terror) as a country with differential ethnic relations with the late President—hopefully through collaborative and democratic processes. Our analysis affirms that the CKSMH is a communicative and commemorative site for (re)negotiating contested memories, histories, and identities for a sense of (un)belonging. Also, the CKSMH highlights that public memory as a concept is discursive, political, historical, ideological, contested, and highly emotional as it can trigger and re-stimulate historical traumas, collective guilt, and perhaps unexpected emotions.

Further, we argue that depoliticizing and neutralizing public memories about Chiang Kai-shek might be a sensible compromise amid long-standing political divisions and polarizations among the different ethnic groups in Taiwan. In the long run, we argue that the "de-Chiang[-]ification" (去蔣化), or the depoliticization of public memories about Chiang Kai-shek, without consensus building could run the risk of widening political polarizations and ethnic divisions in Taiwan. We argue that the healing process of (re)writing public memory about Chiang must begin with honoring peoples' lived experiences, conflicting histories, and differential treatments. In other words, "the public" should be front and center in (re)writing "public" memory about Chiang moving forward. That is, we ask, *what would public memory about Chiang look like with peoples in Taiwan at the center?*

Today, Taiwan is led by President Tsai Ing-wen, the first woman president in Taiwan's history. As the DPP President, we are curious to see if and how she will push the party's political agenda of de-Chiang[-]ification along with issues of human rights, democratization, and others. We end with Luo and Chen's (2017) idea of treating communication as a paradox in that it is possible to embrace simultaneously incommensurate ways of knowing/living/being such as holding paradoxical memories about Chiang Kai-shek as simultaneously a guardian, a dictator, and more.

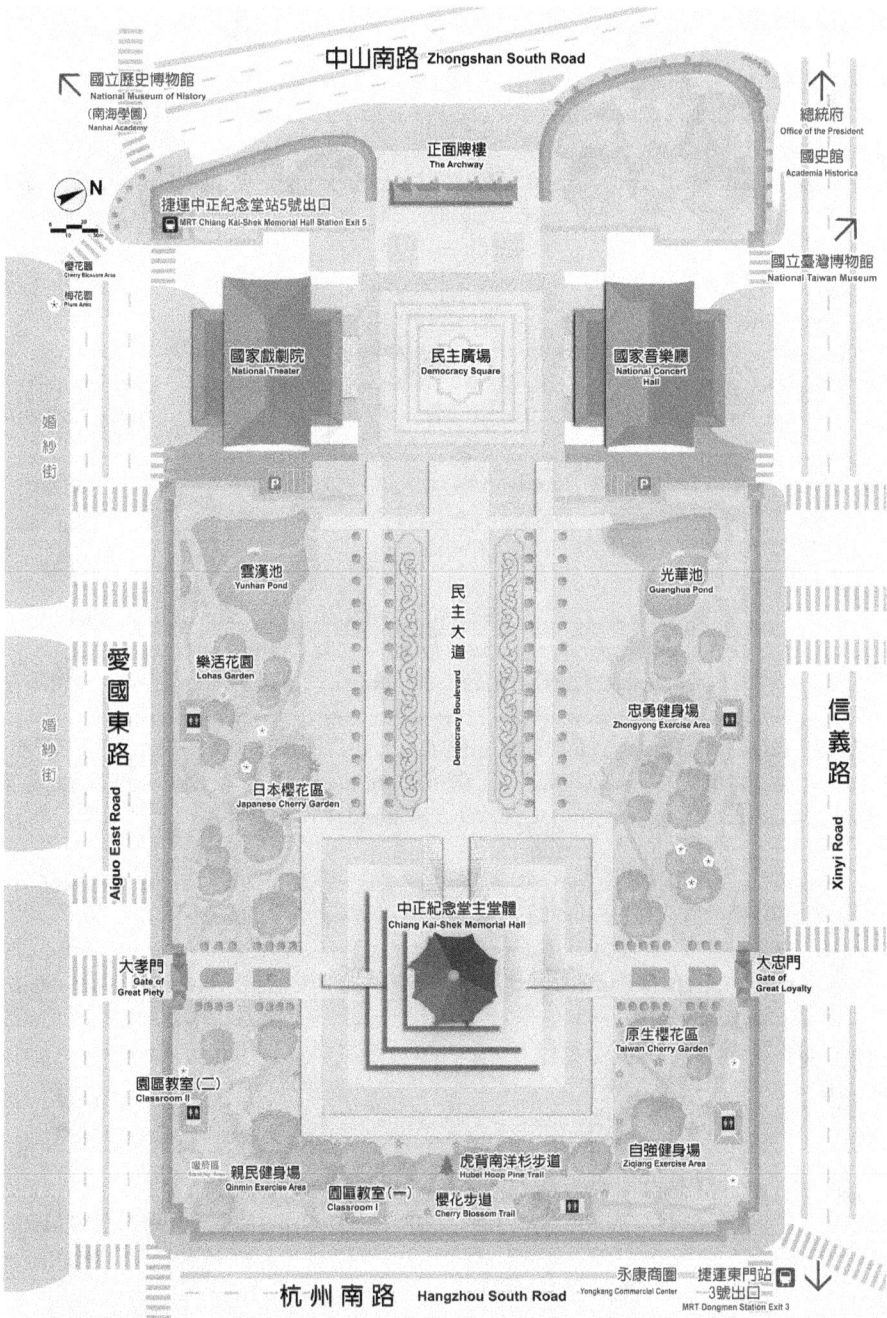

Figure 3.1: Area Map of Chiang Kai-shek Memorial Hall. Source: http://www.cksmh. gov.tw/eng/index.php?code=list&ids=42

References

Blair, C. (2006). Communication as collective memory. In G. Shepherd, J. John, & T. Striphas (Eds.), *Communication as . . . perspectives on theory* (pp. 51–59). Thousand Oaks, CA: SAGE.

Blair, C., Dickinson, G., & Ott, B. (2010). Introduction. In G. Dickinson, C. Blair, & B. Ott (Eds.), *Places of public memory: The rhetoric of museums and memorials* (pp. 1–54). Tuscaloosa, AL: The University of Alabama Press.

Brown, M. J. (2004). *Is Taiwan Chinese? The impact of culture, power, and migration on changing identities.* Berkeley, CA: University of California Press.

Cooper, J. F. (2003). *Taiwan: Nation-state or province?* Boulder, CO: Westview Press.

Dickinson, G., Ott, B., & Aoki, E. (2006). Spaces of remembering and forgetting: The reverent eye/I at the Plains Indian Museum. *Communication and Critical/Cultural Studies, 3,* 27–47.

Diplomatic Allies. (2018). Retrieved on March 14, 2018 from https://www.mofa.gov.tw/en/AlliesIndex.aspx?n=DF6F8F246049F8D6

Fenby, J. (2003). *Generalissimo: Chiang Kai-shek and the China he lost.* London, UK: The Free Press.

Hatfield, D. (2008). Chiang's benevolent smile: Symbolic reduction and national commemoration in contemporary Taiwan. *Harvard Asia Quarterly, 11,* 66–79.

Heylen, A. (2011). Legacies of memory and belonging in Taiwan history. In G. Schubert & J. Damm (Eds.), *Taiwanese identity in the twenty-first century: Domestic, regional and global perspectives* (pp. 17–34). London, UK: Routledge.

Introduction. (2018). National Chiang Kai-shek Memorial Hall. Retrieved from http://www.cksmh.gov.tw/eng/index.php?code=list&ids=3

Ko, S.-L. (2008). National Democracy Hall reopens. *Taipei Times.* Retrieved from http://www.taipeitimes.com/News/front/archives/2008/01/02/2003395260

Long, S. (1991). *Taiwan: China's last frontier.* New York, NY: St Martin's Press.

Luo, G., & Chen, Y.-W. (2017). Communication as paradox and paradox as communication: An interparadigmatic proposal of coexisting cultural epistemologies. *China Media Research, 13,* 71–82.

Matten, M. A. (2011). The Chiang Kai-shek Memorial Hall in Taipei: A contested place of Memory. In M. Matten (Ed.), *Places of memory in modern China: History, politics, and identity* (pp. 51–89). Leiden, Netherlands: Brill.

Ministry of Culture. (2017). Transforming CKS Memorial Hall for transitional justice. Retrieved from http://english.moc.gov.tw/article/index.php?sn=4806

Morris III, C. E. (2004). My old Kentucky Homo: Lincoln and the politics of queer public memory. In K. R. Philips (Ed.), *Framing public memory* (pp. 89–114). Tuscaloosa, AL: The University of Alabama Press.

Nora, P. (1989). Between memory and history: Les Lieux de Mémoire. *Representations, 26,* 7–24.

Rawnsley, M.-Y. T. (2003). Communication of identities in Taiwan. In G. D. Rawnsley, & M.-Y. T. Rawnsley (Eds.), *Political communications in greater China: The construction and reflection of identity* (pp. 147–166). London, UK: Routledge.

Taiwan Thinktank (2016). Transitional Justice Forum Series No.2: From being left-overs of authoritarianism to becoming assets of democracy—perspectives on name change to CKS Memorial Hall. Retrieved from https://globaltaiwan.org/tag/taiwan-thinktank/

The Chiang Kai-shek Memorial Hall Guidebook. (2016). Retrieved from http://www.cksmh.gov.tw/upload/article/effed1279fb4486c4bca75345c6567b7.pdf

Wang, F. (2009). Chiang Kai-shek plaque to return to memorial hall. *Taipei Times.* Retrieved from http://www.taipeitimes.com/News/taiwan/archives/2009/01/22/2003434392

Yearbook of 2016. (2016). Retrieved from http://www.cksmh.gov.tw//upload/article/1a3c9cc490aaf8f92352ba638110d611.pdf

4. Remembering Communism: The Site of Witness and Memory and the House of Leaves Museums in Albania

NINA GJOCI
European University of Tirana

Remembering is a collective activity. The widely accepted definitions of memory as a shared understanding of the past (Halbwachs, 1925) and counter-memory as resistance against the official versions of historical continuity (Foucault, 1994) are largely articulated among contemporary memory scholarship. Places of memory are designated sites of memory that require public discussion, public approval and/or disapproval (Casey, 2004). Understanding public memory requires that memory and place, especially places of memory, be investigated in connection to each other and within the larger social context (Blair, Dickinson, & Ott, 2010). The fundamental changes that took place in former communist countries as they transitioned from a communist system to democracy and pluralism are historical events that call for specific attention to public memory. Such changes during transition periods require a reevaluation of what "it was" and what "it will be." This reevaluation invites present interests, constitutes and requires group identities, attracts various affective investments, and requires material and symbolic support.

Scholarship regarding public memory and memory places, such as memorials, monuments, museums, and sites commemorating communism has been published in Europe as well as in the United States to some degree. Public debates about the communist past, especially related to the European Union project, have produced memory work throughout the former communist bloc. Museums and memorials commemorating victims of communist regimes are built and recognized as such throughout Eastern Europe. Scholarship about traumatic national pasts is significant as well, and has been conducted by scholars across the world, whether dealing with the Holocaust, slavery, apartheid, civil wars, or other forms of oppression. Places that are designated to commemorate the communist and other totalitarian pasts require special attention when critics attempt to understand public memory.

This study investigates how places of memory rhetorically shape and construct the communist past in Albania. I approached two places of memory, the Site of Witness and Memory (SWM) museum in Shkoder and the House of Leaves (HL) museum in Tirana. My rhetorical reading consisted of examining the material and symbolic means of what is addressed, by whom, where, and how the places become legible to audiences, how their display and content primes visitors to particular subject positions, and what public debates they generate. I argue that the best way to explain how these places shape the public memory of the communist past is to classify them into two categories: the counter-memory version and the official version of memory. The SWM museum in Shkoder functions as counter-memory version and the HL museum functions as the official state version of the communist past. The two places of memory I investigated are meaningful when considered in the larger Albanian memory infrastructure. The symbolic and material displays draw their particular meanings as sites of witness to repression. However, their rhetorical force is drawn when they are seen in comparison to the larger communist memory infrastructure. When placed in the larger memory infrastructure they demonstrate the complexity of remembering the criminal regime and the difficulty of staging public memory in the light of political national and international interests.

Scholars have conducted memory studies on former communist countries that were a response to the rise of national consciousness about the past. James (2005) suggests that the monuments in post-communist Hungary are used to make and remake history to serve the ideological purposes of the present by decentering, repurposing, and moving communist visual culture. Vatulescu (2013) investigated the transformation of the infamous Sighet Prison into a memory museum in Romania. She points out "what might have been lost in the creation of the museum's master narrative—alternative stories/histories, tension-ridden differences ..." (p. 317). Atkinson (2016) suggests that the DDR museum exhibits position the East German citizens as hedonistic and juvenile and invite visitors to act in ways that reinforce these positions. Clarke (2017) examined the Leistikowstrabe Memorial Museum conflict between museum professionals and victims' groups representatives over how the museum displayed the victims' suffering. He suggests that the resolution of this conflict was determined beyond the discursive efforts, namely by the interplay of politics, ownership, and museum professionals.

A significant amount of rhetorical scholarship on memory places of national traumatic pasts offer similar approaches to explaining the connection between public memory and place. Dickinson, Ott, & Aoki (2005) outline the material and symbolic ways that history museums function as rhetorical invitations to collective memory and national identity. They investigated the Buffalo Bill Historical Center (BBHC) located in Cody, Wyoming to discover the ways in which these museums create structured invitations to particular meanings about the American Old West. The results for the Buffalo Bill Museum, one of the five museums of the BBHC, show that the four "independent" exhibits work to tell a coherent well-ordered story; a story that suggests that Buffalo Bill's story is not simply *a* history, but *the* history of the West. The second study examined the Plains Indian Museum (PIM) as a key component in the construction of collective memory and national identity (Dickinson et al., 2006). The PIM frames the Western landscape as immense and sublime and positions the visitor to view with respect from a distance. The study of the Cody Fire Museum, which is part of BBHC, focuses specifically on practices of looking and space creation of museums as both selective and biased (Ott, Aoki, & Dickinson, 2011). The authors argue that the Cody Fire Museum mobilizes a Western (Occidental) gaze, which is to engage in surveillance and to see into the distance. It is a timeless gaze. Davis (2013) examined two museums, the American Civil War Center in Richmond, Virginia and the African American Freedom Foundation Civil War Memorial and Museum in Washington DC. She argues that the rhetorical discourses of reconciliation and belonging enabled new "spaces for both, black heritage and civil war tourism" (p. 123).

My investigation of the Site of Witness and Memory (SWM) and the House of Leaves (HL) is informed by rhetorical approaches. Pertaining to public memory, rhetoric is concerned with meaningfulness, legibility, partisanship, consequentiality, and the publicity of discourses, objects, events, and practices (Dickinson, Blair, & Ott, 2010). Public memory is understood as bearing a relationship to the present, narrating shared identities, partial, and possessing a history (Zelizer, 2009). Blair et al. (2010) identify the ways in which place, particularly places of memory, are important to memory. First, place is a symbolic and material vehicle of memory. Because place cannot be transported, read as a narrative, or viewed like a photograph, place affects memory in very special ways. As it is important to identify the various means that memory is understood, represented, shared, and embraced, places are such means. Second, special kinds of places are particularly associated with public memory, the "memory places." Places have survived as a recognizable memory apparatus from ancient times (Yates, 1999).

The relationships between memory and place and time and space are inherently rhetorical as well, (place/space: memory/ time). Just like place is defined from and defines space (Tuan, 1977) so is memory defined in relationship to time. Place is space that is bordered, specified, and locatable by being named, deployed in and deploying space; it is different from open, undesignated, and undifferentiated space. So, memories are differentiated, named "events" marked for recognition from amid an undifferentiated temporal succession of occurrences (Dickinson et al., 2010). So, both memory and place are rhetorical, as they emerge from being "recognizable" as named, bordered, and differentiated by symbolic and material interventions. Their recognizability does not suggest that they are not contestable, because just as there are debates over public memory, there arguments and debates over designations of place.

Places of memory shape the communist past in contemporary Albania based on what is addressed and by whom and where, their partiality and legibility to particular audiences, how they address the past based on display and content, their history of becoming, and the public debates that they have generated. While I focus on the SWM in Shkoder and the HL museum in Tirana, there are three other places of memory. The Spac Prison Memorial site in Miredite, where the infamous political prison and slave labor camp during the communist regime is now turning into a significant place of memory. The two Bunk'Art museums in Tirana, in which the former underground military and security bunkers transformed into museums that are especially geared to tourists.

In the next section, I describe the SWM and the HL museums I investigated for this study and examine how each works to rhetorically shape Albania's communist past. I argue that the ways in which these places shape the public memory of the communist past can be best understood by classifying them into two categories: counter-memory and the official version of memory. The SWM and HL museums are significant elements of the larger national memory infrastructure. These places draw their particular meanings as sites of witnesses and perpetrators based on their symbolic and material display. However, their rhetorical force is heightened when they are positioned in comparison in the larger communist memory infrastructure. I visited the museums several times during the summer of 2017 and followed the public discourse about them.

Counter-Memory: The Site of Witness and Memory Museum in Shkoder

The Site of Witness and Memory (SWM) in Shkoder officially opened in 2014. The SWM museum was the first in the country and the only regional museum to commemorate the victims of communism. The people of Shkoder and civil society took the initiative to convert a place of suffering and torture into a site of memory. The building was originally constructed during the 19th century as a family home. In the 1930s, it was bought and used by the Franciscan Church. In 1946, it was confiscated by the communist regime, which turned the building into the Shkoder Branch of the Ministry of the Interior and the main district jail, a function it served until 1990. After the communist regime ended, the building was returned to the church, which offered it to the citizens in 2012 to be turned into a museum. The museum is on one of the main busy streets of the city, a short walk from the down-town cultural centers. Shkoder is one of the oldest cities in the country and is especially well-known for its contribution to culture and art. The SWM is designed as an educational institution, which is reflected in its mission state-ment written in Albanian and English that hangs in the entrance hall. The mission statement is also printed on flyers that are passed out to visitors when they arrive: "The Site of Witness and Memory museum's mission is to bring the first-hand witness' stories to the new generation, so the troubled painful communist past is never repeated."

When placed into the country's communist memory infrastructure, the SWM museum functions as a counter-memory site of Albania's communist past by transcending from a regional to a national focus, from victim to martyr, and from personal to historical. In the following analysis, I illustrate how the SWM museum tells the story of suffering, and at the same time fosters a spirit of resilience, hope, and freedom in ways that represent new national values.

A Regional Story becomes National. The Site of Witness and Memory museum functions as a counter-memory by narrating a regional story as a national story. The city takes pride in its museums and cultural heritage sites, and the SWM museum is another historical and cultural landmark for all visi-tors. The SWM museum, together with the other museums of national signif-icance, turn this region's resistance to the communist regime into a national symbol. The Site of Witness and Memory was the first place to commemorate the victims of communism in the country and was the first to be established in the remains of a former detention site. The museum's display of regional victims and persecution serves as a template that allows visitors to imagine what the regime was like across the country. A small part represents the whole.

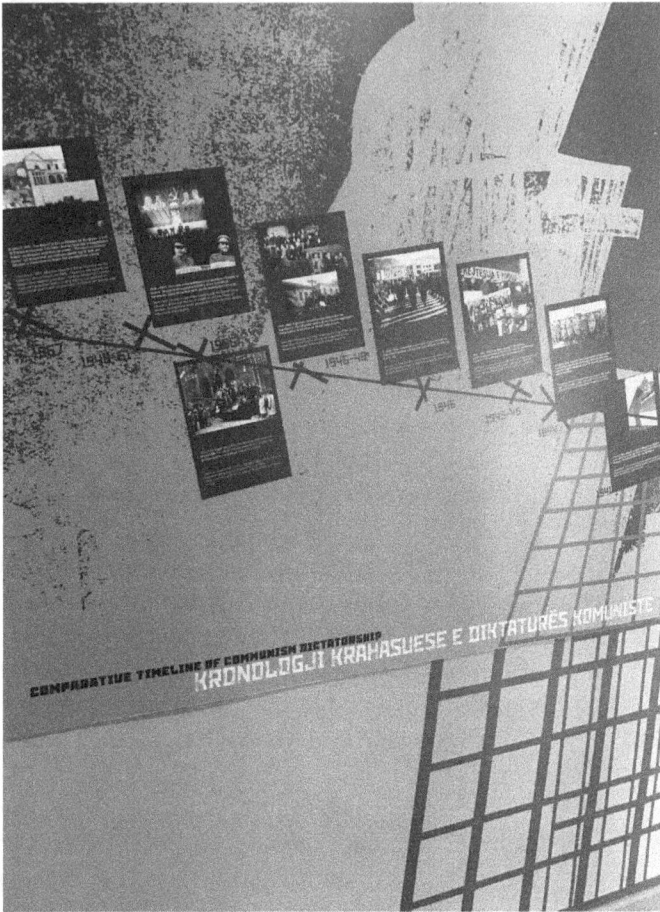

Figure 4.1: Cross-sectional display. Note: All photos were taken by the author at the museum sites.

The museum has two main parts: the museum hall with the exhibition, library, and media room, and the prison section with the prison and jail cells kept in the same condition as they were during the communist era. The entrance hall displays facts about communist persecution in the region. The displays are cross-sectional; local events are accompanied by national and international developments that occurred at the same time (see Figure 4.1). The entrance wall quantifies persecution in the city: 2,890 imprisoned, 1,924 exiled and send to internment camps, 601 executed, 61 religious clerics, and 136 deaths from torture. There is also a map of the city that pinpoints the city's 23 communist prison locations alongside photos of the prisons. The map is displayed on a tall, wall-sized stand that is mounted on a box of barbed wire. The detailed description states that these buildings were family-owned houses and religious institutions that were confiscated by the regime and converted into houses of torture. The history of the museum building's use is described chronologically, from its original use as a family home during the 19th century, to a religious institution during the Albanian Kingdom, to the Central Regional Authority Branch of the Internal Affairs from 1946 to 1991.

The descriptions of the victims, the prisons, and the building's history are regional data that get their significance when placed into the national context. The intensity of the discrimination and the higher number of prisons in the region resulted from the entire city's resistance to the regime (Bushati, 1999). Immediately after the communist state began its operations on December 13, 1944, only two weeks after the fascist liberation, the whole city of Shkoder was under a state of emergency (Qazimi, 2012). The museum's display describes the number of buildings that were turned into detention centers and prisons that mimicked the overall centralized structure of the regime. These places of torture and control were established throughout the country to control, persecute, and oppress any kind of opposition to the communist ideology; however, in Shkoder, the torture sites were a direct response to the open anti-communist movement. It is this region's collective resistance to the oppression that made Shkoder a symbol of anticommunism. The regime had specific directives that the State Security "must increase the number of people in prison" (Dervishi, 2015, p. 77). One of the stories displayed before the interrogation rooms read, "For the prisoner under investigation, the calling up to the office of the investigator would mean a real torture. Prisoners were usually called to be interrogated twice a day. The investigator would insist that the prisoner assert the charges that interested the purpose of the specific process, which the prisoner would sit and think about in the cell, formulating answers to potential investigator's questions. Many prisoners could not resist the tortures and accepted false charges and accusations for themselves and other friends." In many ways, the communist repression started in Shkoder. Names of victims displayed on the museum include nationally recognized intellectuals, writers, priests, scientists, doctors, and teachers. At Zef Pellumbi, a priest who survived communist persecution, was interrogated at this exact prison before his long imprisonment of 27 years. His book, a trilogy, *Rrno per me Tregue (Live to Tell)* was published in 1998, and it has become a legendary story of communist terror and survival in Albania.

The museum's library has an impressive press archive of news articles published in Shkodra's newspaper during the pre-communist era and during WWII, until the publication was banned by the regime in 1945. The press section reopens the national drama of communist oppression and censure. The articles displayed cover national and international topics to provide evidence of the scope of the Shkoder press before communism. Some of this press was restarted in 1992 in an effort to bring back the original editorial and national inspiration it had in the 1930s (Skanjeti, 1994). However, the library's archive provides visitors with first-hand experience of what was able to be published during the communist regime. All democratic reporting of a political, cultural, and regional nature was suspended first in Shkoder, as the communist regime was prepared to prevent any form of communication, media, or art that could interfere with the ideological brain-washing strategy with the regime built the communist ideology (Qazimi, 2012). The closing of democratic media in Shkoder at the regime's start transcends the regional; it becomes part of the national story.

The Victims are Martyrs. The second way the SWM museum works as counter-memory is that it *turns the victims into martyrs*. Starting at the entrance hall and continuing in the exhibits, the visitors are presented with the numbers, facts, photos, dates, places, locations, and descriptions of the victims of communism in Shkoder. The display is not crowded and has room for more than just the names of the victims: it includes the time, the location, and the reason for their arrest, imprisonment, or execution. The following displays grab visitors' attention as they proceed through the museum. The display on the January-February 1946 Postriba revolt, when residents mobilized for a free and democratic country, is detailed: it includes the dates and names of the organizers, how they were confronted by the military and how they were executed in groups, their families were sent to internment camps and their houses and properties were confiscated.

Next are the displays about various communist trials. The names of the persecuted and the reasons for their arrests invite visitors to imagine the consequences of expressing democratic ideals and aspirations during the communist regime. Another significant display shows the first anti-communist revolt in the country. In 1946, Albanian Union groups were charged with treason for propaganda. The Union was created by Catholic priests to work with young people of different religious views towards religious freedom and its vision was based on the values of love for the country, the nation, and religious freedom. The descriptions provide details about how the Union was confronted with arrests, persecution, and executions. Another display shows photos and describes the arrest and persecution of three teenage boys in 1961 who were accused of treason. The description explains how they were arrested for trying to leave the country to visit the forbidden outside world.

These displays are representations of the basic freedoms people were fighting for then and the price they had to pay for resisting the regime. By displaying and describing the victims and their cause, the museum functions to highlight the victims' sacrifices. The display invites visitors to have a sense of gratitude and respect towards the victims' resistance and ultimate sacrifice. The victims at the SWM museum are now depicted as martyrs. As the visitors read the documents about the victims and their corresponding descriptions, they feel a sense of appreciation and approval for the victims' actions. At the SWM museum, the victims are not doomed, rather, it is the communist regime that will meet its inevitable end.

The visual display of the documents contributes to the portrayal of the victims as martyrs. The color, spatial arrangement, and artwork show the painful past, but also imply the spirit of survival and hope. The colors of the display and the walls are light; the display-background ratio invites visitors to appreciate the artifact displayed while highlighting it and prioritizing the people's story. The official documents displayed, the facts and orders of executions, imprisonments, and internments are clearly presented and act as evidence of the events. However, when these documents are juxtaposed with the victims' stories, they are not as significant as the facts that are displayed about victims' responses to the persecutions. The descriptions of the victims' statements at trials, their letters to their family, their public statements on how they survived interrogation, and their photos invite the visitors to construct a past that focuses on overcoming repression. The story is transformed into one about the oppressed rather than the regime, no matter how horrible it was, and those who resisted it are remembered as martyrs.

A sculpture of a young man chained inside a barbed five-point star, the symbol of communism (see Figure 4.2) is displayed in the museum. The sculpture exemplifies the victims of communist repression. As Burke states, "martyrdom is the idea of total voluntary self-sacrifice enacted in a grave cause before a perfect witness" (Burke, 1970, p. 248). Just like Christ was executed on the Cross after being accused of preaching against religious orthodoxy, so this artwork represents the people of Shkoder executed for speaking against the communist ideology. The sculpture symbolizes hope and return as well. This artwork represents the victims of communism turning into martyrs of freedom. The young man of the sculpture exemplifies a martyr who by refusing and resisting the communist regime paid the highest price of self-sacrifice to redeem freedom and democracy.

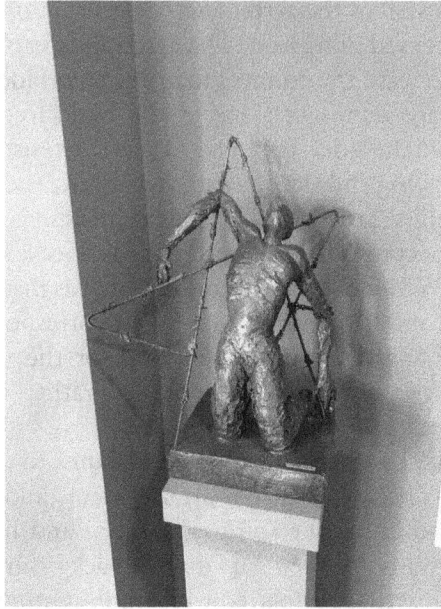

Figure 4.2: The martyr.

Personal Stories become Historical. The third way the SWM museum functions as counter-memory is when the victims' personal stories become historical. The witnesses telling their story allows the visitors to imagine the painful past and create a perception about the context when it all happened as a distinct historical period when the described events could make sense. The consequences of the communist regime are personal and historical. A displayed letter sent home from a prisoner is more than personal; it becomes a historical event when visitors read it. The personal story of the victim becomes concrete—a way for the visitors to experience the past. The exhibition hall offers objects used and manufactured in prison, manuscripts, and personal letters of prisoners sent to the families. The displayed stories about the communist trials and the internment camps become a historical illustration in the museum. The letters from the prisoners to their family offer another way to demonstrate how victims become martyrs at the SWM in Shkoder. The displayed letter from Arshi Pipa sent to his family states, "Physically I have become a corpse, but my thoughts and reasoning are free."

The glass panel, on the next section of the museum, shows original documents of orders given by the regime to punish, torture, and discriminate against the citizens of this region. The execution orders given and signed by the dictator are of special importance. The displayed official order from the military court states the names of the people to be executed and the request to report their last words. The audiovisual room provides videos and short films from the communist time. The personal stories, the official copies of documents related to their cases, and objects and artifacts invite visitors to view the display as historical evidence. Some letters of prisoners displayed were sent home to ask that families send them clothes and shoes, while others want to know why they never received a letter from their family, and still others are mere pieces of paper passed in secret during visits that say things like, "I am being accused of propaganda," or "they think I am a spy," or "please do not worry about me, I will survive." Another piece of artwork, displayed in the Shkodra Remembers section, is a coin. The artist's explanation is next to the artifact and reads "when I asked S. Jera he told me a guard said to him 'we will give you the 70 Albanian *Lek* too.' It was a well-known expression, used by police officers in the prisons of the regime, which meant the prisoner was to be shot. The 70 Albanian *Lek* was not a real piece of currency in the monetary system. I have tried to create it here as a symbol of the devaluation of human life during the communist era and the cynical disregard with which prisoners were treated in that period."

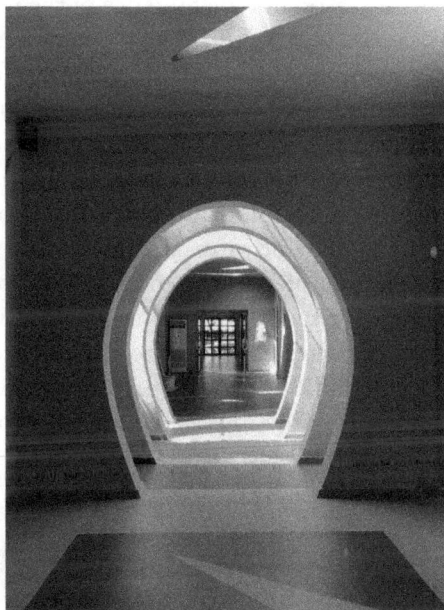

Figure 4.3: Purgatory.

The museum's architecture and spatial organization materially and symbolically contribute to turning personal stories into a historical experience. After the exhibition hall, the corridor that connects the entrance with the prison cells is curated as an art gallery. The gallery is designed as a passage under red circled gates that symbolize the route to a biblical hell: the path to the jail cells. This section of the museum is called *Purgatory* (see Figure 4.3). The gallery contains artwork that symbolizes torture. By giving torture a nuance of holy sacrifice, the passage prepares visitors to reinterpret the past through a historical context in which the content of the exhibition can be imagined and make sense. The display at the entrance states that the building's original design has been maintained. The jail and torture cells are called *biruce* (holes), as they are extremely small with very little light. The two-level cells are kept as they were when in use; the lower level was reserved for political prisoners. At the end of the jail corridor are the torture/investigation rooms containing torture equipment. As the visitors walk through the narrow corridors of the jail cells where the curators have displayed objects and information about the people who suffered in this space, they are positioned to experience these cells as more than personal stories.

The visitors are invited to step into a historical perspective especially when they visit the cells dedicated to the total control of the media and propaganda. The descriptions in these cells explain that these walls are covered in newspapers from the communist period in remembrance of the journalists who were detained here. Another *biruce* is dedicated to women detained and tortured in these cells. The communist propaganda slogans were used to justify and motivate censorship, surveillance, control, oppression, and isolation. Some of the slogans painted on the wall are: "Religion is opium for the masses," "The Party and the People are one," and "The Proletarian Dictatorship is the only way toward progress." These slogans place visitors into a historical perspective, as it is difficult to imagine or make sense of any of them at present. I have explained how the Site of Witness and memory museum in Shkoder functions as public counter-memory of communist past in three significant ways: the regional story becomes national, the victims become martyrs, and the personal stories become historical. The following section illustrates how the House of Leaves museum functions as the site of perpetrators.

Official Public Memory: The House of Leaves Museum in Tirana

Within the national memorial infrastructure, the House of Leaves (HL) museum serve to produce a controlled version of the communist past. The

HL museum is located in Tirana and in local and national news, it is often labeled as "museum of *doom*" (Vokshi, 2015). The following analysis illustrates the ways in which the HL museum function to neutralize/shift the blame regarding the communist regime's crimes and construct a controlled version of the public memory of the communist past for national and international audiences. The House of Leaves museum of the infamous communist State Security Service was fully initiated, designed, and curated under the official supervision of the socialist government, which is the reformed communist party. The analysis shows that the House of Leaves museum is the memorial site of perpetrators and functions to control the public memory of the past, shifting the blame from state oppression.

The House of Leaves: The Site of Perpetrators

The House of Leaves museum opened in May 2007. It is located near the center and in one of the busiest roads of Tirana, behind the Post Office and the National Bank and across from the Orthodox Cathedral. However, the two-story house does not draw much attention from the road. The red brick walls are typical of early 20th century buildings in Tirana. It was first built as a house for a doctor, then he turned it into a maternity hospital. After WWII, the house was confiscated by the communist regime and used for the secret service called State Security Center. From the outside, the building walls were all covered by ivy tree leaves and was perfectly protected from the public eye, hence the name "the House of Leaves." There has been a public debate to whether the House of Leaves will and should be open to the public. In addition, the debate about the House of Leaves has been concurrent with the larger debate on the opening of the communist secret service files.

The wall that separates the building's yard from the street is all covered in a plain metric design that announces the House of Leaves museum. There is only a small door that visitors must get through which takes them directly to the ticket booth. A security guard is on the other side of the room separated by a glass wall. It is a quiet place with a clean yard and preserved as it was during the era of communism. Across from the building's main entrance is a metal horizontal door to an underground tunnel with the description of the interrogation cells. There are two giant binoculars directed at the road, an artistic work symbolizing the surveillance goal of this place during communism. The central aim of the House of Leaves is stated at the entrance: "This museum is dedicated to all the innocent people who were spied on, surveilled on, arrested, persecuted, convicted, and executed during the communist regime," written in Albanian and in English. At the entrance, there is the prologue to the museum's sections and the dedication to the history of the building, which was transformed from a maternity house to a surveillance and political control center. The sections are organized as follows: bugs, live microphones, the internal and external enemy, private and everyday life, voices of the past, and the panopticon illustration. The visitors come to this museum with curiosity, sensitivity, and expectations to visit the place where the communist crimes were designed, initiated, and orchestrated.

Distorted anatomy of a crime scene. The following analysis illustrates how this museum functions to neutralize/shift the blame for the communist crimes and construct a controlled version of the public memory that is "safe" for perpetrators. The extended coverage on how the secret service functioned, the curators enforced interpretations on all the display's content, and the carefully selected facts about the communist regime turns the HL museum into a distorted anatomy of a crime scene. The museum functions not just as a perpetrators' site, but as a perpetrator's story. This sense of control and shift operates in the following three ways: (1) The display and the museum's content are about the system, (2) the visitors are positioned as students and the designers as masters, and (3) the selective and factual display approach.

Focusing on the system. The museums' main approach is the focus on the Security State Service system. The museum's eight sessions all explain how the system functioned. The first section explains how the surveillance system was organized to establish total control. The museum's display invites visitors from the start to focus on the organizational structure of the former State Security Service (SSS). The large displays of the SSS structure, the diagram, and the bug on room-sized black walls with bright white labels invite visitors to concentrate on understanding the structure/system of surveillance control. The operations of the secret service are explained in detail regarding how they covered every aspect and department of the government, with intelligence and counterintelligence in twelve main district branches. In addition to the diagram of the surveillance system, their spying is displayed again with the bug as the structure of total surveillance, with the bug's head as the State Security Center, the two main subdivisions as antennae, and the branches as its legs, see figure 4.4 below. Both the diagram and the bug are taller than a normal person's height, and this positions visitors as small and vulnerable before the large and solid structure. The display is drawn on the wall of the room on a black background with white lighting, and very precise boxes and lines.

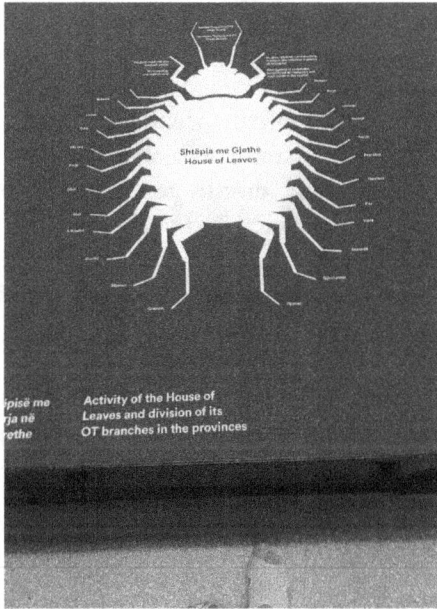

Figure 4.4: The bug.

The following section's display continues with the explanation of how the secret service functioned and how it recruited people. The visitors are invited to focus on the hierarchy within the system, the flow of information and orders from the center, and their execution on the field. The first section displays the scheme of how the secret service files were initiated and planned, and how the surveillance and spying were orchestrated. The section continues with displays and content about how the SSS system operated from "live–microphones," that is, "secret agents among the masses," to e-bugs, that is, the surveillance microphones designed and produced in the State Security laboratory. The description of the communist agitations and propaganda law and the slogan of SSS, which is "for the people by the people," the museum's explanations on how collaborators were recruited invites visitors to perceive the recruiting as inevitable, thus deflecting attention from the perpetrators. The museum display and descriptions position visitors to perceive the SSS regime as one that implicates everybody. In addition, the interpretation label, next to the display reads, "everyone could be a target of secret service ... whether to be spied on or to be recruited for spying." In this way, the perpetrators are neutralized, as they "could be anyone."

The next section continues with displays on how the enemy was created in multiple ways. It was constructed in the movies as well, as part of a state propaganda. Photos from newspapers and films of that time reinforce attention to a system of control and surveillance, demanding that the structure be perceived as the core of the system. The last section of the museum focuses on the symbolism of the regime as the *panopticon*, where everything was surveilled and listen to, a complete rigid and closed structure. As the visitors start with the structure of the system and the bug, the visitors leave the museum with the panoptical visual, reinforcing how the museum reduces the communist past into system and structure.

Designers are the masters. The second key theme evoked at the House of Leaves museum is the positioning of the visitor as "student" and the museum designers as "masters" of explaining and interpreting the totalitarian regime. The visitors are provided with interpretation of every section of the museum from the entrance table. The entrance includes a table that introduces each section and it has an interpretation for each, such as how the dictatorships occur, as if they are introducing a work of art about control and totalitarianism. The museum's interpretations attempt to direct visitors to view the museum as a lecture where the designers explain the communist structure and why it functioned the way it did. The displayed interpretation of surveillance accessories and listening "bugs" states, "the technique is neutral only when it is not used yet …... Each regime uses it differently. It serves the particular needs of the regime, any regime." The displayed interpretation on enemy states, "the perception over the enemy determines the way for repression and control, ways which in turn reinforced who the enemy was, as a vicious cycle of the totalitarian regimes." There is the interpretation on isolation as well, "Self-isolation had the purpose to complete and total control. Claiming to be the only socialist country in the world, all were enemies." The museum designers position themselves as masters of explaining the process of enemy creation in a totalitarian regime. The displayed interpretations on artifacts and objects focus the visitors' attention to the "masters" explanation and creates the perception that the designers are telling it all. This interpretation is presented, "the perception over the enemy determines the way for repression and control, ways which in turn reinforced who the enemy was, - as a vicious cycle of the totalitarian regimes." The rationale of enemy creation continues with the section on surveillance of foreigners as an extension of internal enemies.

Again, the visitors are positioned as students of totalitarian regimes in the sections of the museum that display the everyday social and private life of citizens living during the communist era. The description reads, "surveillance was done on all ... with more intensification on certain groups that were deemed threatening for the party's agenda. Anything any behavior could be labeled/named as enemy action." These sections are authentic displays of artifacts from homes and other private spaces, with the surveillance tools implemented in display as they were used during the communist era. The museum designers' interpretation is that "the communist ideology had a collectivist character and the party-state was ominous and ubiquitous." The displayed interpretations explain how the system is justified by its structure. This is another attempt to distort the past and distance the perpetrators from the crime scene. The museum's interpretation that "the communist ideology had a collectivist character and the party-state was ominous and ubiquitous" invites visitors to see the total surveillance structures supported by communist ideology as so complex that the perpetrators were just the tool it used to operate. The interpretation on the panopticon section reads "the communist did not believe in a perfect society ... so to achieve that, they used absolute control, like the Bentham prison."

Selective factual display. Central to House of Leaves rhetoric is its factual approach and authenticity appeal. The HL museum is built in the former communist secret service center building. The objects displayed are also the original ones used for surveillance, including the secret service files. The visitors are allowed to see but not to touch, which gives the objects the added meaning that they are real, very important, and must be preserved. As Ott, Aoki, and Dickinson (2011) suggest, the contemporary museums emphasize the displayed objects themselves and "operate according to this logic of radical systematization, in which vision is detached from the other senses and visitors' practices of looking are governed by a rationally ordered system of labels" (pp. 223–4).

The House of Leaves is a typical exercise of classification and rationality, which primes visitors to see the museum as an objective description of totalitarianism, surveillance, and control, which in turn, functions to construct a communist past apart from its consequences. The sections are organized to show the structure of surveillance and control. The HL museum displays are clean, sharp, and are carefully classified into categories and subcategories on each of the museum's sections, as in Figure 4.5. Cold facts, graphs, statistics, lighted frames, and labs serve to distance the communist past with its consequences.

Figure 4.5: Spying and surveillance equipment.

In addition to the sophisticated drawings of the State Security Service structure on the backlighted walls and screens, a sense of high importance and worthiness is conveyed by the presentation of the spying and surveillance technology and technique. One large hall is dedicated to communication devices used for secret service, video tapes, computers, printers, radios, microphones on tables and walls, mounted communication cabins in the wall, and a screen that shows pictures and videos from that time. There is much to see in this section, and the technology is classified based on its use and when it was introduced. The large number of objects and the details provided position visitors to see the museum as a technological development. Actually, the visitor is prepared to focus on the Surveillance Bug sections from the first section where the display of the SSS control structure is showed on a form of a bug with branches all over the country (0935). The bug displayed on the operational room techniques shows this photo of a bug with the description "it sucks the blood while people sleep." The emphases on the bug is especially on the surveillance device that was created in Albania with details on its development and use in everything and everywhere. It was called *cimka* (bug) and was developed to counteract surveillance and spying from abroad. Albanian produced spy equipment gives the museum interesting factual and authentic appeal to domestic and foreign visitors and draws

Figure 4.6: The laboratory.

attention to technology. This is reinforced further when visitors check the room where the laboratory of surveillance equipment and spying activity are displayed. The laboratory, as in figure 4.6, was used to fabricate photos and to duplicate documents for spying purposes and fabricate evidence for the "internal enemies, and to check for biological weapons on mail coming to communist leadership from abroad."

The visitors are invited to focus on selected facts about how the surveillance arsenal was administered. The original agreements and former state directives are displayed on lighted frames. The wires that connect these agreements displayed on the walls show structure as well. Everything is clean, well kept, well organized, and connected. The visitor can't help but feel overwhelmed with important objects and clear structure. Also included in this section are the "operational techniques," where documents from that time that show protocol agreements for the purchase of the surveillance equipment from the Soviet Union until 1961, an agreement with China's government until late 1970, other eastern countries, and even with the Western countries afterwards. The focus on internal operational techniques and foreign collaboration on equipment adds to the factual appeal of the surveillance technology. While the museum approach to cold facts works in all the sections, from structure of SSS, to enemy creating philosophy and propaganda, to everyday life, the display of the technology of the surveillance conveys and shifts the attention to facts in a more direct way.

Display rather than consequences. The House of Leaves museum heavily focuses on display and facts about the structure of SSS and surveillance techniques, and operations are an attempt to absolve the former Security State Service from the consequences of their activity. The consequences of the SSS are only mentioned near the exit, with one room all painted in black and with the names of the victims who lost their lives because of the SSS activity. The names are written in white small print and are not easily readable, and on the exit stairs there are falling leaves painted on the walls. The initial dedication to the victims at the entrance and the exit room with names on the wall are the only mentions of consequences. Dark, sharp, and clean are the murderer's display of his own crimes, while the names of victims on one room are some of many – each one is one more. The museum curators have dedicated more space to displaying debatable public surveys on perceptions about spying in communism than to the victims of the regime.

The House of Leaves museum focuses on structure and technology and could not absolve the SSS from the crimes despite the focus on display, facts, and authenticity of the building and the artifacts. The "multiplying levels of authenticity and simulacra cover profound absences" (Dickinson, Ott, & Aoki, 2005, p. 101) and the "absent history is crucial to the museum's rhetoric" (Stolkin, 1992, pp. 13–14). In addition to reduced physical space on the consequences from the SSS activity, the interpretations of introductions to the sections and the on the labels of artifacts displayed the HL museum attempt to re-contextualize the SSS activity and absolve it from its crimes. The interpretation on the technique of surveillance serves to contextualize surveillance anywhere and anytime, as "the technique is neutral only when it is not used yet . . .. The bugs were used for surveillance. Each regime uses it differently and it serves the particular needs of the regime, any regime." Also, the contextualization occurs when the displays describe what was counted as crime and punishable during the era of communism, where more room is given to explain ordinary crimes than to political and ideological crimes. The operational techniques are re-contextualized when details concerning international protocol and agreements about equipment are described in detail. Attempts to provide a context that would shift the focus from the SSS activity are present in every section. One of the descriptions reads "the tortures were recognized by the regime as a way to keep the enemies in check." Sometimes the re-contextualization is done by providing meticulous information on surveillance fieldwork from "live microphone" to "e-spying" and bugs used to create the secret files. Original files are displayed with names erased for the purpose of understanding the administrative process of the SSS.

The House of Leaves museum is the original SSS building, where the surveillance and control were designed and executed, and the authentic surveillance artifacts are carefully displayed and presented. This makes the site as a legitimate crime scene. However, the museum, by positioning visitors to focus on facts in isolation from their consequences, serves as a distortion of the past. The emphasis on structure, facts, original artifact functions, and selective data are "multiplying levels of authenticity" that "cover profound absences" (Dickinson et al, 2005). The memory of the communist crimes is transformed into a lecture on the communist regime structure, the surveillance technology of the era, and an ideological rational for justifying the SSS activity. The museum's claimed dedication to the victims of state surveillance is anything but that; instead the House of Leaves museum serves as the story of perpetrators, whom by attempting to free themselves from guilt offer a distorted version of the communist past.

Conclusion

The SWM museum is best understood as a site of witness and serves as a counter-memory in the larger Albanian national memory infrastructure. This is demonstrated through its transcendence of the communist past story from a regional to national focus, from victim to martyr, and from personal to historical. The House of Leaves museum functions as a site of perpetrators and serves to control the public memory of the communist past in three ways: it focuses on the system, the museum's designers are presented as masters, and it uses a selective and factual display approach. Both the SWM and HL museum invoke particular pasts based on who tells the story, where, and why. The places of memory investigated in this study serve as powerful vehicles of memory of Albania's communist past. The rhetorical examination of these memory places suggests that *who* remembers is key to shaping the communist past. In addition, these places of memory construct a particular story of the communist past based on their specific locations. They engage visitors in particular and powerful ways based on their mission. The SWM museum in Shkoder, as a site of witness, serves as counter-memory and constructs preferred identities for visitors who come to see the atrocities committed by the former regime and the resistance and sacrifices made by those who opposed communism. The HL museum constructs a different past that is also based on who tells the story, where, and why. The story presented by the HL museum is of the perpetrators, at the location where crimes were planned and executed. This museum constructs its visitors' identities as those of students who want to learn how totalitarian regimes functioned. These places of memory construct differing versions of the communist past. When considered as part of the larger memory infrastructure, this variation demonstrates that public memory is weaved into deeper social, cultural, political interests.

This investigation of memory places related to communism makes a significant contribution to the understanding of the workings of public memory. The results of the analysis suggest the manifestation of counter-memory, especially when remembering traumatic national pasts. This study could inform rhetorical scholarship that investigates former state crimes committed by communist regimes or other oppressive regimes. The work presented here is especially important for scholars in the United States and for those in Western Europe when they address communist regimes: As Stephane Courtois has suggested on *The Black Book of Communism*, published in 1999, the Western scholars often neglect the communist crimes regardless of its horrific records of 100 million people killed and the widespread "effect on one-third of humanity on four continents, during a period spanning eighty years" (p. 17). Also, through her research on the Sighet Prison in Rumania, Vatulescu suggests that it is important to revisit and reevaluate Western theoretical discussions about memory, mourning, and representations. The rhetorical investigation of the SWM and HL museums in Albania add to previous studies of memory work on communism. Scholarship on public memory is to be encouraged in an attempt to understand the memory of traumatic national pasts and oppressive regimes. Remembering the communist past means constructing a shared understanding of former state crimes that may be distorted and diffused in various ways.

References

Atkinson, J. (2016). Hiding hedonism in plain sight: Acoustic participatory camouflage at the DDR Museum in Berlin. *Javnost - The Public, 23*(3), 237–254.

Blair, C., Dickinson, G., & Ott, B. L. (2010). Introduction: Rhetoric, memory, and place. In G. Dickinson, C. Blair, & B. L. Ott (Eds.), *Places of public memory: The rhetoric of museums and memorials* (pp. 1–42). Tuscaloosa, AL: The University of Alabama Press.

Burke, K. (1970). *The rhetoric of religion: Studies in logology.* Oakland, CA: University of California Press.

Bushati, H., & Bushati, N. (1999). *Shkodra dhe motet: Tradite, ngjarje, njerez.* Shkoder, AL: Rozafat.

Casey, E. S. (2004). Public memory in place and time. In K. R. Philips (Ed.), *Framing public memory* (pp. 17–44). Tuscaloosa, AL: The University of Alabama Press.

Clarke, D. (2017). Understanding controversies over memorial museums: The case of the Leistikowstraße Memorial Museum, Potsdam. *History & Memory, 29*(1), 41–71.

Courtois, S. (1999). *The black book of communism: Crimes, terror, repression.* Cambridge, MA: Harvard University Press.

Cultural Heritage without Borders (2015). *Spaç Prison on the World Monument Fund's 2016 'Watch' List.* Retrieved from http://chwb.org/albania/news/spac-prison-on-the-world-monument-funds-2016-watch-list/

Davis, P. (2013). Memoryscapes in transition: Black history museums, new south narratives, and urban regeneration. *Southern Communication Journal, 2,* 107–127

Dervishi, K. (2015). *Burgjet dhe Kampet a Shqiperise Komuniste.* Instituti I Studimit te Krimeve dhe Pasojave te Komunizmit. Tirane, AL: Maluka.

Dickinson, G., Ott, B. L., & Aoki, E. (2005). Memory and myth at the Buffalo Bill Museum. *Western Journal of Communication, 69*(2), 85–108.

Dickinson, G., Ott, B. L., & Aoki, E. (2006). Spaces of remembering and forgetting: The reverent eye/I at the Plains Indian museum. *Communication and Critical/Cultural Studies, 3*(10), 27–47.

Foucault, M. (1994). Film in popular memory: An interview with Michel Foucault. In J. K. Olick, V. Vinitzky-Seroussi, & D. Levy (Eds.), (2011). *The collective memory reader* (pp. 249–251). Oxford, UK: Oxford University Press.

Halbwachs, M. (1925). On collective memory. In J. K. Olick, V. Vinitzky-Seroussi, & D. Levy (Eds.), (2011). *The collective memory reader* (pp. 139–149). Oxford, UK: Oxford University Press.

James, B. A. (2005). *Imagining post-communism: Visual narratives of Hungary's 1956 revolution.* College Station, TX: Texas A&M University Press.

Ott, B. L., Aoki, E., & Dickinson, G. (2011). Ways of not seeing guns: Presence and absence at the Cody Firearms Museum. *Communication and Critical/Cultural Studies, 8*(3), 215–239.

Qazimi, A. (2012). *Processi i asgjesimit te fese ne communism.* Instituti I Studimit te Krimeve dhe Pasojave te Komunizmit. Tirane, AL: West Print.

Skanjeti, M. (1994). S'eshte kjo Panorama e Shkodres. *Pishtari, 5*(34), 1–7.

Slotkin, R. (1992). *Gunfighter nation: The myth of frontier in 20th century America.* New York, NY: Atheneum.

Tuan, Y.-F. (1977). *Place and space: The perspective of experience.* Minneapolis, MN: University of Minnesota Press.

Vatulescu, C. (2013). Prisons into museums: Fashioning a post-communist place of memory. In J. Bucker & E. Johnson (Eds.), *Rites of place* (pp. 315–335). Evanston, IL: Northwestern University Press.

Vokshi, I. (2015). "Muzeu i së keqes" – kushtuar Bunkartit dhe Shtëpisë së Gjetheve. *Balkan Insight,* Tirana, Albania.

Yates, F. A. (1999). *The art of memory.* London, UK: Pimlico.

Zelizer, B. (2009). Reading the past against the grain: The shape of memory studies. Competing memories. *Critical Cultural Studies in Mass Communication, 12*(2), 313–339.

Cultural Memory, Identity Politics, and Intersectionality

5. (Mis)Remembering Stonewall: Narrative Authority and the American Monomyth in Queer Public Memory

KATHRYN HOBSON
James Madison University

BERNADETTE MARIE CALAFELL
Gonzaga University

SPENCER B. MARGULIES
University of South Florida

"And so don't ever think that if there were no Stonewall that it would just be like it is Now. Because it was a horrible world before that. We were all runaways and some of them were 14 years old. Some people had scalding water thrown on them by their parents. People that couldn't go back home no matter what. And couldn't go back to school no matter what. And that group of people was the catalyst in the riot. It was the street kids who had nothing to lose. That were the force that got it going" (Kasino, 2012, 16:28–16:45).

"The girls, we had had enough. It was just a momentary thing, no one planned anything there was no pre-rehearsal or getting together —— when this happened it simply exploded. The sad thing about all of that was that the gay and lesbian community took that away from us and just completely white-washed us into the background as if we didn't exist and weren't there ... Like that stupid movie that they made! I mean, he [the main character] was really pretty but he wasn't wearing no dress!" (Nicohls, 2016a, para. 10).

Stonewall (2015), directed by Roland Emmerich and released in 2015, based on the events of the 1969 Stonewall riots in New York City, was met with critical disdain by critics and activists alike for its whitewashing of history and fabrication of a white, cisgender, gay male lead. In a *Buzzfeed* article, Allison Willmore (2015) describes the film as "a movie about a pivotal moment in LGBT history as filtered through the perspective of a fictional hunk of Wonder Bread named Danny" (para. 1). Willmore's (2015) perspective was shared by others, such as Stephen Holden (2015), of the *New York Times*, who wrote, "Its invention of a generic white knight who prompted the riots by hurling the first brick into a window is tantamount to stealing history from the people who made it." Of the film, Maya Stanton (2015), of *Entertainment Weekly*, argued,

> Emmerich and screenwriter Jon Robin Baitz could have focused on real-life participants (the filmmakers have been accused of whitewashing history since the trailer debuted, and deservedly so) or explored any number of themes that would have been more compelling than "pretty white kid comes out, struggles." (para. 3)

With an estimated budget of $13, 500, 000, the film grossed a U.S. total of $186, 354, with $112, 414 of that from its opening weekend (Emmerich, 2015). In addition to low box office numbers, with a 10% critics rating on the website *Rotten Tomatoes*, the film is considered a flop (Stonewall, 2015).

In response to these criticisms, the white openly gay cisgender German director, Emmerich, cried foul suggesting the film was "politically correct" as,

> It had black, transgender people in there. We just got killed by one voice on the internet who saw a trailer and said, this is whitewashing Stonewall. Stonewall was a white event, let's be honest. But nobody wanted to hear that any more. (Nichols, 2016b, para. 4)

Of criticisms of his casting of a white straight actor as an invented "heroic" white cisgender gay male lead, Emmerich further shared,

> You have to understand one thing: I didn't make this movie only for gay people, I made it also for straight people ... I kind of found out, in the testing process, that actually, for straight people, [Danny] is a very easy in. Danny's very straight-acting. He gets mistreated because of that. [Straight audiences] can feel for him. (Keating, 2015, para. 5)

Emmerich further diluted the story, framing it in terms of the struggles of LGBTQ+ youth with homelessness, while deracializing the phenomenon through a generic (read: white, cis, masculine) lead, suggesting,

The problem on the streets hasn't changed since 1969. We may have gay marriage now, but most of these homeless kids come from the small towns where
growing up gay is still terribly difficult, and I wanted this story at the heart of
the film. (Jones, 2015, para. 14)

The controversy over the film is representative of the constant struggle over
queer public and cultural memory; a struggle that consistently erases queer
people of color, trans folxs, and queer feminine folx (Hobson, 2015) in favor
of the politics of white gay male cisgender homonormativity (Duggan, 2002).
This discourse is spread worldwide as a marker of civilizing unruly nations
and unruly people, as marginalized bodies are policed and erased from the
dominant white cis-heterosexual narrative (Calafell, 2017; Pérez, 2015; Puar,
2007). Building on Puar (2007), Pérez (2015) suggests that U.S. imperialist,
white, middle-class, heteronormative and homonormative subjects construct
non-westernized brown bodies as primitive. He adds that "the very notion of
civilization requires a fantasied, primitive space onto which repressed desires
are projected and disavowed" (p. 105).

 Stonewall (2015) becomes a medium to act out a "civilization fantasy
tourism" where the audience is subjected to traumatic historical events for
entertainment purposes. Emmerich has openly acknowledged how his own
identity as a white gay man allowed him as a director to put his own experience in the film (Keating, 2015). However, what remains uninterrogated
is how Emmerich (who as a German filmmaker self-funded a great deal of
the film) draws upon an imperialist script of white gay rights to shape a U.S.
American historical moment of protest, which was actually led by radical
queer and trans people of color. According to Pérez (2015),

The development of an Anglo-American tourism industry to service a growing
leisure class contributed to the formation of a cosmopolitan gay male identity,
making available for consumption both spaces and bodies imagined as pre civilized. (p. 105)

Thus, in this chapter, we examine how the fictionalized character of Danny,
the white cisgender gay male lead, comes to represent the homonormative
imperialist desire to co-opt collective public memories of Stonewall from
queer and trans people of color as a means of spreading discourses of white
cis-gay civility. Viewers are invited to act as voyeurs through Danny's eyes
who are encouraged to identify with his framing as the white cisgender,
masculine man, who is a savior-figure with an active disdain for femininity.
However, Danny strategically uses femininity for his own means of "social
capital" when necessary and then discards it when it no longer suits his agenda
(Bourdieu, 1996). Likewise, queer people of color are used as props for their

ability to help Danny self-actualize and lead him to salvation. Any character of difference becomes a parody of queer existence used as oracles to help Danny find his true identity, while those characters and their lives are shameful and expendable. *Stonewall* (2015) constitutes a certain queer history, yet it does so in problematic ways.

To this end, we ask what are the politics of a white German cisgender queer male having the narrative authority to re-center a white gay cisgender lead at the cost of erasing queer and trans* people of color? How does the material rhetoric he has created to enshrine community memory reinforce a preferred meaning for white homonormative queers?

History of the Stonewall Inn Riots

"What really happened?" History is a contentious concept—can we ever know the truth of what happened in the past? History lies in the liminal space of recollection, documentation, as well as cultural memory. Most commonly, the Stonewall Riots are associated with queer people rising up against police because of dress code and alcohol laws, and thus, beginning the Gay Liberation Movement. While we can never know it all, the following is a conglomeration of historical recollections from several people present at the Stonewall Inn during the protests.

The Stonewall Inn, a bar in the village of New York City was a haven for LGBTQ+ folx who desired a place to dance and drink where they could express their non-normative gender and sexual identities (Lisker, 1969). The bar, owned by the mob, was only one of the places where homosexuals (the term used in 1969) could drink since it was illegal to serve alcohol to members of the LGBTQ+ community at that time (Holland, 2017). In a *New York Times* newspaper article from Saturday, June 29,1969, the unknown author states that "Hundreds of young men went on a rampage in Greenwich Village shortly after 3 A.M. yesterday after a force of plain-clothes men raided a bar that the police said was well known for its homosexual clientele" ("4 Policemen Hurt," 1969). The raids continued throughout the weekend and finally dispersed on Sunday.

The Stonewall Inn riots are often cited as the pinnacle of the modern-day gay rights movement and Gay Pride demonstrations now happen around the same time in June to commemorate the riots. Scholars are critical of elevating Stonewall because it was one of many incidents happening around the country at the time (Armstrong & Crage, 2006). Events like The New Year's Ball Raid, in San Francisco, January 1965; Compton's Cafeteria Disturbance, August 1966; and the Black Cat Raid in Los Angeles, January 1967, were happening around the same time, and yet, are not revered in the same way as Stonewall (Armstrong & Crage, 2006). The reasons for this devaluation are multiple, with other historical events happening at the time, that is, the Civil Rights Movement; a lack of national traction, with most of the events being seen as more localized; and thus they did not become as notable as "the shot glass heard 'round the world'" at Stonewall.

While some news sources credit young gay men for starting the riots at the Stonewall Inn, queer folxs present at the riots had different recollections of that night. Jerry Lisker's (1969) piece published in *The Daily News*, writes:

> Queens, princesses, and ladies-in-waiting began hurling anything they could get their polished, manicured fingernails on. Bobby pins, compacts, curlers, lipstick tubes and other femme fatale missiles were flying in the direction of the cops. The war was on. The lilies of the valley had become carnivorous jungle plants. (para. 9)

Elements of femininity embraced by many at the Stonewall Inn were cloaked in overtly racialized overtones in Lisker's (1969) piece, which reflects his observations during the riots—that most of the folx rioting were people of color. Drag queens and transgender women, mainly Puerto Rican and African American used feminine accouterments as weapons against the white cisgender police force attempting to quell the riots and restrain rioters. Various queer, primarily transwomen of color formed barrier lines to prevent police from attacking the rest of the rioters (Levine, 2010). On Saturday, during the riots, a group of young queer people began cheering, "Gay power" and a group of cheerleaders began to chant, "We are the Stonewall girls/ We wear our hair in curls/ We have no underwear/ We show our pubic hairs!" (Truscott IV, 2003, p. 570). Embracing femininity was a distinctive element of the Stonewall rioters, and the right to express their femininity was a top priority of the transwomen and drag queens who started and participated in the riots.

In the interview with Keating (2015), Emmerich said that he consulted with historians and veterans and concluded that "there were only a couple of transgender women in the Stonewall ever. They were like a minority" (para. 5). However, not all Stonewall veterans agree with that assertion. According to Calafell (2019), histories of the colonized, transwomen of color, are erased to privilege more palatable white, cis narratives of queer history. Even in the case of Marsha P. Johnson, a black transwoman, her story was co-opted by directors assuming narrative authority over her life and framing her as a trauma victim, although her life was more multifaceted than that (Calafell, 2019). In an interview with Mey Rude (2015) in Autostraddle, Miss Major Griffin-Gracy, a black transwoman present at the time of the riots, remembers that it was actually cisgender people in the minority that night. She recalls:

> I'm sorry, but the last time I checked, the only gay people I saw hanging around [the Stonewall] were across the street cheering. They were not the ones getting slugged or having stones thrown at them," she said. "It's just aggravating. And hurtful! For all the girls who are no longer here who can't say anything, this movie just acts like they didn't exist. (paras. 3–4)

Griffin-Gracy explains in the interview with Rude (2015) that she is not surprised that such a film was being made again because it had been done just a few years prior, and it was whitewashed, too. She explains, "I sent them [the filmmakers] a note, who I was, I wanted to talk to them for a minute. No one even acknowledged the fact that I came [to the riots]" (para. 15).

In regards to different perceptions of the same events, the concept of cultural memory circulates through communities in various ways, providing narratives of "what really happened." Emmerich's decision to consult with historians over transwomen and drag queens of color present illustrate his perpetuation of imperialist discourses, choosing to consult those with the financial capital and power to create and narrate the history of a movement, rather than discussing what happened with the marginalized folx who were present.

As Griffin-Gracy explains in her interview with Huffpost writer James Nicohls (2016a), "You know, it's a matter of white people already feel like they rule the world and make history anything they want it to be, as they have done for years" (para. 8). She suggests that history is not just systematic facts, but rather something written and circulated by those in power, which perpetuates marginalization. However, it is not just white people Griffin-Gracy is critical of, but the mainstream LGBTQ+ community who co-opted Stonewall's history, while erasing the contributions of trans people, especially transwomen of color. Two of the transwomen were Marsha P. Johnson and Sylvia Rivera; yet their narratives are misconstrued to fit the director's vision of Danny as instigator and white savior.

Both Marsha P. Johnson and Sylvia Rivera were influential drag queens, transwomen of color, and gay liberation activists before, and after the Stonewall Inn riots. While Johnson does have a significant role in the film, Rivera is absent from the film altogether. Erasing her from the film perpetuates the myth that transwomen were insignificant in the riots, and in queer liberation organizing altogether. Rather, a white, cisgender male representing the filmmaker becomes the pinnacle of LGBTQ+ organizing in the 1960s and 1970s. Sylvia Rivera's absence in the film further perpetuates a mis(re-membering) of the Stonewall Riots in favor of a dominant cis white male framework.

While always incomplete, the following details the events of that June evening as remembered by Johnson and others present at the Stonewall Inn. Marsha P. Johnson arrived at the Stonewall Inn on the evening of the riots to celebrate her 25th birthday. She was one of the first queer people to come to Stonewall in drag (King, 2015). In a documentary about Johnson's life, the filmmaker explains that after the Stonewall Inn had been raided multiple times in one month, and the LGBTQ+ people were feeling especially targeted, although the raids were supposedly due to mob activity, the girls had gotten fed up. He heard from Robin Sousa [another drag queen activist] that Johnson yelled " 'I got my civil rights!' and then threw a shot glass into a mirror. And that started the riots" (Kasino, 2012, 15:52–17:00). Thus, began a riot when trans people, (men, women, and gender non-conforming folx) fought back against the police, refusing to succumb to law enforcement, and breaking free of the paddy wagons. As Griffin-Gracy recalls, "The police got so scared they backed into the club and locked the doors!" (Rude, 2015, para. 11). While there are various recollections of how the riots started, several popular press items state that it was Johnson's "shot glass heard round the world" that got the ball rolling.

Whether or not it was the absolute peak of all the gay rights movements at the time, it is obvious that the Stonewall Riots played a significant role in queer history and in public memory. While "what really happened" will linger unanswered, how we make sense of remembering the Stonewall Inn riots is what matters. This is what scholars refer to as public memory, and like history, it is also contentious.

The Struggle Over Public Memory

Matthew Houdek and Kendall R. Phillips (2017) define public memory as "the circulation of recollections among members of a given community" that are:

> [im]perfect records of the past; rather, they entail what we remember, the ways we frame, and what aspects we forget. Broadly public memory differs from official histories in that the formal is more informal, diverse, and mutual where the latter is often *presented* as formal, singular, and stable. (p. 1)

Writing about queer memory, Dunn (2009) argues for the importance of studying material rhetoric that represents memories, such as statues. He suggests,

> Material rhetoric simultaneously provides an opportunity to further detail the role materiality plays in queer public memory more generally. Constrained by

heteronormative forces and erased by historical arbiters, queers have often relied upon the most ephemeral forms of memory - like gesture, performance, and intergenerational storytelling - to maintain their shared pasts. While many of these memory rhetoric's have important material qualities, rarely have queers been afforded the means to enshrine their memories in material forms as enduring as monuments and commemorative sites. Thus, highly material memory projects ... provide substantial opportunities for queers to disrupt the forgetting and erasure that has so contributed to GLBTQ marginalization. (Dunn, 2009, p. 437)

However, Dunn (2009) cautions that "the inclusion of such rhetoric's into the queer memory repertoire simultaneously produces unintended consequences for how historical and contemporary GLBTQ identity is conceptualized" (p. 437). He posits that material rhetorics may represent the "preferred means by which official community memories have been enshrined" (p. 437). As a national historic landmark/monument and New York State monument, *Stonewall* (2015) operates as a site of public memory, similar to a memorial statue. It is a site of material rhetoric that many read as telling the "official story" of the start of the Gay Liberation Movement. In the case of the riots at Stonewall, it is central to ask, who owns public memory of Stonewall, the location, the events of the riots, and the erasure of central participants?

Stonewall (2015) itself is a site of cultural memory and material rhetoric in which distorted historical narratives contorts the public perception of past events. In her discussion of films that focus on the struggles of African and African American folx, Kelly J. Madison (1999) argues "Because these films are 'historical' (if not historically accurate)" it is important to understand "the role of the mass media in the construction of 'collective memory'" (p. 400). Madison (1999) defines collective memory as

the shared memories and recollections of social groups. Both individual and collective memory may at times be in error; both may be distorted and biased. However, distortion and bias in collective memory is of much greater consequence because ... Shared memories of the past are constructed, nurtured, and invoked as tools to defend political aims, objectives, and realities of the present. (p. 400)

Madison's work is central as it helps us frame the political stakes of memory, particularly as it finds its way into films, which often become cultural master narratives or shorthand references for a historical event. Films, as visual narratives connected to and contributing to public and collective memory, also tell us who are the central players in history. Thus, we are interested in how *Stonewall* (2015) frames the collective and public memories of the Stonewall riots.

Danny: Cisgender, Homonormative, Color-Blind, White American Monomyth

Madison (1999) examines how the collective memories of the cultural struggles of African and African American people filter through the lens of the "anti-racist-white-hero-film which reproduces white supremacist ideology and re-legitimates white domination and identity" (p. 401). More recently, Megan D. McFarlane (2014) builds on Madison's (1999) work to examine how gender informs the anti-racist-white-hero film's framing of race and racism, to ostentatiously offer critiques of racism all the while sustaining white supremacy. Griffin (2015) contributes to this discourse in her analysis of the film, *The Help* (2011), arguing though the film masquerades as a critique of white supremacy through the stories of African American women domestic workers, it is really a story about the redemption of white women at the expense of black women. In their analysis of *Too Wong Foo, Thanks for Everything, Julie Newmar*, Brookey and Westerfelhaus (2010) discuss how the film queers the western or frontier narrative of the American monomyth so that the lead characters, drag queens, are deified as they come into a town to restore justice and then leave. The American monomyth as noted by Jewett and Lawrence (1977) "portrays a hero with superhuman powers who enters an isolated community in order to save it from some threat" (p. 144). However, this deification is marginalizing, as is the assumption that the drag queens need to leave. Madison (1999), Brookey and Westerfelhaus (2010), Griffin (2015), and McFarlane's (2014) arguments are central to unpacking the framing of collective and public memory in *Stonewall* (2015) as Danny fulfills the role of a color-blind white savior who is plagued by internalized homophobia (Eguchi, 2006). Simultaneously, he is also critical of the homophobia that the queer folx on Christopher St. experience without recognizing his role in homophobic discourse. When juxtaposed with the gender-non-conforming Ray, Marsha, and other queer folx, Danny stands in for white supremacist capitalist cis-homonormative patriarchy.

Furthermore, Danny's story fits within the American monomyth as he comes in, restores justice and order, and then leaves. However, it is the drag queens and transwomen who are on the periphery and remain marginalized in his absence. The public memory of Stonewall through a white homonormative patriarchal lens is accomplished through the strategic negation and use of femininity and by having queer characters of color act as guides in Danny's road toward self-actualization and queer activism.

Disgusted and Enabled by the Feminine

The audience is first introduced to Danny when he steps off the bus in New York City. He appears scared and overwhelmed as he stares at two men kissing. He is quickly noticed by a transwoman who tells him, "Hey. Don't be scared. Don't be scared. They're not going to bite you. Come back you. Come back little lost sheep. I could be your shepherd" (Emmerich, 2:45). Viewers are encouraged to identify with Danny early in the film as he is rhetorically presented as safe or "normal" in comparison to the gender non-conforming and feminine queer folx. These out and highly visible queer characters disrupt the respectability of the streets by asserting themselves upon white, middle-class heteronormative people and businesses.

Immediately after this encounter, Danny is hit on by an older transwoman (Emmerich, 3:30). Danny plainly is uncomfortable as he is presented with gender expressions different than those he has ever been privy to. Amidst all of this Danny meets Ray, a Puerto Rican gender non-conforming individual, who decides to take Danny under his wing (Emmerich, 5:30). Danny's difference from Ray and the other unapologetically queer characters is further marked in terms of not only race but also class, as he is quick to tell his new friends that he will be starting school at Columbia in the fall (Emmerich, 6:00). Ray jokes with him about being from Kansas, symbolic of middle America; the heartland or Americana, while later introducing a black transwoman, Queen Conga as being "straight off the boat from some godforsaken island" (Emmerich, 7:00).

While some queer folx who were present at the Stonewall Inn interpolate that Ray is meant to signify Sylvia Rivera, others suggest that Ray is Raymond Castro, a Puerto Rican gay man also present at the Stonewall Inn riots (Segel, 2015). Castro and Rivera both overlap in the characterization of Ray, despite their different gender identities. Regardless, the film erases Sylvia Rivera's name from the film and with it, her identity. If this film is to be taken with an iota of seriousness, then the expectation that the characters in the film would be named after their real-life inspirations, is not, to us, an unreasonable one. In disregarding Rivera, in both characterization and namesake, the audience loses the influence of trans femininity within the queer community of the time, as well as the role femininity played in beginning the riots.

As the story progresses, viewers are given Danny's backstory. He was a football player on the high school team his father coached. He became sexually involved with the star quarterback, Joe, unbeknownst to everyone. However, one night as he is performing oral sex on Joe, he is caught by two friends who quickly spread the news of the relationship across the school and his small Indiana town. This results in Danny being kicked out of his house, uncertain about his future at Columbia because his father will not sign the necessary paperwork for his scholarship.

Alongside their race and class, "the girls," as they refer to themselves, are constructed as abject because of their performances of femininity and desire. For example, Danny is first introduced to crime when Queen Conga breaks a store window and steals a garment. Similarly, Marsha P. Johnson is introduced as "the only drag queens that's nice to us" (Emmerich, 10:25). To which, Johnson replies, "Those other bitches don't know one day Jesus is going to punish them for their sins and fuck them up good" (Emmerich 10:32). Not only did the writer and director force the narrative of Danny, the American monomyth, but they also write similarly misogynistic and femmephobic lines for those characters who embrace femininity. This creates an incongruous narrative where it seems like all gay male culture is femme and transphobic, even when there are characters who identify as she/her, wear feminine clothing, and perform an androgynous or more feminine relational style.

Danny's negation of femininity is best evidenced in his relationships with Ray and Trevor, a white, cisgender, middle-class, gay rights "activist" who comes to represent the respectability politics Ray and his friends do not. While Ray imagines a life away from Christopher Street with Danny, as his (white) knight in shining armor, he is quick to ignore his desire as he feigns sleep after he tells him about the life they could have.

As the film progresses, the group goes to the Stonewall Inn where Ray instructs Danny to use a fake name to sign in, and as such, Danny scrawls John Wayne and walks into the bar. The irony that Danny signs in as John Wayne, the frontier hero, is not lost here. It encourages the audience to view Danny as the quintessential American monomyth, a character identifiable to a predominantly heteronormative audience. In writing the name John Wayne, he conjures the concept of the American monomyth, as the name creates an identifiable framework that makes Danny palatable to a heterosexual audience who is now able to view him as the white savior coming in to save the feminine and gender non-conforming characters in the events to follow.

Ray is further shut down by Danny as he emerges in a glittery dress, with freshly applied lipstick seductively asking him to dance to "Venus" with him (Emmerich, 43:47). Though he claims he does not feel like dancing, moments later he is slow dancing with Trevor, an ambiguously raced, cisgender gay man he just met. As they talk, Trevor is quick to point out that neither he nor Danny really belong in the "shithole" that is Stonewall (Emmerich, 46:58). He identifies himself as a member of the Mattachine Society, "an organization that fights for gay rights" (Martin, 2018, para. 11). As the police raid the bar, Trevor tells Danny not to worry because, "They only arrest the trannies. It's the 'three article of clothing' rule. They're also going to arrest the dykes because they're wearing men's clothes" (Emmerich, 49:27). This once again positions Trevor and Danny as rhetorically similar, yet different from the rest of the patrons, particularly as Trevor uses offensive language to describe the transwomen. This is classic cissexism as defined by Julia Serano (2007), where cisgender individuals and their gender identities are viewed as normal and authentic, whereas people view trans identities as specious and abnormal. However, as Trevor shows an officer his identification card and leaves, an example of his racial, class, and cisgender privilege, it is Ray who helps Danny by providing him with a fake ID card. It is also Ray who takes several hits from a billy club.

The positioning and normalizing of Danny and Trevor, through homo and cisnormativity at the abjection of the transwomen, happens again after Danny, who performs sex work for money with the help of his new friends, runs into Trevor. As Trevor disparages the group by referring to them as "your little street gang," Danny asks what he has against them (Emmerich, 59:42). Trevor responds, "You don't seem like the type of guy who wants to hang out at the Stonewall and turn tricks with your girlfriends. You know, wear red lipstick, nail polish" (Emmerich 59: 54). Danny retorts, "Well that's because red's not my color. They've been better friends to me than most of the people I thought were my friends my whole life" (Emmerich, 1:00:00). Suggesting that Danny only feels this way because he "didn't have the right friends," the two go their separate ways; Danny retreating to a violently assaulted Ray, before meeting up with Trevor to attend a Mattachine Society meeting, of which Trevor is a part.

In the meeting hosted by the Mattachine Society, a white cisgender gay man in a suit and tie speaks, suggesting:

> We have to fight in a peaceful way and resist the radicalism that I see starting to take hold in some quarters. Don't forget, wearing a suit and tie will make them understand you're just like them ... That's how we win!" Pushing back against this discourse, Danny asks Trevor, "Is that really what you want? To blend in? I mean, we are different, right? You know I'm beginning to realize just how different we really are." Trevor scoffs, "Yeah? Like wearing a dress and prancing up and down Christopher Street? (Emmerich, 1:05:01)

Suddenly a savior and advocate for the femininity of "the girls" of Christopher Street, while rejecting it for himself, Danny retorts, "Hey, it takes a lot more balls to wear a dress than it does a suit and tie. What would you have me do? Be a fuckin' florist or decorator? Come on. What, are these—the options open to me?" (Emmerich, 1:06: 38). Although Danny claims that he sees how different queer people are from those in the assimilationist Mattachine Society, Danny still blends into heteronormative culture because of his cisgender identity and homonormative performance. While he may sense himself as different, and same-sex sexuality certainly is an element of the diversity of experience, Danny is learning more about the experiences of radically being different because he stepped outside of his typical bubble of white civility. However, it primarily is the homeless, queer people of color on Christopher Street who ultimately give Danny insights into their lives and try to help him understand the reality of living a radically queer life—one not predicated by suits and ties, rationality, and assimilation.

As the conversation with Trevor continues, Danny suggests that he feels like he wants to break something, gesturing to the idea that he is taking on political consciousness and foreshadowing the audience a sense of what is to come. In telling his own story of coming out, Trevor explains that he won over his parents through logic. Rationality is juxtaposed against the abject and unruly bodies of the transwomen and drag queens on Christopher Street. In contrast to Trevor, when Ray describes his family, he does so almost naked, beat up, curled in a ball on a bed in a dark hotel room. Through sobs, Ray describes a possible father in Sing-Sing, a correctional facility in New York State, not knowing where his mother is, a sister in foster care, and a dead grandmother in Ponce, a city in Puerto Rico. "Happy fuckin' family!" Ray exclaims (Emmerich, 1:02:03). There is no reasoning within Ray's circumstances, no winning over his family through logical explanations because he does not have any family other than his chosen family on Christopher Street. Desperately he wants Danny to understand this so that Danny will take Ray away to start a life together.

Unfortunately for Ray, his desires are never actualized. Danny eventually moves in with Trevor and takes a job at a local grocery store, where he tries to live a "normal" law-abiding life. However, when he catches Trevor cheating on him, they break up and he returns to his friends on Christopher Street. His return coincides with the beginning of the Stonewall Riots as Danny is depicted as the first person to throw a brick through the window at the Stonewall as a means of resisting police raid and their ensuing violence. Soon Danny is leading everyone into fighting back while Trevor tells him that this is not the (respectable) way to fight for social justice. As police in riot gear arrive, Danny (centered) and the transwomen arm in arm around him chant, "We are the baddest girls. We wear our hair in curls. We wear no underwear. We show our pubic hair" (Emmerich, 1:40:28).

Danny is situated throughout the film as being disgusted by femininity, in some ways echoing the misogyny performed by some gay men (Eguchi,

2011), with a growing political consciousness that is tied to understanding the transgressive possibilities of queer rather than homonormative politics, and femininity, in particular (Hobson, 2015). However, in this moment he appropriates femininity to enable his performance of great white savior who is bringing justice to Christopher Street. Like the American monomyth, he is quick to distance himself once justice was restored. Thus, the film masquerades as a critique of homophobic violence, injustice, and homonormativity, arguing for the transgressive possibilities of transfemininity; however, it simply re-centers white homonormativity, while femininity is trivialized and quickly discarded.

This distancing and rejection of femininity is most evident in the conversation Danny has with Ray after the riots. Ray tells Danny, "I guess everything is different now. Things are changing, like ... We could really get a place, you know. I could get a real job. Screw this!" (Emmerich, 1:45:15). Danny looking disgusted by Ray's proposition says, "Ray, come on. Don't you understand?... That I can't love you. You and me ... I mean, different isn't even the word ... Thank you for showing me New York" (Emmerich, 1:45:28). As he tells Ray he will always be "his sister," he departs. We learn that Danny is able to attend Columbia because his mother signed the necessary paperwork, and he returns home to reunite with his family after his first year of college. However, Danny is still rejected by his father. Viewers are encouraged to feel the pain of Danny's rejection and his homelessness throughout the film, all the while normalizing the homelessness, racism, and misogyny experienced by the gender non-conforming, transwomen, and drag queens. They are simply props or guides through which Danny is able to realize his role as an activist; thus, at the end of the riots, he must leave them.

The centering of Danny as the hero of the film is complete when Danny returns to Christopher Street for the Gay Liberation parade. It is immediately clear that he has not seen Ray and his other friends for some time. Ray tells Danny, "You know you can bring your country ass downtown more often" (Emmerich, 1:56:42). As Danny marches he sees his sister and mom who smile proudly as they watch him. The scene fades to black and white to create the effect of archival footage as it transitions to brief blurbs about the real people at Stonewall, such as Marsha P. Johnson and Bob Kohler. Yet, Sylvia Rivera, and other trans activists remain absent.

As the film closes, the screen reads, "This film is dedicated to the unsung heroes of the Stonewall Riots. Today, still 40 percent of all homeless youth in America are LGBT. Homosexuality remains a crime in 77 countries" (Emmerich, 2:00:28). The irony of the film making some political statement while whitening and cis-gendering the portrayals of the riots weighs heavy.

Additionally, the fact that it is many trans and queers of color who make up the homeless population of queer youth is glossed over. Finally, in ending with the decontextualized statement that "homosexuality remains a crime in 77 countries," the film positions the U.S. and white queerness as exceptional, progressive, and civilized in comparison to other countries that are seen as underdeveloped and primitive (Emmerich, 2:00:40). The transwomen and drag queens in the film function in ways similar to "the magical negro," a term coined by Spike Lee in his 2001 college tour (Zoller Seitz, 2010). The magical negro is

> a saintly African-American character who acts as a mentor to a questing white hero, who seems to be disconnected from the community that he adores so much, and who often seems to have an uncanny ability to say and do exactly what needs to be said or done in order to keep the story chugging along in the hero's favor. (Zoller Seitz, 2010, para. 3)

Examples of this figure in films include Harriet Tubman (Donella, 2019) as well as Laurence Fishburne in *The Matrix* and Will Smith in *The Legend of Bagger Vance* (Zoller Seitz, 2010). These characters function primarily as supporting characters to help or enable the white male hero self-actualize or act in some way. While characters, such as Ray or Queen Congra, do not take on "saintly" characteristics, they do act as mentors for Danny to reach political consciousness. For example, as the film ends it wraps up the story by focusing on Danny's resolution through his return home and the acceptance by his mother and sister. The audience is reintroduced to Ray and the others only as they briefly enter when Danny is back for the march. Despite the fact that we learn from Bob, a local, middle-class, white, cisgender, gay veteran who acts as a guardian for the group, that, "Ray started trickin in Times Square when he was 12," we are left uncertain about Ray's future (Emmerich, 1:14:17). Throughout the film, Ray lives on and off the street, must prostitute himself to survive, and is attacked by police and johns alike. There is no redemption for Ray. Ray and the other transwomen and gender non-conforming folx are there to help Danny learn to survive on the street and lead him toward the path of self-discovery. While Danny is positioned as the American monomyth, even he cannot save Ray and the other fictional characters, who continue to live on the streets turning tricks and surviving day by day.

Conclusions

Released forty-six years after the riots at the Stonewall Inn, *Stonewall* (2015) and its ensuing controversy demonstrate the fight over social justice activism and its collective, and public memorialization. While *Stonewall* (2015) certainly is not an official material manifestation of public memory, it still holds weight as an international film, through the pedagogy of popular culture. Its creation by a white cisgender gay German filmmaker provides us an important moment to reflect on the use of memory and popular culture as means to reproduce ideologies of white queer exceptionalism and civilization worldwide. The right to narrative authority of queer history must not be predicated to the continual recreation of the American monomyth and white cis-gay man savior complex, when the center foci should be on trans folx, people of color, and gender non-conforming folx (Calafell, 2019).

Queer scholars of color Anzaldúa (1987), Moraga and Anzaldúa (2015), Johnson (2001), Lorde (2007), and Eguchi and Asante (2016) have long critiqued the whiteness of queer cultures, and as we can see from this case study public memory becomes yet another site where the struggle remains. How might imperialist nostalgia guide the (re)storying of historical struggle and the framing of events such as these? *Stonewall* (2015), contorts history and memory in ways that reshape the color-blind, cisgender white man as the savior and queer activists of color into "magical negros" as both victims and oracles.

References

4 policemen hurt in 'village' raid (1969, June 29), *New York Times*. Retrieved from https://www.nytimes.com/1969/06/29/archives/4-policemen-hurt-in-village-raid-melee-near-sheridan-square-follows.html

Anzaldúa, G. (1987). *Borderlands La Frontera The New Mestiza*. San Francisco, CA: Aunt Lute Books.

Armstrong, E. A., & Crage, S. M. (2006). Movements and memory: The making of the Stonewall myth. *American Sociological Review, 71*(5), 724–751.

Bourdieu, P. (1996). On the family as a realized category. *Theory, Culture & Society, 13*(3), 19–26. https://doi.org/10.1177/026327696013003002

Brookey, R. A., & Westerfelhaus, R. (2010). Pistols and petticoats, piety and purity: To Wong Foo, the queering of the American monomyth, and the marginalizing discourse of deification. *Critical Studies in Media Communication, 18*(2), 141–156.

Calafell, B. M. (2017). Brownness, kissing, and U.S. imperialism: Contextualizing the Orlando massacre. *Communication and Critical Cultural Studies, 14*(2), 198–202.

Calafell, B. (2019). Narrative authority, theory in the flesh, and the fight over the death and life of Marsha P. Johnson. *QED: A Journal in GLBTQ Worldmaking, 6*(2), 26–39.

Donella, L. (Speaker). (2019, November 3). *Harriet Tubman "visions"* [Audio Podcast]. https://www.npr.org/2019/11/03/775818750/harriet-tubmans-visions

Duggan, L. (2002). "The new homonormativity: The sexual politics of neoliberalism". In R. Castronovo & D. D. Nelson (Eds.), *Materializing democracy: Toward a revitalized cultural politics* (pp. 175–194). Durham, NC: Duke University Press.

Dunn, T. R. (2009). Remembering "A Great Fag": Visualizing public memory and the construction of queer space. *Quarterly Journal of Speech, 97*(4), 435–460.

Eguchi, S. (2006). Social and internalized homophobia as a source of conflict: How can we improve the quality of communication? *Review of Communication, 6*(4), 348–357.

Eguchi, S. (2011). Negotiating sissyphobia: A critical/interpretive analysis of one "femme" gay Asian body in the heteronormative world. *The Journal of Men's Studies, 19*(1), 37–56. https://doi.org/https://doi.org/10.3149/jms.1901.37

Eguchi, S., & Asante, G. (2016). Disidentifications revisited: Queer(y)ing intercultural communication theory. *Communication Theory, 26,* 171–189.

Emmerich, R., (Director) & Baitz, J. R. (Writer). (2015). *Stonewall* [Motion picture]. USA: Roadside Attractions. Retrieved from http://www.imdb.com/title/tt3018070/?ref_=nv_sr_1

Griffin, R. A. (2015). Problematic representations of strategic whiteness and "post-racial" pedagogy: A critical intercultural reading of The Help. *Journal of International and Intercultural Communication, 8*(2), 147–166.

Hobson, K. (2015). Sue Sylvester, Coach Beiste, Santana Lopez, and Unique Adams: Exploring representations of queer femininity on Glee. In B. C. Johnson & D. K. Faill (Eds.), *Glee and new directions for social change* (pp. 95–107). The Netherlands: Sense Publishers.

Holden, S. (2015, September 24). Stonewall doesn't distinguish between facts and fiction. [Review of the film *Stonewall*, directed by Roland Emmerich, 2015]. *New York Times.* Retrieved from https://www.nytimes.com/2015/09/25/movies/for-stonewall-an-indiana-born-avatar.html?partner=rss&emc=rss

Holland, B. (2017, December 22). How the mob helped establish NYC's gay bar scene. *The History Channel.* Retrieved from www.history.com/news/how-the-mob-helped-establish-nycs-gay-bar-scene

Houdek, M., & Phillips, K. R. (2017). Public memory. In *Oxford Encyclopedia of Communication.* Retrieved from https://www.oxfordreference.com/view/10.1093/acref/9780190459611.001.0001/acref-9780190459611-e-181

Jewett, R., & Lawrence, J. S. (1977). The American monomyth. Garden City, NY: Anchor Press.

Johnson, E. (2001). "Quare" studies, or (almost) everything I know about queer studies I learned from my grandmother. *Text and Performance Quarterly, 21,* 1–25.

Jones, E. (2015, September 24). Roland Emmerich defends 'personal' Stonewall movie. *BBC News.* Retrieved from www.bbc.com/news/entertainment-arts-34340260.

Kasino, M. (2012). Pay it no mind – The Life and Times of Marsha P. Johnson. [Video file]. Retrieved from www.youtube.com/watch?v=rjN9W2KstqE

Keating, S. (2015, September 22). Director Roland Emmerich discusses 'Stonewall' controversy. *Buzzfeed News*. Retrieved from www.buzzfeed.com/shannonkeating/director-roland-emmerich-discusses-stonewall-controversy?utm_term=.sjM-JE6j8A#.pcbNABGx8

King, J. (2015, June 25). *Meet the trans women of color who helped put Stonewall on the map*. Retrieved from https://mic.com/articles/121256/meet-marsha-p-johnson-and-sylvia-rivera-transgender-stonewall-veterans#.Hq6PHoOHp

Levine, M. (Speaker). (2010, June 25). *Personal view of history: "Stonewall Did That for Me"* [Audio Podcast]. www.npr.org/templates/story/story.php?storyId=128085183

Lisker, J. (1969, July 6). Homo nest raided queen bees are stinging mad. *New York Daily News*. Retrieved from https://www.pbs.org/wgbh/americanexperience/features/stonewall-queen-bees/

Lorde, A. (2007). *Sister outside: Essays and speeches*. Berkeley, CA: Crossing Press.

Madison, K. J. (1999). Legitimation crisis and containment: The 'anti-racist-white-hero' film. *Critical Studies in Media Communication, 16*(4), 399–416.

Martin, K. (2018, Sept 8). The Mattachine Society & LGBTQ history. *Magellan TV*. Retrieved from https://www.magellantv.com/articles/the-mattachine-society-lgbtq-history

McFarlene, M. D. (2014). Anti-racist white hero, the sequel: Intersections of race(ism), gender, and social justice. *Critical Studies in Media Communication, 32*(2), 81–95.

Moraga, C., & Anzaldúa, G. (2015). *This bridge called my back*. Albany, NY: New York Press.

Nichols, J. M. (2016a, July 23). Miss Major is a trans elder and Stonewall icon . . . and she's changing the world. *HuffPost*. Retrieved from www.huffingtonpost.com/entry/miss-major-transgender-elder_us_57927351e4b01180b52ef264

Nichols, J. M. (2016b, June 22). Roland Emmerich: "Stonewall was a white event let's be honest." *Huffpost*. Retrieved from https://www.huffpost.com/entry/roland-emmerich-stonewall-white-event_n_576ab781e4b09926ce5d493b

Pérez, H. (2015). *A taste for brown bodies: Gay modernity and cosmopolitan desire*. New York, NY: NYU Press.

Puar, J. (2007). *Terrorist assemblages*. Durham, NC: Duke University Press.

Rude, M. V. (2015, August 10). How dare they do this again: Stonewall veteran Miss Major on the "Stonewall" movie. *Autostraddle*. Retrieved from https://www.autostraddle.com/how-dare-they-do-this-again-miss-major-on-the-stonewall-movie-301957/

Segel, M. (2015, September 23). I was at the Stonewall riots. The movie "Stonewall" gets everything wrong. *PBS NewsHour*. Retrieved from www.pbs.org/newshour/art/stonewall-movie/

Serano, J. (2007). *Whipping girl a transsexual woman on sexism and the scapegoating of femininity*. Berkeley, CA: Seal Press.

Stanton, M. (2015, September 28). Stonewall: EW review. *Entertainment Weekly*. Retrieved from www.ew.com/article/2015/09/28/stonewall-ew-review/

Stonewall. (2015). *Rotten Tomatoes*. Retrieved from www.rottentomatoes.com/m/stonewall_2015#contentReviews

Truscott IV, L. (2003). View from the outside: Gay power comes to Sheridan Square. In P. McCarthy (Ed.) *The radical reader* (pp. 568–576). The New Press.

Willmore, A. (2015, September 30). Oscar movies are still apologetic about LGBT Characters. *Buzzfeed*. Retrieved from www.buzzfeed.com/alisonwillmore/the-oscarfication-of-lgbt-pain?utm_term=.bno5o7x3l#.kqnVkqgB7

Zoller Setiz, M. (2010, September 14). The offensive movie cliché that won't die. *Salon*. Retrieved from https://www.salon.com/test/2010/09/14/magical_negro_trope/

6. *Queer Fantasy: A Memory of Michael Sam's* Big Gay Kiss

SHINSUKE EGUCHI
University of New Mexico

In the evening of May 10, 2014, the ESPN (Entertainment and Sports Programing Network) and NFL (National Football League) network broadcasted the last minutes of NFL's draft. The first openly gay Black cisgender male football player Michael Sam from the University of Missouri was yet waiting to be drafted by a team. Sam's draft received great media coverage because no other football players had been out as a gay man at the time of their NFL drafts. American football continues to represent manhood and masculinity through which the excessive displays of U.S. American nationalism are performed (Butterworth, 2008). Such nationalistic framing of masculinity that reinserts the superiority of cisheteronormativity almost always constructs the NFL players as *cisgender* and *hyper-heterosexual* regardless of their racial and ethnic backgrounds. As McCune (2014) reminds, "sexuality outside of heterosexuality is, still indeed, a taboo subject in American society. Sexual taboos undeniably facilitate and encourage comfort in more normative sexualities" (p. 28). Given this socio environment, there were some uncertainties around Sam's possible draft because he was an out gay man. However, toward the end of draft, Sam received a phone call; the St. Louis Rams just drafted him. So, Sam immediately burst into tears as he had been waiting for this news for last two days. Then, Sam suddenly moved to kiss his cisgendered White male boyfriend Vito Cammisano in front of camera.[1]

Not long after Sam's big gay kiss scene aired nationally and transnationally throughout media networks, the audience's reactions to Sam kissing Cammisano heated up. According to Yan and Alsup (2014, May 13) writing in CNN (Cable News Network), a former NFL's running back and super bowl champion Derrick Ward commented on twitter, "I'm sorry but that

Michael Sam is no bueno for doing that on national TV." He continued to say, "Man U got little kids lookin at the draft. I can't believe ESPN even allowed that to happen." In addition, a strong safety Don Jones, who played for Miami Dolphins at that time, tweeted negative phrases, such as "OMG" and "horrible." However, Miami Dolphins immediately responded to Jones' tweet by fining and restraining him from team activities. On the Sunday, May 11, 2014, Jones delivered the public statement of apology. Even though many unsupportive comments from former and current NFL players in social media continued, some public figures, such as President Barack Obama, started to release supportive comments on Sam kissing his boyfriend. This public man-on-man interracial intimacy known as *Sam's big gay kiss* aroused much public controversy.

Now that it has been a few years since then, possibilities of queerness surrounding Sam as a first openly gay Black male football player have seemingly lost. By queerness, I mean the politics of anti-normative sexual and gender transgression. That is, "truly liberating, transformative, and inclusive of all those who stand on the outside of the dominant constructed norm of state-sanctioned white middle-and upper-class heterosexuality" (Cohen, 2005, p. 25). However, the logics of cisheteronormativity almost always discipline, control, and constraint possibilities of queerness. In August 2014, St. Louis Rams did not add Sam into the roster after his debut in the preseason game against New Orleans Saints. An undrafted rookie Ethan Westbrooks was picked over Sam. Then, he transferred to the Dallas Cowboys where he also did not make it to play. In May 2015, Sam signed the two-year deal with one of the Canadian Football League (CFL) teams, Montreal Alouettes. However, he left the team in August 2015 because of his concern with mental health. Since then, Sam has been active as a media personality and LGBT (Lesbian-Gay-Bisexual-Transgender) equality advocate. With such career shifts, Sam is no longer idolized as the first openly gay Black NFL football player in the field. As a matter of fact, he has never really played for NFL's official games. Thus, I am concerned with the way in which Sam's big gay kiss now seems to be just a *footnote* of NFL's history.

In this essay, I critique the performative rhetoric of queerness around Michael Sam after his big gay kiss was aired live on 2014's NFL's (National Football League) draft. I approach Sam's big gay kiss as a memory of queer fantasy. Muñoz (2009) defines, "Queer fantasy is linked to utopian longing, and together the two can become contributing conditions of possibility for political transformation" (p. 172). Queer fantasy is a politically transgressive form of imagination through which queerness is fully embraced. However, what accompanies with queer fantasy is the material reality of queer failure.

Queer failure allows us to recognize what is missing from the present time (e.g., Halberstam, 2011; Keeling, 2019). The present is almost always structured to normalize the power of heterosexuality. Accordingly, queerness is only a possibility in the present (e.g., Abdi & Calafell, 2017; Chambers-Letson, 2018; Eguchi, Files-Thompson, & Calafell, 2018). Thus, queer failure "rejects the normative values of ideas" in order to imagine and reimagine the futurity of queerness (Muñoz, 2009, p. 172). Thus, I am interested in critiquing Sam's queerness through an ongoing interplay of contradictions between fantasy and failure. In so doing, my overall goal of this essay is to create a platform to rewrite and restore the Sam's big gay kiss event as a queer cultural production of memory that resists the logics of cisheteronormativity.

In what follows, I contextualize the issue of Black masculinity in NFL. Then, I situate my critique in the genealogy of queer intercultural communication. The presentation of my critique is organized according to three themes; *homonationalism*, *homoerotic interracialism*, and *anti-queerness*. After demonstrating my critique, I end this essay by discussing the implications of Sam's big gay kiss as a memory of queer fantasy.

Black Masculinity and NFL

In order to carefully unpack queerness around Michael Sam after his big gay kiss, I turn my attention to the issue of Black masculinity in NFL first. Sam's big gay kiss is only a queer possibility in the cisheteropatriarchal and hypermasculinist landscape of NFL. American football represents cisheteronormative displays of U.S. American nationalism rooted in whiteness. This is a cultural and intercultural context where no other players had been openly out as a Black gay man at the time of their NFL drafts.

The Black male body is a social and performative site of public and private contestations in which complex and messy layers of racism, classism, heterosexism, and homophobia are simultaneously represented and materialized. Neal (2013) argues that "the most 'legible' Black male body is often thought to be a criminal body and/or a body in need of policing and containment – incarceration" (p. 5). For example, hip-hop music has been increasingly mainstreamed in contemporary media. Such mainstreaming perpetuates the racialized gender imaginations of "thug life" or "pimping" associated with Black men as irresponsible figures (Watts, 2005). At the same time, such representation of Black masculinity has been also serving as a strategic vehicle of resistance for the Black men to overcome the emasculation of Black men influenced by the institutional legacy of slavery. So, they can survive under the nation-state control and surveillance of the Black male body rooted in White supremacy (e.g., Collins, 2004; Connor, 1995; McCune, 2014; Snorton, 2014). Accordingly, patriarchal masculinity has functioned as an ideality for most Black men during the twentieth-century (hooks, 2004). Still, social and performative aspects of patriarchal masculinity reproduce and reconstitute the repudiation of femininity rooted in the logics of misogyny, cisheterosexism, and homophobia (e.g., Eguchi, Files-Thompson, & Calafell, 2018; Means Coleman & Cobb, 2007).

The heteropatriarchal productions, constitutions, and negotiations of Black masculinity always already take place behind the superiority of Whiteness as a property. Nakayama and Krizek (1995) argue, "The construction of discursive space of whiteness has material effects on the entire social structure and our places in relation to it" (p. 305). For example, the Black male thug aesthetic is a material consequence of the Black male body as the *problem* in the historical continuum of racial formation. White supremacy has almost always subordinated Black masculinity as backward, unprogressive, and sexually barbaric. What remains invisibly sustained is the centrality of whiteness that maintains the inferiority of people of color in and across local, national, and global contexts. The shapes, forms, and visions of whiteness may change over time for meeting the interest, need, and concern of the center mostly occupied by White, cisgendered male, heterosexual, able-body, and affluent (e.g., Eguchi & Ding, 2017; Griffin, 2015; McIntosh, Moon, & Nakayama, 2019). Indeed, this changeableness is a discursive strategy that help reproduce the invisible superiority of whiteness in and across different times, spaces, and contexts. In so doing, whiteness serves to defend and protect the invisible territory of the center.

Such strategic working of whiteness explicates the material realities of NFL. In fact, NFL is a historical and contemporary space of racial struggle that sustains the superiority of whiteness and the inferiority of people of color. Griffin and Calafell (2011) maintain, "The history between blacks and whites in U.S. sports is replete with notions of white supremacy and inequality" (p. 119). According to Rhoden (2011, December 11), there has been a long history of racial segregation and exclusion in the NFL that coincided with the nation-state and its policy. Even after NFL had been desegregated in 1946, unwritten quotas limited the ratios of Black players to White players. Also, Black players were subjected to compete against one another for the same positions. Such racist practices have gradually changed over the time while anti-racist movements gained the visibility. At the same time, the historical superiority of whiteness embedded in the material realities of NFL continues to be strategically self-defended and self-protected. For example, NFL's positions of power, such as owners, head coaches, and coaches, continue to be overwhelmingly occupied by White cismen (see, Kimes, 2016, January 12; Smith, 2017, January 14). The large number of Black men are yet relegated to physically work in the field, that is, they are "owned" and "controlled" by White men in the corporate ladder of NFL.

Indeed, the Black male body is commodified for the interest of people of power, who invest in and get benefits of the national and transnational endorsement of American football as "combat sport" (Oates & Durham, 2004). The Black male body functions as an athletic form of entertainment, exploitation, and appropriation for White pleasure and consumption driven by the logics of master-slave relationship (Griffin & Calafell, 2011). The prominent media stereotype is the physically fit, athletic, hypermasculine, and hypersexual Black man. At the same time, Black players experience harsh burdens of surveillance, punishment, and discipline when they violate the cultural code of NFL. Such White symbolic ownership of the Black male body insinuates the historical relationship between race and crime. Ahmed (2012) reminds us that "people of color in White organizations are treated as guests ... people of color are welcomed on condition they return that hospitality by integrating into a common organization culture, or by 'being' diverse, and allowing institutions to celebrate their diversity" (p. 43). This racial inequality, organizing the material realities of NFL, is structured to sustain the superiority of whiteness at the expense of people of color.

Simultaneously, it is important to note that the logics of cisheteronormativity also play behind such racialized scripts of the Black male body. The default of NFL's players is almost always *hyper-heterosexual*. The performative characteristics of patriarchal masculinity are expected to eradicate any signs of male effeminacy including homosexuality (Means Coleman & Cobb, 2007). However, there has been an emerging discourse of anti-normative sexualities challenging the heteronormative assumptions of NFL players. According to Buzinski (2017, June 20), some players worked in a regular season, such as Kwame Harris[2] and Esera Tuaolo,[3] have come out as a gay man after their retirements. Also, there have been ongoing gossips around some NFL players who are alleged to discreetly engage in same-sex sexual and intimate relations. However, the logics of cisheteronormativity, creating patriarchal and hypermasculinist images of American football players, almost always marginalize emerging possibilities of queerness in NFL. The usual and ordinary assumption about NFL players is that they must be *hyper-heterosexual* regardless of their racial and cultural backgrounds. Under such technology of cisheteronormativity, NFL continues to signal and affirm a performative space and power of U.S. American nationalism rooted in the patriarchal masculinity intersecting with whiteness, capitalism, and consumerism.

Methodology

To interrogate the performative rhetoric of queerness around Michael Sam, I ground my critique within the genealogy of queer intercultural communication. Chávez (2013) has proposed the field of queer intercultural communication as a critical qualitative inquiry to complicate the circumference of theorizing about intercultural communication. The overall goal of queer intercultural communication is to highlight anti-normative modes of sexualities and genders as conceptual lens to identify with and critique complex and dynamic natures of intercultural interactions, relations, and contexts. Queer intercultural communication examines culture-specific and text-specific nuances of raced, gendered, sexualized, classed, and nationalized knowledge embedded in the material realities of LGBT people of color in and across local, national, and global contexts (e.g., Alexander, 2010; Eguchi & Calafell, 2020; Morrissey, 2013; Snorton, 2013).

Queer intercultural communication actively decenters the *whiteness* of mainstream queer theorizing that emphasizes on the western, U.S. American—hence preferred—logics of selfhood, individual agency, and sexual freedom. As Cohen (2005) addresses, "queer theorizing that calls for elimination of fixed categories seems to ignore the ways in which some traditional identities and communal ties can, in fact, be important to one's survival" (p. 34). Indeed, the historical and contemporary realities of relationships, communal ties, and collective resistance are highly significant to identity negotiation processes of LGBT people of color who come from raced and classed communities (e.g., Johnson, 2016; Johnson & Henderson, 2005; McBride, 2005;). At the same time, LGBT people of color, while dealing with interlocking power relations, also develop the intellectual, aesthetic, and political nuances of queerness that creatively work on and against the majoritarian codes of belonging (e.g., Johnson, 2001; McCune, 2014; Means Coleman & Cobb, 2007; Muñoz, 1999; Snorton, 2014). Otherwise, queerness remains, as Puar (2007) has argued, as *an intercultural communication process of whitening* sexualities and genders represented by LGBT people of color. For that reason, intellectual and political intersections between the queer and the intercultural require a careful and nuanced critique of often invisible power relations in and across the lines of differences, such as race, ethnicity, gender, class, nation, and the body.

Queer intercultural critics who work on the intersections of queer and intercultural must pay attention to specific needs and concerns of non-White, non-U.S. American middle/upper class sexualities and genders (e.g., Atay,

2020; Chávez, 2013; Eguchi & Asante, 2016; Eguchi & Calafell, 2020; Yep, 2013). They need to evaluate critically the historical continuities and contemporary realities of whiteness that standardize social and performatives aspects of sexualities and genders for people of color. Today's queer liberalism, fostering the capitalistic inclusions of White middle/upper-class gays and lesbians into the nation-state, serves as the logics of color blindness (Eng, 2010). Thus, queerness, as performed through a raced, gendered, and classed body, necessitates a careful and nuanced reading.

Drawing from this methodological perspective, I critique the performative rhetoric of queerness surrounding Sam's Black male body as an analytical site. My critique, inspired by the genealogy of queer intercultural communication, elaborates Pérez's (2015) call that "queer critique must investigate the circulation of homosexual desire within the erotic economics of both capitalism and the nation in order to guard against its cooptation into neoliberal and colonial projects" (p. 3). I take it into consideration when I offer my reading of Sam's queerness because it is simultaneously racialized, gendered, sexualized, classed, and nationalized in the intersected webs of larger structural contexts. Before showcasing my critique, I contextualize the background of Sam's big gay kiss.

Michael Sam's Big Gay Kiss

According to Drape, Eder, and Witz (2014, February 11), Sam was born and grew up in Galveston, Texas. He experienced some life and family obstacles while growing up. He attended the high school in Hitchcock, Texas, where he started playing football. Then, he attended University of Missouri between 2009 and 2013. There Sam played as the defensive end for the football team. During his college football career, he began sharing the small group of the teammates that he was gay. By August 2013, he told the whole team including coaching stuff about his sexuality. On February 9, 2014, Sam announced that he was gay during his interview on the ESPN's Outside the Lines. He became the first openly gay identified cisgendered Black male football player waiting to be drafted into the NFL. His team, well-known athletes, fans, and notables, including President Obama and First Lady, celebrated him coming out in the public outlet. Accordingly, this coming out story brought many popular media attentions to Sam during the NFL's 2014 draft held in Radio City Music Hall in New York between May 8th and May 10th. In this context, Sam's big gay kiss was aired live. Now, I demonstrate my critique of queerness around Michael Sam. It is consisted of three themes; *homonationalism, homoerotic interracialism*, and *anti-queerness*.

Homonationalism

Sam's big gay kiss event, aired on the 2014's NFL's draft, signals macro-structural negotiations and adjustments of intimacy, family, and kinship that attempt to incorporate gay and lesbian citizens-subjects (who are mostly White, cisgender, able-bodied, and affluent) into the nation-state. So, profitable and valuable connections between capitalism, consumerism, and American football continue to be flourished. Eng (2010) maintains, "Our current moment is marked by the merging of an increasingly visible and mass-mediated queer consumer lifestyle with recent juridical protections for [White] gay and lesbian rights to privacy and intimacy" (p. 3). Sam is temporarily positioned to perform a Black gay male football player, who helps secure the technologies of sexual exceptionalism intersecting with homosexuality and empire in the period when same-sex marriage is institutionalized. This form of sexual exceptionalism—"the emergence of national homosexuality" (Puar, 2007, p. 2)—affirms how progressive, liberal, and exceptional U.S. America is. The nation-state legally and representationally accepts homosexuality. This rhetoric of homonationalism is a democratic and capitalist strategy of U.S. American nationalism rooted in whiteness. Puar (2007) claims that "this brand of homosexuality operates as a regulatory script not only of normative gayness, queerness, or homosexuality, but also of the racial and national norms that reinforces these sexual subjects" (p. 2). Consequently, Sam's Black male body becomes an additional key for the ideological advancement and structural sustainability of homonationalism that supports the nationalist production of American football.

Under the discursive and material effects of homonationalism, Sam is constructed as a *good, progressive,* and *responsible* Black gay male player, who subscribes the normative ways of gay life rooted in whiteness. This is particularly important because Black men who engage in discreet queer sexual activities have been framed as the *irresponsible* source of spreading sex problems in the media and popular culture (McCune, 2014; Snorton, 2014). For example, during his ESPN interview that took place in February 2014, Sam announced, "I am an openly proud gay man." By saying so, he came out of the closet. This paradigm of coming out implicates the individualistic logics of self-discovery, self-fulfillment, and progressiveness rooted in whiteness (Ross, 2005). At the same time, the closet indicates the site of queer oppression through which sexual minoritarians are thought to conceal their same-sex desires. However, this epistemology does not account the ways in which people of color work with their anti-normative sexualities and genders under the structural constraints every day. The coming out of closet paradigm cannot easily measure the raced, gendered, and classed nuances of queerness. Accordingly, sexual discretion known as the closet may serve as an alternative space through which sexual minoritarians of color perform the simultaneous technologies of race, gender, sexuality, class, and nation. Snorton (2014) maintains, "The closet is a site structured by queer oppression, yet the rhetoric of the closet cannot fully capture what queer oppression looks like or the way the closet acts as both shelter from and a manifestation of domination" (p. 18). However, Sam's public announcement of being gay shuts down any queer possibilities of the closet. Instead, Sam's coming out helps minimize the potential framing of Sam as a sexually irresponsible Black man who endangers sexual health, family, and kinship.

In addition, a successful narrative of Sam, who got out of his "ethnic ghetto," represents his *good, progressive,* and *responsible* Black male image that points to the cultural myth of American dream. By American dream, I mean a normative individualistic value through which anyone, regardless of race, gender, and/or class, can achieve their own versions of success through hard work, discipline, and positive attitude. For example, Sam appeared in ABC's *Dancing with Stars Season 20*, aired from March 16 to May 19, 2015. His dancing partner was an Australian Latin Dancer Peta Jane Murgatroyd, who was born in New Zealand. Sam and Murgatroyd got eliminated from the contest during the week four titled, "Most Memorable Year," aired on April 6, 2015. Going with this week's theme, the show specifically featured Sam's *successful* narrative of coming out of the closet and overcoming his tough upbringing. Sam started off this special segment by saying his memorable year was 2014 when he came out as a gay man. Sam commented that the year of 2014 was when both positive and sad things happened to him. Then this segment moved to geographical image of Hitchcock, Texas where Sam started playing football. He said, "When I was growing up, we did not have a lot of money. My oldest brother was killed by the gunshot. And that was very hard for my family. I just remember a lot of fights between my mom and my dad. Then my dad just left." Sam also commented that his father was not present when he needed him the most. Here, ABC's *Dancing with Stars Season 20* reproduces and reconstitutes a stereotypically raced and classed narrative about young Black men whose fathers are absent. Then the segment focused on Sam's present relationship with his father. While applauding sounds played behind the images of Sam's coming out, Sam said, "What people do not know is, it [coming out] cost my relationship with my father." Sam explained how hurtful it was to know his father's interview with *New York Times* discussing his disapproval of Sam's coming out. Sam said, "I called him. And I said, you lost another son again . . . .. And I haven't talked to him since." Then the segment immediately moved on to Sam's dancing practice.

This particular segment of Sam implicates the logics of homonationalism as it maps "out the intersections, confluences, and divergences between homosexuality and the nation, national identity, and nationalism" (Puar, 2007, p. 49). ABC's *Dancing with Stars* strategically presented as if Sam magically overcame life obstacles as he focused on becoming a football player. This American dream narrative of getting out of ethnic ghetto through an athletic program implies the nationalist and color-blinded belief that "success depends on one's attitude" (Halbertsam, 2011, p. 3). It ignores the commodification and consumption of the Black male body that maintain the superiority of whiteness in tough sports like football. At the same time, the U.S. is also framed as a globally exceptional society of sexual freedom through which coming out of the closet leads to one's success. Coming out of the closet that reinforces the individualized logics of merit, responsibility, and choice is the material reality of colorblindness that sustains the superiority of whiteness as a property. Such strategic function of whiteness that privileges the logics of individualism organizes and reorganizes the homonationalist imagination of Sam's background story aired on ABC's *Dancing with Stars*. In so doing, Sam can become and be an exceptional Black gay male public figure.

Simultaneously, ABC's *Dancing with Stars*' story about Sam only focused on his Black family and kinship relation as his *problem*. Sam's father's homophobia serves as a measurement indicating how Black families and kinship relations remain "backward" and "unprogressive." Sam's father symbolically becomes the *homophobic suspect,* who deteriorates the nationalist agenda and progressiveness of homonationalism rooted in whiteness. It is also worthwhile to mention that this segment made the presence of homophobic and racist White families and kinship relations invisible. Doing so color-blinds ongoing structural problems of race, racism, and property that materially affect the theorization of gay lifestyle as a White problem among Black communities. This logic ignores, erases, and marginalizes other intercultural interactions, relations, and contexts including high school, college, and NFL where Sam might have actually struggled with technologies of racism, heterosexism, and homophobia. In so doing, Sam is once again framed as a good, progressive, and responsible Black gay male football player who has exceptionally exceeded his *racial hang-ups*. The media displays of Sam's queerness are strategically used not to challenge the nationalist propaganda of homonationalism that color-blinds ongoing racial disparities.

Ultimately, Sam's public relation image is produced for the American football corporate interest of profit making. The politics of homonationalism closely operates with the advancement and suitability of capitalism (Puar, 2007). Cultivating LGBT markets plays a key role in promoting consumerism in and across local, national, and global contexts. Affluent White cisgender gays and lesbians are particularly known to be the major consumers in today's U.S. (Eng, 2010). However, American football is historically constructed as hyper-heterosexist and homophobic. Openly gay and bisexual male players are rarely present. American football remains such a nationalist and heteropatriarchal sports that is "the affirmation of American civil religion" (Butterworth, 2008, p. 318). Bellah (1969) defines that civil religion is "concerned that America be a society as perfectly in accord with the will of God as men can make it, and a light to all the nations" (p. 18).

Yet, a visible incorporation of growing LGBT markets has the potential to bring uncertain profits to the American football corporation where is not known as a queer friendly environment. Ferguson (2005) suggests that "sociological arguments about the socially constructed nature of (homo) sexuality index the contemporary entrance of White gays and lesbians into the rights and privileges of American citizenship" (p. 53). The performative rhetoric of queerness around Sam hints the ways in which American football attempts to include gay men of color into their corporation where gay and bisexual players of color actually and already labor in the field. So, these men like Sam can serve as faces of American football to attract potential LGBT market consumers.

Homoerotic Interracialism

The performative rhetoric of queerness around Sam during his big gay kiss event explicitly suggests the colonialist logics of homoerotic interracialism. That is "the foundation of sexual modernity and shared trait of white colonial masculinity – both homosexual and heterosexual" (Pérez, 2015, p. 53). Sam's athletic, muscular, and built cisgendered Black male body signifies an ideal center of homoerotic desire rooted in the gaze of whiteness reinforcing the secret history of U.S. Americans' interracial desire. The Black male body has been an ideological and material site of racialized fetishism where the White male exercises the displays of sexual power to control, desire, and eroticize (Stockton, 2006). The large Black male penis has been a major source of discourse through which Black male sexuality is considered as the threat to the sustainability of White racial purity. This points to the historical legacy of lynching of Black men. As Pérez (2015) argues, "this White desire for a Black male body, alternately manifested as love, disgust, fear, and murderousness, resides at the heart of U.S. sexual cultures, straight and queer" (p. 115). In this context, the colonial dyad of Sam and Cammisano aired on the 2014's NFL's draft aesthetically appeals to the White male gaze as a referencing point of media consumerism.

Sam as a big Black masculine man moved to hold a smaller framed White male Cammisano in the kiss scene. At the same time, Cammisano's arms moved onto Sam's big shoulder reinforcing his upper body force. Then, Sam kissed Cammisano. This aesthetic of interracial same-sex intimacy resembles the stereotypical image of a man kissing a woman, which is often circulated through romantic movies and TV programs. Puar (2007) echoes, "Intimacy in its liberal fantasy form is the historically the providence of heteronormativity and now, as I have argued, homonormativity" (p. 164). The aesthetic of kissing, performed through Sam and Cammisano's same-sex interracial coupling on the screen, appropriates the logics of heteronormativity because the existing but illusive binaries such as masculinity-femininity, straight-gay, and top-bottom represent the Black-White colonial dyad. Had Sam not come out, he could easily have passed as a hypermasculine Black straight man. He performs such Black straight image of patriarchal masculinity really well. Simultaneously, Cammisano's White male body signifies the invisible centrality of homonormative standard that racially marks the Black male body as the hypersexual object. A former college swimmer Cammisano is well-toned, not as effeminate as stereotypical feminine gay men often portrayed in media. He is much more like "the contemporary White gay male clone, the type that populates certain neighborhoods in major U.S. cities" (Muñoz, 2009, p. 60). This body image of Cammisano further reconfigures Sam's athletic, muscular, and built Black male body as the (homo)sexually desired object. This romantic dyad of Sam and Cammisano works within the colonialist logics of homoerotic interracialism intersecting with whiteness, patriarchy, and capitalism.

To further clarify my argument, I share my own curiosity here. When I watched Sam's big gay kiss on the screen, I said to myself, "Why do the Black male (like Sam) date the White male (like Cammisano)?" My reaction emerged from my everyday participation in the gay sexual cultures. Diverse men of color are subjected to the brand value of whiteness embedded in the material realities of homonationalism. Puar (2007) reminds, "The American flag appeared everywhere in gay spaces, in gays bars and gay gyms, and gay pride parades became loaded with national performatives and symbolism: the pledge of allegiance, the singing of the national anthem, and floats dedicated to national unity" (p. 43). Such hegemonic citizenship is a discursive product of whiteness in the historical continuities of racial formation. Consequently, finding a White man as a sexual and romantic partner signifies an ideality for men of color in and across gay sexual cultures (McBride, 2005). Here, I do not essentially suggest that all men of color desire the White male. However, I question and critique the colonialist logics of homoerotic interracialism that locally, nationally, and globally reproduce a homonormative path for men of color to desire the White male. At the same time, I remain wondering if Sam's boyfriend was the Black male. What kinds of public reactions could such intra-racial coupling attract? How does such intra-racial coupling serve as the racialized mode of queer transgression in the age of (White) homonationalism? The romantic dyad of Sam and Cammisano implicates complex and contested technologies of homonormative desire, intimacy, and relationality.

Anti-queerness

Thus far, I have argued the way through which the discursive and material effects of homonationalism and homoerotic interracialism shape the performative rhetoric of queerness around Sam. Under such conditions, a memory of Sam's big gay kiss remains to be a queer fantasy. This explicitly points at the historical continuities of anti-queerness that marginalize a moment of transgression in which Sam's big gay kiss could have offered. Indeed, it is noteworthy to mention that no other NFL players publicly kissed their same-sex partners during their drafts since Sam. Thus, NFL's interest of profit making constrain possibilities of Sam's queerness.

For example, a celebrity news website TMZ (Thirty Mile Zone), owed by Time Warner, published a two-minutes-and-31-seconds interview with Sam on December 3, 2014. This was when Sam did not make it play for the Dallas Cowboys after being transferred from St. Louis Rams and New Orleans Saints. In this interview titled *"I'm Not in the NFL ... Because I'm Gay,"* a TMZ reporter found Sam in the baggage claim area in an airport.[4] He asked Sam, "What's the next step for Michael?" While looking at his cellphone, Sam replied, "Everybody is curious. I am curious. What's up?" After a couple of exchanges between the reporter and Sam, Sam confirmed that he absolutely wanted to stay in the NFL. Then, the reporter asked Sam if his coming out or his level of talent he went up against after the college had to do with him. With his frustration, Sam immediately made a response, "I think I was a SEC player of the year[5] last year. So, I don't think it has to do with that." Then, Sam turned away from the reporter. This ending showcases Sam alluding to the homophobic condition of NFL working environment.

Here, I emphasize Sam's queer praxis of calling out NFL's homophobia. Sam's response hints how simultaneous technologies of racism, (hetero)sexism, and homophobia are deeply ingrained in NFL. From this perspective, I critically celebrate how Sam challenged the NFL in the TMZ's interview. Indeed, Sam's big gay kiss represented a possible space of queer fantasy where public man-on-man interracial intimacy can be displayed in the heteronormative and patriarchal environment like NFL. A queer fantasy became the reality for a second during 2014's NFL draft. Still Sam had to take the material consequence of being unable to become the first openly gay NFL player in the field. American football continues to represent the ideal U.S. American citizenship rooted in whiteness, patriarchal masculinity and heteronormativity. Accordingly, American football may be going to remain anti-queer forever.

In this social context, I worry if gay, bisexual, and queer men of color also buy into the national myth that American football players should be straight. For example, because sexuality is a fluid and contradictory concept (e.g., McCune 2014; Snorton, 2014), desiring the straight male is one of the typical homoerotic imaginations embedded in and across gay sexual cultures. Bailey (2016) maintains, "FOR MANY PEOPLE, sexual pleasure is experienced through our apparent contradictions" (p. 239, emphasis in original). He continues to reflect, "I am an out and proud Black gay man who loves heterosexual sex ... I am turned on by straight-identified men, sometimes even the mildly homophobic ones" (p. 239). This kind of sexual contradiction indicates complex and messy technologies of homoerotic desire, intimacy, and fantasy. Accordingly, I call into question gay, bisexual, and queer men of color who may be comfortable with the powerful sustainability of heteronormativity intersecting with patriarchal masculinity, whiteness, and capitalism ingrained in the NFL. Gay, bisexual, and queer men of color are always already subjected to anti-queerness in the current political, economic, and cultural climate. The logics of cisheteronormativity, intersecting with whiteness, patriarchy, and capitalism, control, discipline, and punish the shapes, forms and vision of queerness. Anti-queerness is the material reality. Thus, I call to the need of collectively rewriting and restoring Sam's big gay kiss event as a queer cultural production of memory.

In Closing: Rewriting Sam's Big Gay Kiss

In this essay, through a queer intercultural communication lens I have attempted to critique the performative rhetoric of queerness around Sam especially after his big gay kiss was aired live on 2014's NFL's draft. I am particularly concerned with the discursive and material effects of homonationalism and homoerotic interracialism that constraint queerness of Sam. Simultaneously, Sam's queerness has also served as a temporal moment of transgression in the context of NFL through which the technology of cisheteronormativity intersecting with patriarchal masculinity is powerfully maintained. Therefore, I reiterate that Sam's big gay kiss should never be forgotten before ending this essay.

After reading this essay, some readers may still find that Sam's big gay kiss is still just a *footnote* of NFL's history. Because no one really talks about Sam's big gay kiss today, they may also think Sam has not really challenged and shifted the heteronormative and patriarchal landscape of American football, in general, and NFL, in particular. However, as Muñoz (2009) said, queerness is an ideality in the present. It is almost unattainable in the present straight time. This is the paradox for the subject performing queerness like Sam in and across cultural and intercultural contexts. The colonialist logics of cisheteronormativity working with whiteness, patriarchy, and capitalism easily ignore, erase, and marginalize whatever sexual minoritarians of color do to transgress the present. However, such temporal moment of transgression, performed by sexual minoritarians of color, is indeed a possibility for the future through which everyone can become and be whom they want to become and be. Morris and Sloop (2006) suggests that the public display of man-on-man public kissing is an absolute political performance "understood accordingly by those who see it as a chief threat to heteronormativity and seek its discipline" (p. 2). Thus, Sam's big gay kiss should never be simply translated as a footnote of NFL's history. The intercultural memory of Black male football player kissing his White boyfriend in the NFL draft, aired on the national television, is quite transgressive. Sam's big gay kiss undeniably violates the historical and ongoing expectations of the Black male football player rooted in the technology of anti-Black racism working with patriarchy, cisheteronormativity, and capitalism. Such memory of temporal transgression is a possibility of Sam's racialized and gendered queerness that intellectually and politically creates an additional and alternative paradigm of the present.

Therefore, I end this essay by reiterating Sam's big gay kiss as a memory of queer fantasy that moves toward the future of sexual freedom. With this assertion, I once again recall for ongoing queer intercultural communication critiques to collectively promote shared critical dissatisfactions in and across power lines of differences. So, we will work toward the future where queerness is no longer an ideality. Queerness must become the material reality we live in.

Notes

1 Sam is no longer romantically with Cammisano.
2 As a Jamaican-born Black male, Harris was a former offensive tackle who played in six seasons for San Francisco 49ers and Oakland Raiders between 2003 and 2008. In 2010, he retired after being cut by United Football League's Florida Tuskers.
3 As a Samoan born in Honolulu, Hawaii, Tsaolo was a former defensive tackle playing for NFL teams such as Green Bay Packers, Minnesota Vikings, Jacksonville Jaguars, Atlanta Falcon, and Carolina Panthers between 1991 and 1999. With Atlanta Falcon (1998), he made it to Super Bowl XXXIII.
4 I assumed it to be LAX (Los Angeles International Airport). However, the location of an airport was not explicitly stated in the interview.
5 Sam was recognized as a consensus All American and the Southeastern Conference (SEC) Defensive Player of the Year while he was a senior at the University of Missouri.

References

Abdi, S., & Calafell, B. M. (2017). Queer utopias and a (Feminist) Iranian vampire: A critical analysis of resistive monstrosity in A Girl Walks Home Alone at Night. *Critical Studies in Media Communication, 34*(4), 358–370.

Ahmed, S. (2012). *On being included: Racism and diversity in institutional life.* Durham, NC: Duke University Press.

Alexander, B. K. (2010). Br(other) in the classroom: Testimony, reflection, and cultural negotiation. In T. K. Nakayama & R. T. Halualani (Eds.), *The handbook of critical intercultural communication* (pp. 364–381). West Sussex, UK: Wiley-Blackwell.

Atay, A. (2020). Intercultural queer slippages and translations. In S. Eguchi & B. M. Calafell (Eds.), *Queer intercultural communication: The intersectional politics of belonging in and across differences* (pp. 141–156). Lanham, MD: Rowman & Littlefield.

Bailey, M. M. (2016). Black gay (raw) sex. In E. P. Johnson (Ed.), *No tea no shade: New writings in black queer studies* (pp. 239–261). Durham, NC: Duke University Press.

Bellah, R. (1969). Civil religion in America. *Daedalus, 96*, 1–21.

Butterworth, M. (2008). Fox sports, Super Bowl XLII, and the affirmation of American civil religion. *Journal of Sport & Social Issues, 32*(3), 318–323.

Buzinski, J. (2017, January 20). There have been 11 known gay players in NFL history. *Outsports: A Vehicle For LGBT Athletes.* Retrieved from https://www.outsports.com/2017/6/20/15842796/gay-nfl-players-history-kopay-ocallaghan

Chambers-Letson, J. (2018). *After the party: A manifesto for queer of color life.* New York: New York University Press.

Chávez, K. R. (2013). Pushing boundaries: Queer intercultural communication. *Journal of International and Intercultural Communication, 6*(2), 83–95.

Cohen, C. J. (2005). Punks, bulldaggers, and welfare queens: The radical potential of queer politics? In E. P. Johnson & M. G. Henderson (Eds.), *Black queer studies: A critical anthology* (pp. 21–51). Durham, NC: Duke University Press.

Collins, P. H. (2004). *Black sexual politics: African Americans, gender, and the new racism*. New York: Routledge.

Connor, M. (1995). *What is cool?: Understanding Black manhood in America*. New York: Agate.

Drape, J., Eder, S., & Witzfeb, B. (2014, February 11). Before coming out, a hard time growing up: Michael Sam's troubled upbringing in Texas. *The New York Times*. Retrieved from https://www.nytimes.com/2014/02/12/sports/football/for-nfl-prospect-michael-sam-upbringing-was-bigger-challenge-than-coming-out-as-gay.html?mcubz=0

Eguchi, S., & Asante, G. (2016). Disidentifications revisited: Queer(y)ing intercultural communication theory. *Communication Theory, 26*(2), 171–189.

Eguchi, S., & Calafell, B. M. (2020). Introduction: Reorienting queer intercultural communication. In S. Eguchi & B. M. Calafell (Eds.), *Queer intercultural communication: The intersectional politics of belonging in and across differences* (pp. 1–16). Lanham, MD: Rowman & Littlefield.

Eguchi, S., & Ding, Z. (2017). "Uncultural" Asian Americans in ABC's *Dr. Ken*. *Popular Communication, 15*(4), 296–310.

Eguchi, S., Files-Thompson, N., & Calafell, B. M. (2018). Queer (of color) aesthetics: Fleeting moments of transgression in VH1's *Love & Hip-Hop: Hollywood Season 2*. *Critical Studies in Media Communication, 35*(2), 180–193.

Eng, D. L. (2010). *The feeling of kinship: Queer liberalism and the racialization of intimacy*. Durham, NC: Duke University Press.

Ferguson, R. A. (2005). Race-ing homonormativity: Citizenship, sociology, and gay identity. In E. P. Johnson & M. G. Henderson (Eds.), *Black queer studies: A critical anthology* (pp. 52–67). Durham, NC: Duke University Press.

Griffin, R. A. (2015). Problematic representations of strategic whiteness and 'post-racial' pedagogy: A critical intercultural reading of *the Help*. *Journal of International and Intercultural Communication, 8*(2), 147–166.

Griffin, R. A., & Calafell, B. M. (2011). Control, discipline, and punish: Black masculinity and (in)visible Whiteness in the NBA. In M. G. Lacy & K. A. Ono (Eds.), *Critical rhetorics of race* (pp. 117–136). New York: New York University Press.

Halberstam, J. (2011). *The queer art of failure*. Durham, NC: Duke University Press.

hooks, b. (2004). *We real cool: Black men and masculinity*. New York: Routledge.

Johnson, E. P. (2001). "Quare" studies or (almost) everything I know about queer studies I learned from my grandmother. *Text and Performance Quarterly, 21*(1), 1–25.

Johnson, E. P. (2016). Introduction. In E. P. Johnson (Ed.), *No tea no shade: New writings in black queer studies* (pp. 1–26). Durham, NC: Duke University Press.

Johnson, E. P., & Henderson, M. G. (Eds.). (2005). *Black queer studies: A critical anthology*. Durham, NC: Duke University Press.

Keeling, K. (2019). *Queer times, Black futures*. New York: New York University Press.

Kimes, M. (2016, January 12). New study exposes the NFL's real coaching diversity crisis. *The ESPN News*. Retrieved from http://www.espn.com/nfl/story/_/id/14549971/study-nfl-coaching-diversity-crisis

McBride, D. (2005). *Why I hate Abercrombie and Fitch: Essays on race and sexuality.* New York: New York University Press.

McCune Jr., J. Q. (2014). *Sexual discretion: Black masculinity and the politics of passing.* Chicago, IL: University of Chicago Press.

McIntosh, D. M. D., Moon, D. G., & Nakayama, T. K. (2019). Introduction: Introducing twenty-first century whiteness or "everything old is new again." In D. M. D. McIntosh, D. G. Moon, & T. K. Nakayama (Eds.), *Interrogating the communicative power of whiteness* (pp. 1–12). New York: Routledge.

Means Coleman, R. R., & Cobb, J. (2007). No way of seeing: Mainstreaming and selling the gaze of homo-thug hip-hop. *Popular Communication, 5*(2), 89–108.

Morris, C. E., & Sloop, J. M. (2006). "What lips these lips have kissed": Refiguring the politics of queer public kissing. *Communication and Critical/Cultural Studies, 3*(1), 1–26.

Morrissey, M. E. (2013). A DREAM disrupted: Undocumented migrant youth disidentifications with U.S. citizenship. *Journal of International and Intercultural Communication, 6*(2), 145–162.

Muñoz, J. E. (1999). *Disidentifications: Queers of color and the performance of politics.* Minneapolis, MN: University of Minnesota Press.

Muñoz, J. E. (2009). *Cruising utopia: The then and there of queer futurity.* New York: New York University Press.

Nakayama, T. K., & Krizek, R. L. (1995). Whiteness: A strategic rhetoric. *Quarterly Journal of Speech, 81*(3), 291–309.

Neal, M. A. (2013). *Looking for Leroy: Illegible black masculinities.* New York: New York University Press.

Oates, T. P., & Durham, M. G. (2004). The mismeasure of masculinity: The male body, 'race' and power in the enumerative discourses of the NFL Draft. *Patterns of Prejudice, 38*(3), 301–320.

Pérez, H. (2015). *A taste for brown bodies: Gay modernity and cosmopolitan desire.* New York: New York University Press.

Puar, J. (2007). *Terrorist assemblages: Homonationalism in queer times.* Durham, NC: Duke University Press.

Rhoden, W. C. (2011, December 11). At Some N.F.L. Positions, Stereotypes Create Prototypes. *The New York Times.* Retrieved from http://www.nytimes.com/2011/12/12/sports/football/at-some-nfl-positions-stereotypes-reign.html?pagewanted=all&_r=0

Ross, M. B. (2005). Beyond the closet as a raceless paradigm. In E. P. Johnson & M. G. Henderson (Eds.), *Black queer studies: A critical anthology* (pp. 161–189). Durham, NC: Duke University Press.

Snorton, C. R. (2013). Marriage Mimesis. *Journal of International and Intercultural Communication, 6*(2), 127–134.

Snorton, C. R. (2014). *Nobody is supposed to know: Black sexuality on the down low.* Minneapolis: University of Minnesota Press.

Smith, M. D. (2017, January 14). NFL will have at least eight minority head coaches in 2017. *NBC Sports*. Retrieved from http://profootballtalk.nbcsports.com/2017/01/14/nfl-will-have-at-least-eight-minority-head-coaches-in-2017/

Stockton, K. B. (2006). *Beautiful bottom, beautiful shame: Where 'black' meets 'queer'*. Durham, NC: Duke University Press.

Watts, E. K. (2005). Border patrolling and "passing" in Eminem's 8 Mile. *Critical Studies in Media Communication, 22*(3), 187–206.

Yan, H., & Alsup, D. (2014, May 13). NFL draft: Reactions heat up after Michael Sam kisses boyfriend on TV. CNN news. Retrieved from http://www.cnn.com/2014/05/12/us/michael-sam-nfl-kiss-reaction/index.html

Yep, G. A. (2013). Queering/Quaring/Kauering/Crippin'/Transing 'other bodies' in intercultural communication. *Journal of International and Intercultural Communication, 6*(2), 118–126. doi:10.1080/17513057.2013.777087.

7. Photographs as Diasporic Memories: Turkish Cypriots, Home, and Memory

AHMET ATAY
College of Wooster

Lately, I feel as though I am stuck in a nexus of the past and the present, constantly having a hard time moving forward. Sometimes, moving forward and leaving the past behind is not an option, and it can be rather painful. Often, the only things we have from our past are the memories of what we have left behind, gently reminding us who we were and where we have been. Every so often, we realize that we can only exist by standing next to our memories. At the end of the day, we only have memories and photographs of the people we loved, the places we visited and to which we belonged, the places we called home, and finally, the places we can never get back to.

We often remember our past fondly despite our dark or bleak moments and hurtful experiences, and it is possible that the past was not as spectacular as we make it out to be in the present. After all, we try to hang on to the happy times of our youth, our past, and who we were, which possibly explains why people in exile, immigrants, and the members of different diasporic communities often story their past and relive their memories in order to belong to, feel connected to, and make sense of their in-between experiences that have been shaped by their colonial past, imperialistic agendas, and the outcomes of globalization processes. Sometimes, a photograph, a sudden smell in the air, or a rhythm or motif in a song takes us back to times that are often buried in our deepest memories. We might recall things, experiences, or stories that others might not remember. Occasionally, we might be the only one left behind to remember something of our past.

This essay is about memory. It is about negotiating and making sense of intercultural, diasporic, and cosmopolitan memory. It is also about remembering the past, keeping it alive, and not letting it go. Hence, in this diasporic autoethnography, I write about in-between experiences and remembering the past through the liminal spaces that we perpetually step in and out of as dislocated and planted bodies. My memories are partial, and some of them are worn out because of my desire to constantly remember them. In this essay, I present three interrelated stories, and I use pieces from the past to a construct a larger story as a way not only to remember these stories but also to immortalize them. Hence, I employ autoethnographic writing to connect personal to cultural. Autoethnography "is an approach to research and writing that seeks to describe and systematically analyze (graphy) personal experience (auto) in order to understand cultural experience (ethno)" (Ellis, Adams, & Bochner, 2011, p. 273).

Stories help us make sense of our experiences and our past, and they are often preserved in photographs and films. We sometimes write about these stories in the form of poetry. We might turn them into a canvas or make art out of them. We sing about them. We use them as an ingredient in our cooking. We move with them as if they are our dancing partners, hand in hand, cheek to cheek.

Stories, Home, and Belonging

When I began to make sense of the idea of home, something that I consciously refused to do for the longest time, I turned to theory—the theories of home, belonging, and memory—to make sense of my own journey of finding home, or the home that exists in my memories. As I began to make sense of home, I chose to story the theories about home and belonging with the hopes of having an emotional reaction so I could finally begin to make sense of their meaning. This paper is about narrated theories and theories in narration about home, belonging, and memory.

A significant portion of this essay was written during the COVID-19 pandemic in lockdown, away from people and human contact. My interactions have been limited to communication on new media platforms. Hence, I created cyber memories in Zoom, Skype, and Microsoft Teams. I created new memories of home and of being at home. I revised my existing memories of home and tried to make sense of my transnational experiences about home in lockdown at my home away from home. However, this is essay is not about being in lockdown or about the cyber memories I have recently created. It is about digging into the archives and revisiting memories. It is about remembering. Perhaps because I have been alone at home for several months now, I have had time to think about the past. I have had time to watch online videos about popular songs from my childhood, old films, and decades-old episodes of my favorite soap operas. I have taken the opportunity to look at older photos. I have had to remember, thus the reason I am currently caught in the middle of the past and the present, remembering the past because I cannot move forward.

As Devika Chawla (2014) claims, "Stories begin in memories" (p. 1). I am a diasporic body whose understanding of home is fractured, incomplete, fluid, ever-changing, and patched together with a mixture of locations, feelings, images, and memories. These stories I have knitted together are about remembering the past as well as the role and the importance of photographs, and these stories are about people who are caught in between "here" and "there." They are about that liminal space where our only friends are our own memories.

Background

As a child, London was a faraway place where some of my relatives lived. It was so far away that some of them never visited us, and some of them I only met once. They only existed in photographs or in the form of "once in a while" telephone conversations for me. Eventually, England became a part of me when I went to a school that was built on the British education system. As a former colony, after 1960, Cyprus still had a significant number of expats living on the island (both on the Greek and Turkish sides). There were also common practices rooted in the colonial past, such as driving on the left-hand side of the road, which were part of our everyday reality. Moreover, I grew up watching British TV shows, using British products, speaking English, and finally, learning about British history and culture. There was a part of England in me, that faraway place I had always desired to visit.

***

Following the Russo-Turkish war, the British occupied the island of Cyprus in 1878, and as a result of the Ottoman Empire's actions, the British protectorate began. Once WWI began in 1914 and the Ottoman Empire joined the Central Powers (which also included Austria-Hungary, Bulgaria, and Germany), Britain declared the annexation of Cyprus and incorporated it into its empire. A decade later in 1925, the Crown Colony of Cyprus was proclaimed. Cyprus remained under British rule until 1960 (British Rule in Cyprus). Currently, there are two military bases on the island, both known as a British Overseas Territory: the Sovereign Base Areas of Akrotiri and Dhekelia. While providing an in-depth discussion about Cyprus and its history in the empire is beyond the scope of this essay, I have to note that this particular part of history greatly impacted the island and its people. Many generations grew up under British rule and became accustomed to British ways and cultural practices.

Following WWI, Greek Cypriots began immigrating to Britain to work in the catering industry in Soho, London (Cypriot London, 2008). Around the beginning of WWII, there were 8,000 Cypriots living in London. During the mid-1950s, more Cypriots arrived in the UK as the Greek National Organization of Cypriot Fighters (EOKA) campaigned for the independence of Cyprus. An average of 4,000 Cypriots left the island every year during this period (Winder, 2004). Robert Winder (2004) suggests that migration peaked following the independence in 1960, and roughly about 25,000 Cypriots left the island to join their relatives in the UK. Due to the ethnic conflict on the island between Greeks and Turks, a second wave of migration began in 1974. During this time, roughly 10,000 Turkish and Greek Cypriots immigrated to the UK.

Even though Greek Cypriot migration began earlier, the Turkish Cypriot migration began due to intercommunal conflicts during the 1950s and 1960s (Robins & Aksoy, 2001). Before the independence of Cyprus, approximately 8,500 Turkish Cypriots were living in Britain (Humayun, 2004). Turkish Cypriot migration continued during the 1970s due to unresolved ethnic conflicts and during the 1980s because of economic reasons. Since 2004, when Cyprus joined the EU, the holders of Republic of Cyprus passports, including the Turkish Cypriots who live in the Turkish Republic of Northern Cyprus (TRNC), have been able to migrate to the UK. Because of the UK's departure from the European Union, the migration patterns of Cypriots to the UK are now subject to further fluctuations.

Sixty years and much political turbulence later, the memory of the past is still present. One can see this past in our architecture and in the way our lives were organized and lived. Some of our past was in the British stores, such as Debenhams and Marks & Spencer. Some was in the media we consumed, such as Benny Hill Show or other British TV shows and films. Some was destroyed by or disappeared with each political conflict. The physical signs might not be that easy to find any more even though the vibes and essences of British culture were embodied for generations. Today, there are at least 50,000 Brits living on the island, and Cyprus is still considered a summer destination for many vacationers from the UK. Similarly, there are roughly 80,000 Greek and Turkish Cypriots living in the UK who were born in Cyprus. There are also second-, third-, and fourth-generation British Cypriots who were born into their diasporic families or into mixed-family compositions. Hence, the memory of our British past is quite present in Cyprus today in so many different ways.

Photograph 1: Diaspora

I learned the definitions of "diaspora" long before I was exposed to the theoretical materials on diaspora studies and postcolonial theory in my graduate courses. Diaspora for me as a child represented my relatives who lived in faraway places, such as in Istanbul, London, or other parts of the world. They were not only my relatives; they were Cypriots who had left the island for a number of reasons before I was even born. I thus understood that there was a direct relationship between "home" or "homeland" and diaspora. According to Hall (1995), diaspora is "the long-term settlement of peoples in 'foreign' places which follow their scattering or dispersal from their original homeland" (p. 193). Similarly, Anthias (1998) defines diaspora as "the process of settlement and adaptation relating to a large range of transnational migration movements" (p. 557). Finally, in my previous research, I (2015) defined the concept of diaspora as "a community or a group of people who live outside of their homeland, and [who] try to accommodate to a host culture while simultaneously trying to maintain cultural beliefs, practices, and norms of their homeland" (p. 31). Hence, diasporic communities consistently engage in intercultural communication practices in order to define home, make sense of their belonging, and understand complexities of their cultural identities (Atay, 2015; Carlson 2001; Safran 1991).

***

I met my aunt (my father's older sister) through photographs of her. I also met my great aunt (my fraternal grandmother's younger sister) for the first time in our family album. As a child, I remember going through our photograph albums, which people had back then. These albums were possibly some of the most precious belongings of any household. I remember looking at pre-1974 photos and imagining how things were before the interethnic conflict in Cyprus. I also remember looking at photos of happy people in happy occasions, people who I had never met—some of them relatives who had passed away and others the people who lived in faraway places.

Summers are always hot and sunny in Cyprus. As on most summer days, I was staying at my grandparents' house until my parents could pick me up after work. I was taking a break from playing under the tall grape vines that covered the back yard. My grandmother was inside, taking a break from cooking and making yogurt. After she was done, she decided to spend the afternoon cleaning out one of her closets. As a child, one of the things I enjoyed about cleaning closets was the possibility of finding all sorts of treasures. This closet contained mostly boxes of photographs and old items, tucked away and waiting to be remembered. While my grandmother pulled things out, I picked up one of the family albums. Inside were some black and white photos and some color ones, captured either by professional photographers in studios or by a family member. Cameras were not very common until the 1960s or 1970s, and most of these photos were from those eras.

Since my grandmother already knew that I was going to ask "Who is this person?" over and over again, she sat by me and began telling me about the people in the photographs. They were her children: my dad and his siblings. There were also photos of her grandchildren. In one of the black and white photos, there was my aunt with her five children, my older cousins, arranged by their age and height, standing in front of each other. The last person was my aunt. I remembered her because my parents had the exact same photo in our family album. Like so many others in Cyprus after 1974, my aunt and four of her younger children joined her husband, who was working in London at the time, only leaving behind one child who was already married and working. Years later, I looked at the same photo at my cousin's house in London. One of the things we do after not seeing each other for a long time is to go over family albums and retell family stories.

After looking at my aunt's photos, we moved to those of my grandmother's relatives. Some had passed on and some were away. As usual, I quickly asked "Who is she?" when I saw the photo of my grandmother's sister, who left Cyprus in 1975 with most of her children to join her husband in London. She only existed in the photos for me until I met her once in Cyprus when she visited in the mid-1980s.

***

Looking at those photos might have been a sad yet cherished experience for my grandmother. Having family members who live in different parts of the world was not easy at that time. Even though the improvements in transportation technologies made international travel easier, the cost of traveling, on the other hand, made things more difficult, especially for diasporic individuals who needed more financial means to constantly travel between countries. Most Cypriots thus did not see their relatives for long periods of time, sometimes even decades, especially between 1950 and 1980. Hence, most of these people only existed in photos for us, the members of the new generation who did not know our relatives in person, and for others, they were but memories, often existing in stories, other times materializing in photographs. Photographs became part of the diasporic memory.

Photograph 2: Photo of the Homeland

The notion of home is a complex one that carries different meanings for different groups of people. For some, it is a physical place, and for others, it can be a source of happiness or fear. For diasporic individuals, the concept of home represents a number of things. These definitions or explanations often blend current reality with memory and nostalgia. For some, home represents something they can never return to. Hence, home for diasporic individuals is a very convoluted concept that often captures or defines their in-between experiences and stands for a part of history that exists only in the memory, stories, or photographs.

Diasporic communities leave their homeland and migrate for various reasons, such as political struggles or social and cultural restlessness in their homeland, lack of economic opportunities, the appeals of Western lifestyles, or the urge to move to a former colonizer's land for a better life. In the case of the Cypriots, leaving the homeland was directly tied to economic issues as well as the island's ethnic and political conflicts. While diasporic individuals physically change geographic locations and create new homes in new locales, they often remain emotionally, mentally, and culturally rooted in their homeland. This connection may be less intense for second or third generations. For example, after the ethnic conflict, in 1975, because of rough financial realities, my great aunt and her family moved to London to seek a better life, make enough money and eventually return back to the island. This was the reality of thousands of Cypriots at the time.

James Clifford (1994) maintains that the transnational connection between diasporic communities and their "real or symbolic homeland" should be carefully examined. Home not only refers to homeland as a geographical locale, but it can also mean the idea of home or "homes away from home" as well as the illusion of a homeland. This illusion is the mixture of the past and how the "homeland" is currently storied for or by the diasporic individuals. Clifford also argues that diasporic individuals experience a constant struggle as they try to adapt to a new culture while also trying to maintain their communities—their collective homes away from home. This constant push and pull helps them to define and understand the notion of home as well as maneuver between multiple homes and negotiate the meaning of belonging.

***

It was one of those hot summer days during the summer of 1991. My dad and I drove to Nicosia, the capital city of Cyprus (Nicosia is a divided city and the capital of the Greek and Turkish side of the island). We were going to apply for a visa for my parents and me to travel to England to visit my uncle and my cousins from both my father's and mother's sides of the family. After finding a parking spot for our Renault, we walked to the very crowded British representative office. The hot and steamy room was packed with people who were hoping to travel to London to visit their relatives. My dad found the necessary forms and filled them out. At that time, Turkish Cypriots needed visas to travel to England with their TRNC passports. Additionally, the government required bank statements, proof of property or land, and a letter from the travelers' workplace saying that the applicants had a secure job and intended to come back. We presented the paperwork, and after a restless waiting period that felt like forever and a day, we returned to the consulate for the interview. Upon finishing the interview, we were approved and given our visas to travel.

We left the island on a Cyprus Turkish Airlines plane, landing in Istanbul and waiting two hours on the plane before taking off to go to London. After the long journey, we arrived at Gatwick airport, passed through customs, and were picked up to be taken to our family friend Ceylan's Victorian house located on the south side of London. Ceylan lived on the ritzier south side of the city while most of the Greek and Turkish Cypriots lived in places like Harangey or Edmonton.

I was finally in London. I had waited for this moment for such a long time, to be in the city where my relatives had come to search for their dreams. We climbed the steep stairs to the top of the stairwell, where Ceylan welcomed us with a warm hug. As we settled in, she made us each a cup of tea (British style with a touch of milk). The living room was full of photos in frames. Some were her family members, and some were photos of her distant relatives. There was a photo of her remembered Cyprus, our capital city. It was the photo of her street where she lived as a child. She cherished this photo because at the time we visited her, she had only returned to Cyprus twice since leaving in 1955. Even though she was in her home, the photo constantly reminded her of her "homeland" and what she had left behind. This photo was her way of being connected or feeling at home and encapsulated everything she had left behind yet still yearned for. The street in that photo looked very different in the early 1990s. However, in her mind, that street still looked the same as it did in the photo. That photo froze time for her and made everything more present even though everything in the photo was now absent. She felt at home when she looked at the photo, yet it only represented her memory of a place to which she could go back. Home was different. Returning to that street was physically impossible, whenever she felt alone and wanted to have a piece of Cyprus with her. That photo was her home.

***

Anjali Ram (2004) argues that the "most important vehicles of memory, both collective and personal," are media (p. 122). Photographs as part of the visual culture enable us to remember but also to return to that memory, albeit for a short period of time, even though this return only exists through the celluloid that the image or the memory is captured on. David Bate (2010) claims,

> While the capacity of individuals to remember and recall things varies enormously, it is true that the invention of devices to support and extend the human ability of remembering has meant that humans no longer have to carry everything around with them in their heads, or like the character in *Gulliver's Travels* who has to carry actual objects on his back of the things he wishes to remember. (p. 244)

Ceylan was not Gulliver nor was she traveling between homes, but she needed a photo, an image of her home, to feel connected and to ponder her in-between experiences as she made sense of belonging to that street and of feeling at home in London.

Photograph 3: Return

We take photos for a number of reasons, but most of us take photos to remember people, places, and events, and to capture how we feel at a given moment in time. Kotkin (1978) argues that "We tend to take photos according to how we want to preserve, remember, and be remembered . . .. [F]amily photos represent a stylized reality" (p. 5). While family photos help us to remember, they also catalogue our lives and establish connections among people from different generations. For example, we may get to know our great-grandparents through photos of them. Similarly, we can observe family events that happened in our absence. Hence, photographs have the power tell us something about the people we have in common as well as the moments and events we share, and these images help us fill the gaps or provide knowledge that we cannot otherwise obtain. They also help us to construct a narrative about our past and our experiences.

As a diasporic body who lives alone practically in the middle of Nowhere, Ohio, I lack the privilege of having any family albums. I am not the keeper of these particular family treasures, which is possibly the reason why I do not have any photos of my childhood here with me in the U.S. That part of me is in the homeland along with my photos. In the absence of photos, I only have the memories of those days. Perhaps because of this, in my mind, everybody is still as young as the day I last saw them. Even though digital albums provide an opportunity to archive our memories, surely they do not create the same feeling that physical albums do. Nonetheless, these digital memories still provide possibilities for diasporic individuals to remember the past and reconnect with their homelands.

***

Lately, I feel like I am stuck in a nexus of the past and the present and lost somewhere in between, maybe because we are living in the era of COVID-19 pandemic lockdowns, and I have not seen anyone for a while. Or maybe because this summer, I was planning to visit Cyprus and Britain, but due to these extraordinary circumstances, I am not able to go and have been feeling a little melancholic. Maybe deep down, I have been yearning for familiarity, or perhaps I have simply been missing home. Though I never considered London home, I always feel at home when I visit.

Click. I opened one of my digital folders full of photographs from London when I was living there during my sabbatical. I was part of the Turkish Cypriot diaspora even though it was only for four months. I browsed through the photographs, reliving the recent past and remembering all those moments when I was stuck in a time vortex, where the past mingled with the present, and the present was really becoming the past as soon as I was about to leave London to come back to the states. I was an immigrant, a diasporic and cosmopolitan body moving between continents and locations, and maneuvering between cultures. I was a pedestrian, entering into the stories of other Turkish Cypriots living in London, and creating new memories before exiting. Even though our lives and locations were different, as Turkish Cypriots we all knew what it meant to be living away from the homeland and away from family members. For a while, our stories intersected and merged. As we revisited the past, we exchanged stories. They told me about their childhood homes, homes don't exist anymore. They told me about family members who are long gone. In each story, someone always ask "do you know her/him or them." As if we are all connected like a spiderweb and as if we know the characters from our stories. Most of these stories were about home, our childhood, or our individual and collective ancestors. They were about food, places, and sometimes about the hot summers in Cyprus. They were about family and belonging. These stories were all fragmented, mostly mixed with "here" and "there," and the people in these stories were familiar to some of us and unfamiliar to others. We told stories about the "same" location, but there was nothing the same about it. We lived in different periods of time in the same city without having any continuity. Hence, our stories were simultaneously connected yet disconnected. We embodied diasporic storytelling where the past intersected with the present, characters in our stories were disjointed, and there was nothing cohesive about it. It was a large narrative threaded together with different pieces of memories.

After looking at a number of photos, I paused. My eyes were captivated by the simplicity of a particular photo. It was the photo of Ceylan's house and the same street I had walked up and down roughly three decades earlier. I remembered it vividly. The photo took me back to 1991 when I saw this house for the first time. I was stuck on Memory Lane.

I arrived at Ceylan's home on a sunny summer day. This was my fifth time staying at this beautiful old Victorian house on the south side of London. It had been twenty-five years before that I had stayed with her for the first time. She was younger, then. She now looked tired, but she smiled at me as soon as she saw me on the doorstep. She gave me a hug and said "Welcome home." London and this house have been her home since the 1950s as it had been mine every time I stayed for a long period in London. She gave me the key to the door, saying, "Keep this key, and remember, this is your home as long as you are in London, and as long as I live in this house."

Her garden was in blossom with roses of all kinds. Her loquat tree was heavy with fruit, and even though it was in her garden, it grew large enough to cross to the other side of the fence. Her neighbor Kristina, a Greek Cypriot who grew up in Famagusta and had left the island in the 1960s to come to England, stepped outside to join our conversation.

"Kalimera!"
I responded, "Kalimera, Kristina!"
Ceylan quickly followed, "Do you remember Ahmet? Ahmet and his family stayed with me 25 years ago, and now he is back for another visit."
Kristina responded, "Of course! He came back a couple of years ago, and we talked about Cyprus, our homeland."

We carried out our conversation by that tree that connected two gardens, two cultures, two languages. None of us live in Cyprus any longer, but the land we once lived on created a bond among us even though we neither knew each other in Cyprus nor were we contemporaries with similar memories. While we ate our loquats, we chatted about the sunny and warm days of Cyprus. Despite the ethnic conflict and decades-long segregation on the island, the Greek and Turkish Cypriots managed to create civil and respectful relationships in their new homelands. We narrated our different recollections of Cyprus. The women told me about a Cyprus I had never experienced. They spoke about different ethnic communities living together peacefully until the conflict. Their Cyprus was different than mine. The notion of family was at the heart of their stories. Their stories were about their childhoods because that's what they remembered about their home. They talked about food they ate, places they visited with their families, and sometimes events that they remembered. For example, they talked about playing with other children on the street during the hot summer afternoons. They *talked about how people used to sit outside during the warm summer evenings inhaling the faint smell of jasmines. They talked about familial relationships and about times when people cared about each other, times when people had time to look at the blue Mediterranean Sea and hear the waves on a hot Wednesday afternoon. Their home was different from mine.*

Kristina told us she had decided to sell her house and move to a village north of London. She said she was ready to create a new episode in her life where she could feel at home. Ceylan and I left Kristina standing by the loquat tree in the garden. Three months later, I heard she had sold her house and moved away. A part of me moved with her. A part of us moved with her. And a part of me felt sad for Ceylan, who considered Kristina to be more than just a neighbor; she considered her a friend.

I left London and Ceylan's Victorian house to go back home to Ohio, but I promised Ceylan I would visit next year and spend several months carrying out my research on diaspora. During my journey back to Ohio, it felt much like what Devika Chawla (2014) had articulated; I was leaving one home and arriving at another.

Conclusion

Decades later, the Turkish Cypriots in the UK still maintain close ties to their "homeland," even though the notion of "homeland" might refer to different geographical and emotional spaces for the members of the second or third generations of Cypriots. Many see themselves as British Cypriots, loosely connected to Cyprus. For others, Cyprus is what they left behind; it is but the memory of a place that none of us can physically return to, the *idea* of Cyprus. For these British Cypriots, Cyprus is what it used to be in 1960s or 1970s. For me, Cyprus is what it was during the 1980s and 1990s. We are all attached to the idea of the land that is no longer there. Every time we return as diasporic bodies, we return to something new and different. Even though we might be searching for what we remember, this return is never possible. We can only return to our memories and the idea of Cyprus through the photos we have and the stories we tell about those days. Cyprus and the people who still live there have moved on as did we in our diasporic homes, but in our minds and hearts, we are stuck in the vortex of the then and the now. We are somewhere in the middle. There is no return, and moving forward is only possible as long as we have our diasporic memories.

Photos and stories often function as communicative forms, especially in the context of intercultural communication, to evoke emotion and trigger memories. Especially their role in the lives of diasporic communities should be carefully examined since they have personal and cultural significance and they also facilitate archiving lived experiences, places, and people. They are the constant link between "here" and "there," between home and "home" and between now and the past. Stories like Ceylan and Kristina's also testify how similar lived experiences could bring people from different backgrounds together despite the political conflicts. As I illustrate in this chapter, intercultural communication and memory research should be concerned with diasporic stories, and especially the role of visual representation, such as photographs, in keeping the past alive, presenting ways to remember, also making sense of diasporic, immigrant, and in-between identities.

***

In the fall of 2016, I returned to stay at Ceylan's for four months until January 2017. This photograph is from that time period. That was the last time I saw the house. A year or so later, Ceylan fell down the stairs and had to be moved to a nursing home. Soon after her move, the house was sold. My experiences with her became distant memories, as if they had never happened and we had never been there at the same time. Sometimes I look at this photo to remember Ceylan's and my "good old days." I was only a pedestrian coming in and out of her life while she lived there for decades. The only thing that is left behind are the photos and our collective memories about the house, partially familial, partially diasporic, and partially digitalized. In April 2020, Ceylan passed away. We have her memories, her diasporic, in-between, happy and sad, partial, and fragmented memories. Even though her house, her diasporic home, is no longer hers, we still have those memories. Photos and our stories are what is left behind. She used to have the photo of her childhood street in her house. Now, I have the photo of her diasporic home and the long road that connects the past and the present, diaspora and the homeland, and stories and memories. They are all fragmented and in between, like the lives of so many diasporic Turkish Cypriots in London.

References

Anthias, F. (1998). Evaluating 'diaspora': Beyond ethnicity? *Sociology*, 32(3), 557–580.

Atay, A. (2015). *Globalization's impact on cultural identity formations: Queer diasporic males in cyberspace*. Lanham, MD: Lexington Books.

Bate, D. (2010) The memory of photography. *Photographies*, 3(2), 243–257. doi: 10.1080/17540763.2010.499609.

British Rule in Cyprus. http://cypnet.co.uk/ncyprus/history/british/index.html

Carlson, D. (2001). Gay, queer, and cyborg: The performance of identity on a transglobal age. *Discourse: Studies in the Cultural Politics of Education*, 22(3), 297–309.

Chawla, D. (2014). *Home, uprooted: Oral histories of India's partition.* New York: Fordham University Press.

Clifford, J. (1994). Diasporas. *Cultural Anthropology, 9*(3), 302–338.

Cypriot London. BBC London. 13 May 2008. Retrieved June 14, 2020.

Ellis, C., Adams, T., & Bochner, A. (2011). Autoethnography: An overview. *Historical Social Research, 36*(4), 273–290.

Hall, S. (1995). The whites of their eyes: Racist ideologies and the media. In G. Dines & J. M. Humez (Eds.), *Gender, race and class in media* (pp. 18–22). Thousand Oaks, CA: Sage.

Humayun, A. (2004). *The infidel within: Muslims in Britain since 1800s.* London, UK: C Hurst & Co.

Kotkin, A. (1978). The family photo album as a form of folklore. *Exposure, 16*(1), 4–8.

Ram, A. (2004). Memory, cinema, and the reconstruction of cultural identities. In M. Fong & R. Chuang (Eds.), *Communicating ethnic & cultural identity* (pp. 121–134). Lanham, MD: Rowman and Littlefield.

Robins, K. & Aksoy, A. (2001). From spaces of identity to mental spaces: Lessons from Turkish-Cypriot cultural experiences in Britain. *Journal of Ethnic and Migration Studies, 27*(4), 685–711. doi: 10.1080/13691830120090458.

Safran, W. (1991). Diasporas in modern societies: Myths of homeland and return. *Diaspora, 1*(1), 83–99.

Winder, R. (2004). *Bloody foreigners: The story of immigration to Britain.* London, UK: Abacus.

8. Displaced Memorials: Commemorating the "Comfort Women" in the United States

MARIKO IZUMI
Columbus State University

Why Break New Ground?

"No understanding of history is innocent," writes critical theorist Steven Best (1995) (p. xvi). And the same can be said of memory. The differences between the Marine Corp War Memorial located in Virginia and the Vietnam Memorial in Washington D.C. in their designs and people's responses to them, for example, show how memorials and monuments are created out of diverse needs and desires. When visualized, collective memories tend to be "conventionalized, because the image has to be meaningful for an entire group; simplified because in order to be generally meaningful and capable of transmission, the complexity of the image must be reduced as far as possible" (Fentress & Wickham, 1992, pp. 47–48). "By creating common spaces for memory," as James Young points out, these public memorials and monuments "propagate the illusion of common memory" (Young, 1992, p. 6). Together with annual commemorative ceremonies and shared calendars, they often work as what Marita Sturken (1997) calls "technologies of memory," rhetorical loci around which the national identity is often produced and reproduced.

Because these public memorials require considerable resources, they are often considered as the conduits for "official" narratives about the past. Concerned about the ways in which these official memorials perform continuous oppressions of the marginalized through conventionalizing and simplifying of memories, many scholars began exploring alternative sites of remembering beyond traditional and formally dedicated memorial spaces. For example, Smith and Bergman (2010) explore Alcatraz Island as "recalcitrant memory space," and Elizabethada Wright (2005) explores cemeteries as rhetorical memory space. Blair and Michel (2007) examine AIDS Quilt as a site of public commemoration; Eves (2005) explores cookbooks as rhetorical site where collective memories of African-American women are generated.

If "[m]emory is never shaped in a vacuum [and] the motives of memory are never pure," as James Young says (1993), an exploration of alternative memory space beyond official sites of commemoration requires critical inquiry into the underlying motives and the presumed benefits (p. 2). Recalling Nietzsche's genealogical advice for assessing different moralities, we may ask why broadening our understanding of memory space is desirable or beneficial, and for whom. By asking these questions, I do not mean to be a flat-footed consequentialist, insisting on tangible "pay off" for academic inquiry. Rather, I am interested in raising a question about the unstated *ethos* that informs such impulses toward breaking new ground, in the context of contemporary initiatives for extending or tweaking the familiar sites of memory. In the name of intellectual curiosity, one may argue that it is always a good idea to broaden our proverbial horizon, but that may not be enough to explain why we should strive to open new vistas for re-mapping memory.

In the following, I will discuss the memorials for the "comfort women," the victims of sexual servitude and atrocities perpetrated by the Japanese Imperial Military during the Asia-Pacific War (1930–1945).[1] As logistics of war and colonialism, these women were shipped from various Asian countries and systematically administered as an essential part of the so-called comfort system, in which they were subjected to sexually "comfort" the soldiers in occupied territories and battle fields. The term "comfort women" has been contested by many. For example, scholars like Fujimaki (2006) argues that the term embodies a masculinist viewpoint, and the use of the term "comfort women" will make the researcher unwittingly complicit in further circulating such viewpoint. On the other hand, others like Park (2010) use the term "comfort women" because "the discomfort of the reader vis-à-vis the ironic term can alert him or her to its inadequacy" (p. 206). I do not disagree about the masculinist ideology that produced the very term "comfort women" and hence the danger of reproducing the ideology. However, I chose to use the term "comfort women" with quotation marks, following Trinh T. Minh-ha's idea that quotation as a textual displacement that challenges the system of subordination and creates a new space for creative production through its mobility.

Over the last five years, the United States has become a major site for commemorating the former "comfort women." Since 2010, more than 10 "comfort women" memorials have been built in U.S. towns and cities.

But, why in the United States? The controversies and discourses about memories of the "comfort women" have been most actively animated in the Asia-Pacific region, particularly as issues concerning Japan's responsibility for its wartime and colonial past. These memorials appearing in the United States seem out of place, without any obvious connection between the site and the act of commemorating. Some of these memorials are replicas of a memorial in Soul, South Korea, appearing only in different geographical and cultural context of the United States. Do memorials "work" beyond national borders?

At first glance, memorials that travel across national boundaries look very attractive, for they seem to cash in the cosmopolitan idea that the nation-state, though far from obsolete, has reached its limits with respect to ethical inspiration under the current conditions of globalization. For example, Mary M. McCarthy (2014) writes,

> By moving this topic [of "comfort women"] into larger contemporary contexts, such as human rights, women's rights, and human trafficking, it is possible to erase national and historical specificities. . . . Ultimately such efforts . . . can wind up exerting significant influence over the way all of us, including policymakers, view and react to these issues. (p. 2)

Yet, because memory plays a precarious role at the contested intersection of people's historical, political, and moral vision, certain aspirations toward re-mapping memory may turn out to be worthwhile, while others may go awry. To what extent can transnational memorials as an alternative space of displaced memory promise (or threaten) to generate new political vibrancy and take on a life of their own?

Transnational Memorials and the "American Present"

Since early 1990s, Japan's "comfort women issue" received strong attention both domestically and internationally. A number of former "comfort women" began coming forward to the Japanese public in 1991 demanding reparations and a state apology, breaking their silence since the end of the Asia-Pacific War in 1945. With an air of scandalous-ness and novelty, the ensuing discussion and controversy during the last several decades showed an intensity that stood in contrast to the previous past treatment of the issue in Japan as well as in many Asian countries, where the ordeals of the "comfort women" constituted a part of a cultural/historical knowledge that was familiar, if not transparent or resolved. The Asian Women's Fund, a non-profit and non-partisan organization established by the Japanese government, describes this historical moment as follows:

It cannot be said that people in Japan were completely unaware that there were comfort women during wartime. Those who went to the war knew, at least to some extent, that they existed. But there was almost no awareness of the issue as a social problem. Beginning around 1965, those interested in Japan-Korean relations generally knew that there had been comfort women, and that their experiences were the cruelest outcome of Japan's colonization of Korea. But the victims were thought of only as people who were part of history. (The Asian Women's Fund, 2004, p. 14)

When the victims began coming forward to the Japanese public, this cultural/historical knowledge gained face and body. While the victims urged the Japanese government to take legal responsibility by issuing an official state apology and pay reparations, the Japanese government responded with a moral remedy. While denying its legal responsibility, the Japanese government established the Asian Women's Fund (AWF) in 1995, the 50th anniversary of the end of the Asia-Pacific War, "from [a] moral standpoint [. . .] to fulfill its responsibility for the wartime 'comfort women'" (The Asian Women's Fund, 2009).

This response from the Japanese government fueled, rather than settled, the international controversies over women's rights, justice, and reparations. Scholars, artists, and non-governmental organizations began organizing events and protests in many countries to raise international awareness about the plight of the former "comfort women" and pressure Japanese government to take legal responsibility for its colonial sexual atrocity. A Japanese NGO hosted Women's International War Crimes Tribunal on Japan's Military Sexual Slavery in Hague, Switzerland. South Korean activists began their Wednesday protests in front of the Japanese Embassy in South Korea. Museums and universities began curating traveling exhibits of the former "comfort women" across the U.S., and Korean and Korean-Americans began dedicating memorials for the former "comfort women" in the U.S.

James Young has distinguished two types of monument as a way to bring to the fore the political nature of collective memory. Traditional monuments tend to be representational and didactic in that they tell viewers what to remember and how. Counter-monuments, on the contrary, return the "work" of remembering back to the visitors by violating their expectations and "literacy" about monuments. Like Bertolt Brecht's "epic theatre," counter-monuments challenge our own frame of reference and push us to unlearn the customary ways in which memory is framed by historical narratives, often in tandem with ethical sanctions (Izumi, 2014). It is an attractive concept because it makes room for creative, interpretive diversity. By the same token, it may effect freedom from a paradigmatic historical vision, which places hegemonic or ideological constraints on our political imagination.

Counter-monument, then, is generally capable of fostering hermeneutic liberty in our practice of recollection. As such, it has informed an important strand of scholarship on collective memory in our discipline. As Carol Blair and Neal Michael (2001) puts it, "[s]uccessful commemoration spaces engage us by asking us to think. Rather than tell us *what* to think, they invite us *to* think, to pose questions, to examine our experiences in relation to the memorials' discourse" (p. 189).

From this perspective, the "comfort women" memorials are more monumental than counter-monumental in that they embody specific historical messages and instruct viewers how to remember. The memorial erected in Glendale, California, for example, is a replica of a statue in Seoul, South Korea. It is a life-size bronze statue of a very young Koran girl. She looks about 14 years old, wearing a traditional Korean dress, her hair cut short and straight right along her chin, which was typical for school girls in Japan and colonial Korea during the period of the Asia-Pacific War. Sitting next to an empty chair, which could easily be taken for a school chair, she has both hands clenched into a fist and placed on her lap. She is barefooted, and there is a little bird on her left shoulder. Her shadow is composed of shattered pieces from a dark stone, with a white butterfly-shaped open space around her heart. Next to the statue is a plaque that informs the viewer of the symbolic meanings inscribed in each detail of the statue and the reason for the dedication.[2] The replica was also placed in Detroit, Michigan, in 2014, and another one was unveiled in front of the Fullerton Museum in Orange County, California in the fall of 2015.

The creation, placement, and subsequent viewer-encounter of these memorials are intended as acts of resistance or counter-hegemonic gestures against prevalent historical views of WWII and the Asia-Pacific War, which have often excluded and suppressed the victims' ordeals as part of Imperial Japan's war crimes. The original statue in Soul is positioned on a sidewalk facing the Japanese Embassy, where Korean survivors and activists have been holding a ritual-like demonstration every Wednesday, demanding an official apology and reparations from the Japanese government. I chose "ritual-like" rather than "ritualistic" here in order to off-set common associations which reduce ritual to a more or less rigorously controlled performance. While rituals are certainly rule-governed, I also wish to underscore the fact that rituals, qua instances of social practice, remain vulnerable to practical subversion or "upset" beyond the obvious cases of direct violation rules. Like all other rituals, rituals of commemoration may get derailed, even if those performing them seem to be doing everything by the book. My understanding of ritual is influenced by Luc Boltanski's insightful and provocative discussion of this topic, as well as by Grand David Bollmer, to whom I will refer later. Memorials like this one center on "an ideology of stolen youth and innocence that had become the popular lens through which the survivors were seen in South Korean public culture" (Pilzer, 2012, p. 24). Such iconography tends to exclude many other victims, such as sex workers, whose background and experiences may be considered "impure" by contrast (Ueno, 1999). It has also become a trope of ethnic-national identity for Korea as a raped nation. Invoking a sense of shame and humiliation inflicted by Japanese colonial imperialism, the "comfort women" memorials help to circulate the counter-hegemonic discourse, which has already turned into a common national currency (such as the Korean critique of Japanese imperialism) (Choi, 1993). Such conflation of individual experiences with that of the nation risks stripping victims of their political agency, because it enables impositions of national desire onto the victims, as some of the activist organizations have done by directing the victims in their response to the Japanese government's initiatives.

Yet, when relocated in the U.S., the memorial functions like a counter-monument. The U.S. residents' encounter with the memorial is likely to be guided by a string of questions: What is this? What is this for? Who are they? Why here? The plaque placed next to the statue may answer some of these questions, but the absence of an obvious connection between the respective site (be it in California, Michigan, or another state) and the act of commemoration is bound to remain somewhat disorienting. As noted earlier, disorientation may well prove stimulating under certain conditions. Thus, the overarching location of the United States could enable these displaced memorials to perform as "atopos," that is, to enact a "provocative and novel rhetoric" that can bring about a "temporary 'displacement' " in its audience (Reeves, 2013, p. 308).

The inquiries prompted by such string of questions, then, may open the viewers to the stories of the victims' lives, alert them to the historical record of Japan's war crimes, and draw them into one or several of the contemporary discourses concerned with redress and reparation. More importantly, these questions may lead the visitors to inquire about the complicity of the U.S. in silencing the victims by deliberately overlooking Japan's colonial atrocities and imperialist offenses. Choi (1997) writes, "Under the assumption of Western humanism, which was the philosophical basis of the Nuremburg and Batavia Trials, Asians did not belong to the category of humanity and women were all the more excluded therefrom" (p. vi). The out-of-place character of the "comfort women" memorials, therefore, seems to be an effective stimulus for opening new emancipatory vistas for re-mapping memory. The creative and performative "work" of the memorial disrupts the viewers' hermeneutic habits and thereby offers some critical distance or differentiation from the hegemonic patterns of historical vision and pre-formatted political alliances. As such, the "comfort women" memorials in the U.S. offer the potential to engage the viewers in what Joshua Reeves explicates as "suspended identification," a process of "working out of a common ground that will allow one to get back into place *with* the object of his or her displacement" (Reeves, 2013, p. 316). But, who is the new solidaric "we" that is supposed to emerge from the counter-monumental workings of the displaced "comfort women" memorials?

The transnational constitution of these memorials defies any naïve celebration of remembrance as a form of critical resistance. In the United States, solidarity with the victims takes on a different but no less problematic ethos. Lisa Yoneyama (2003) writes:

> [T]he U.S. war against Japan is remembered as a "good war." According to this dominant way of remembering, the U.S. war against Japan (1930–45) not only liberated Asians, including Japanese themselves, from Japan's military fanaticism, but also rehabilitated them into free and prosperous citizens of the democratic world. Put differently, dominant American war memories are tied to what might be called an imperialist myth of "liberation and rehabilitation," in which violence and recovery are enunciated simultaneously. (p. 58)

Placed on the U.S. ground, the encounters with the "comfort women" memorials might unwittingly feed a hegemonic postwar myth that Americanizes the idea of justice. On the one hand, Asian/Americans who have been historically positioned as "unassimilable" and "ambiguously nationalized others" might welcome the encounter with transnational memorials as an opportunity for engaging in joint moral discourse, inside the U.S., and thus for rehabilitating themselves as legitimate citizen-subjects. On the other hand, the encounter with the "comfort women" memorials may well be seen as an invitation to viewers to partake in writing history from the position of *American* subjects, regardless of their ethnic origins. As Barbara Biesecker (2012) points out, "WWII was one of the means by which what I call 'pedagogies of citizenship' take place" (para. 19). Such pedagogies "teach persons, individual citizens, how to lead their lives, how to take the measure of the present" (para. 19).[3] By "becoming" *American* subjects through a discursive gesture of transnational solidarity, Asian/Americans also run the risk of participating in a project of (re-) writing an American postwar myth that erases their historical-cultural specificity.

In terms of reshuffling discursive positions (including the positions for ethical subjects opposed to war crimes), transnational memorials seem to share significant features with counter-monuments. Yet on this new transnational register, the counter-monumental capacity for sparking public controversy appears strangely attenuated. The displaced memorials do not seem to generate the kind of political vibrancy that was intended by the activists who promoted these memorials. To form solidarity not only with other Asian/Americans (such as Chinese/Americans, Japanese/Americans) but also with non-Asian/Americans, one would have to de-emphasize the ethnic-cultural frame of one's past histories. But it is not clear how this can be done without thereby blurring the specific cultural landscape and association space in which the "comfort women" gained their distinct profile as victims and survivors of history. Such overcoming of an "Asia/Pacific past" may result in an uncritical celebration of the "American present." This American present ought to be seen as a dangerous political myth, for it tacitly places the United States at an implausible historical distance from "Asian conflicts." As critics like Biesecker have rightly stressed, we ought to be suspicious of any neat separation as well as of any hasty conflation of WWII and the Asia-Pacific War.

The Vicissitudes of Ritual: Memory as a Cosmopolitan Movement?

The tension running through the transnational "comfort women" memorials discussed above speaks to a concern Biesecker (2012) voices in the context of contemporary museum and memorial culture in the United States. Observing trends that "steal" the "rhetoric of pain" from traditional identity politics and absorb this rhetoric into an emergent "conservative hegemonic discourse formation," she discusses the dangers of enlisting sites of memory (particularly monuments and war memorials, but also war movies) for generating certain anachronistic effects of empathy. In particular, Biesecker (2012) examines how the discourses surrounding the 9/11 tragedy as "our new Pearl Harbor" reinscribe new traumas back into the familiar historical frames of World War II. In this process, Americans are invited to reinterpret their historical wounds by translating them into a patriotic idiom of proud victimhood. What is at stake here is an ominous competition over trauma as the new source of moral authority within the increasingly unstable landscape of globalism haunted by questions about aggressive nationalist backlashes and possible cosmopolitan alternatives. The consequence of channeling empathy through these pre-formatted interpretive pathways is a disconcerting combination of re-ignited nationalism coupled with political "melancholia"—a form of enthusiasm without agenda, which makes people feel morally excited, while keeping them politically impassive.

Following Biesecker, one of the most urgent issues for memorial studies, then, is to test the new "technologies of memory" for their capacity to help us break out of this dialectic of new trauma–old trauma (Sturken, 1997, pp. 9–12). Under conditions of global capitalism, this dialectic usurps the moral pathos of traditional identity politics by turning trauma into a cultural good of sorts. While it seems politically correct to pay tribute to the suffering of "global others" (like the "comfort women" encountered by U.S. citizens), unqualified calls for empathy with the victims run the risk of converting commemoration into a self-referential exercise of proud victimhood, where the suffering of other groups basically reminds people of their own tragedies. How, then, can the freedom effected by the counter-monumental quality of the memorials be converted into political vibrancy without such re-cycling of historical trauma?

While I do not have a ready-made answer to offer, I think Grant David Bollmer's (2011) re-theorization of collective memory as action offers a point of departure in exploring the potentials and limits of the transnational "comfort women" memorials. Sharing certain assumptions with Young's conception of counter-monument, Bollmer suggests that the work of memory in its creative modes is animated in the first instance by movements of differentiation rather than by statements of political self-assertion.[4] Importantly, Bollmer adds, for such differentiation or unlearning to have any kind of lasting impact or societal ripple effect, it has to be converted into ritual.

According to Bollmer (2011), the dynamics of memory-in-action with the power to organize and mobilize new collectives does not start (or end, for that matter) with solid political identities or interest groups. In other words, even if those who promote transnational monuments have clearly articulated humanitarian agendas (be it in terms of human rights or historical reparations), these agendas do not govern the actual affects generated by these monuments.[5] Rather, the kind of ripple effects these monuments either produce or fail to produce is to do with the "partial objects" out of which these monuments are assembled. The phrase "partial object," inspired by Gilles Deleuze, indicates the fluidity of the ontological boundaries of certain cultural referents, in that they cannot be fully separated from the cultural activities or spaces in which they occur. In this sense, "partial objects" do not designate a static assembly of physical things lumped together. For instance, the presence and meaning of a hairstyle incorporated in a bronze statue (like the one featured in the aforementioned memorial in Glendale, CA) is not reducible to a certain amount of metal. Rather, it belongs to a specific association space, from within which it may resonate with different viewers differently.[6] It is not so much a question of who feels provoked or left out. Rather, the partial objects out of which a monument is composed simply may not resonate when memorials are transplanted or displaced. Those partial objects, such as visual and aesthetic features charged or invested with cultural meanings, may remain mute within a displaced association space.

This notion of variable resonance returns us to the question of whether transnational memorials can generate any political vibrancy. Following Bollmer (2011), this potential would depend on the memorial's capacity to inspire the kind of rituals, which allow fleeting acts of commemoration to leave more long-lasting material traces within the life of a community or society. In terms of political affect, such "traces" include a new sense, or senses, of solidarity. By analyzing the emergence of the Tea Party as a strikingly schizophrenic movement (in the Deleuzian sense of schizophrenic), Bollmer illustrates that movements of such novel solidarity are not a matter of clearly or even consistently articulated ideological commitment. The impetus of this movement is different from traditional protest movements, for it is no longer grounded in a set of clearly stated values or political demands. Rather, this schizophrenic motility is actualized through rituals that perform memory. Bollmer does not want to say that the Tea Party is either good or bad, but he seems to welcome the way in which a hard-to-pin-down movement like the Tea Party can shake up the political scene as a catalyst for genuine political reform.

In exploring the political potential of the "comfort women" memorials in the U.S., Bollmer's perspective raises the following key questions: What would be the *transnational* equivalent of the Tea Party, taken as a blue print for the innovative, subversive movement to be stimulated by transnational monuments? And what kind of commemorative rituals could sustain such a movement and give it social staying power? It is worth noting here that the dynamic assemblages of partial objects which animate the Tea Party (including the American Constitution, select writings of the American Founding Fathers, and the Lincoln Memorial, among others) seem to resonate within a cultural space of association that is still nationally coded. Even if the Tea Party is interestingly incoherent, it seems to draw its political energy from cultural referents that are very much U.S.-American. In other words, there seems to be an understated national frame or repertoire that undergirds Bollmer's analysis. To be fair, Bollmer's discussion does not present the U.S. cultural context as anything like an ideologically unified horizon. Thus the destabilizing presence of the Tea Party within the American political landscape can be appreciated without presenting this landscape as a monolithic set of meanings or homogenous values. Still, it does seem that the Tea Party is gaining its "upsetting" momentum from within a limited association space of cultural goods.

By no means do I wish to lessen the merits of Bollmer's rich discussion, which remains compelling within its scope of analysis. Rather, I think Bollmer's re-theorization of collective memory may help us bring the potentials and limits of transnational memorials into sharp relief. Following Bollmer's cautionary remarks about the largely unpredictable flows of political affect, it is perhaps misguided to ask for a universal ethical formula to which transnational memorials would have to answer. Still, as we learned from Biesecker, this does not absolve the memory scholar from working out critical differences between memorials, which tend to re-cycle trauma and thus support a self-referential cult of proud victimhood, and those that do not. In the absence of any guidelines for imagining what a successful cosmopolitan ritual might look like, the elusive invitation to empathize with global others at the site of displaced transnational memorials may be anything but salutary.

Notes

1 The "comfort system" had been in practice since early 1930s, when Japan began its invasion into China. In order to include these victims during this period prior to WWII, I use Asia-Pacific War to segment the historical period.
2 In other cities, such as Fairfax, VA and [other city] has dedicated memorial stones or granite tablet with text that explains pretty much the same or the similar texts. NY's regulative resolution tablet also provides factual info.
3 In light of this insight, it is it is revealing how much of the news reports and commentaries in the US refer to the "comfort women" as victims of the Japanese military *during World War II*, rather than during the Asia-Pacific War.
4 Here "movement" is used as an overtly double-voiced expression, connoting both the motion of tangible objects as well as the trajectory and orientation of social movements. However, Bollmer will want to qualify any such reference to social movements. His working conception of movement does not dovetail with the traditional notion of socio-political initiatives like the Civil Rights Movement, for example.
5 Taking my bearings from William Connolly and Sharon Crowley, I use the term "affect" to refer to a broad range of emotional proclivities, which put a particular spin on the communicative exchanges among groups and individuals. These emotional tendencies are not necessarily in harmony with each other and often influence people below the level of conscious awareness and rational self-reflection. William Connolly (1995). *The Ethos of Pluralization*. Minneapolis: Minnesota University Press. Sharon Crowley (2006). Toward a Civil Discourse: Rhetoric and Fundamentalism. Pittsburgh: University of Pittsburgh Press.
6 The notion of resonance here is informed by Connolly's Deleuzian conception of a "resonance machine." William Connolly (2008). *Capitalism and Christianity, American Style*. Durham and London: Duke University Press. See Ch. 2.

References

Best, S. (1995). *The politics of historical vision: Marx, Foucault, Habermas.* New York, NY: Guilford Publications.

Biesecker, B. A. (2012). Interview with Barbara Biesecker. Memories, technologies, rhetorics (T. Hoag, Interviewer). *Currents in electronic literacy.* Retrieved from https://currents.dwrl.utexas.edu/2012/interview-with-barbara-biesecker.html

Blair, C., & Michel, N. (2001). Designing memories ... what? Reading the landscape of Astronauts memorial. In J. Wolscheke-Buhlman (Ed.), *Places of commemoration: Search for identity and landscape design* (pp. 185–214). Washington, DC: Dumbarton Oaks Research Library and Collection.

Blair, C., & Michel, N. (2007). The AIDS memorial quilt and the contemporary culture of public commemoration. *Rhetoric and Public Affairs, 10*(4), 595-626. http://www.jstor.org/stable/41940327

Bollmar, D. (2011). Virtuality in systems of memory: Toward an ontology of collective memory, ritual, and the technological. *Memory Studies, 4*(4), 450–464.

Boltanski, L., & Elliott, G. (2011). *On critique: A sociology of emancipation.* Malden, MA: Polity Press.

Choi, C. (1993). The discourse of decolonization and popular memory: South Korea. *Positions: East Asia Cultures Critique, 1*(1), 77–102.

Choi, C. (1997). Guest editor's introduction. *Positions: East Asia Cultures Critique, 5*(1), 1.

Connolly, W. E. (1995). *The ethos of pluralization.* Minneapolis, MN: University of Minnesota Press.

Connolly, W. E. (2008). *Capitalism and Christianity, American style.* The United States of America: Duke University Press.

Crowley, S. (2006). *Toward a civil discourse: Rhetoric and fundamentalism.* Pittsburgh, PA: University of Pittsburgh Press.

Eves, R. S. (2005). A recipe for remembrance: Memory and identity in African-American women's cookbooks. *Rhetoric Review, 24*(3), 280–297.

Fentress, J., & Wickham, C. (1992). Social memory. Cambridge, MA: Blackwell.

Fujimaki, M. (2006). "Gjyenda to komyunicashion: Seisa no rinkaiten de kangaeru 'watashitachi' to karada no kankei," In R. Ikeda (Ed.), *Gendai Komyunikeshongaku.* Tokyo: Yuhikaku.

Izumi, M. (2014). Museums as our new epic theatre. *Poroi, 10*(2), 1–12.

Kang, H. Y. (2003). Conjuring "comfort women": Mediated affiliations and disciplined subjects in Korean/American transnationality. *Journal of Asian American Studies, 6*(1), 25–55.

McCarthy, M. M. (2014, August 12). US comfort women memorials: Vehicles for understanding and change. *Asia Pacific Bulletin, 275,* 1–2.

Nietzsche, F. W., & Kaufmann, W. (1989). *On the genealogy of morals and Ecce Homo.* New York, NY: Vintage.

Park, Y. (2010). Compensation to fit the crime: Conceptualizing a just paradigm of reparation for Korean 'Comfort Women.' *Comparative Studies of South Asia, Africa and the Middle East, 30*(2), 204–213.

Pilzer, J. D. (2012). *Hearts of pine: Songs in the lives of three Koran survivors of the Japanese "comfort women."* New York, NY: Oxford University Press.

Rafu Staff. (2014, August 24). Fullerton Council Approves 'Comfort Women' Resolution. *The Rafu Shimpo Los Angeles Japanese Daily News.* Retrieved from http://www.rafu.com/2014/08/fullerton-council-approves-comfort-women-resolution/

Reeves, J. (2013). Suspended identification: *Atopos* and the work of public memory. *Philosophy and Rhetoric, 46*(3), 306–323.

Smith, C. D., & Bergman, T. (2010) You were on Indian land: Alcatraz island as recalcitrant memory space. In G. Dickinson, C. Blair, & B. L. Ott (Eds.), *Places of public memory: The rhetoric of museums and memorials* (pp. 160–188). Birmingham, AL: The University of Alabama Press.

Sturken, M. (1997). *Tangled memories: The Vietnam war, the aids epidemic, and the politics of remembering* (pp. 9–12). Berkeley, CA: University of California Press.

The Asian Women's Fund, Events Leading up to Establishment of the AWF (English original), accessed July 1, 2009, www.AWF.or.jp/english/about/leading/html.

Ueno, C., & Sand, J. (1999). The politics of memory: Nation, individual and self. *History & Memory, 11*(2), 129–152.

Wright, E. A. (2005). Rhetorical spaces in memorial places: The cemetery as a rhetorical memory place/space. *Rhetoric Society Quarterly, 35*(4), 51–81.

Yoneyama, L. (2003). Traveling memories, contagious justice: Americanization of Japanese war crime at the end of the post-cold war. *Journal of Asian American studies, 6*(1), 58–59.

Young, J. E. (1992). The counter-monument: Memory against itself in Germany today. *Critical Inquiry, 18*(2), 267–296.

Young, J. E. (1993). *The texture of memory: Holocaust memorials and meaning.* The United States of America: Yale University Press.

9. "Funk Isn't a Trend; It's a Necessity": Favela Funk's Vernacular Discourse and the Struggle for Cultural Legitimation

RAQUEL MOREIRA
Graceland University

"It is now decided that funk is a musical and cultural movement," states the text of a 2009 statutory law, proposed and promoted by favela funk artists and supporters (ALERJ, 2009). Rio de Janeiro's favela funk is a musical genre and cultural movement poor folks of color developed in the 1980s. The characteristic beats, lyrics, dance moves, and clothing suggest a "social practice that is historically situated" (Lopes, 2011, p. 19): favela funk is the product of continuous unequal and violent conditions poor people of color face inside Rio's slums. The movement has been the target of various government sanctions, most of which prohibit parties in favelas with the justification that they promote drug trafficking and promiscuous practices, among other morally condemnable reasons (Facina, 2009). When the 2009 bill was voted in the state's legislature, supporters who were present sang and danced to the 1990s hit "Silva's Rap," a song about favela funk being a necessity for its poor people, and not just a cultural trend. This was an odd occurrence given the history of criminalization and persecution that same House promoted against the movement (Lopes, 2011). That day, many poor Afro-Brazilians walked into Rio's state capitol for the first time with the goal of defending favela funk against the government's historical maltreatment (Lopes, 2011). As a result of the positive vote, authors and supporters of the bill celebrated the fact that, like samba, funk would no longer be a police matter, but a legitimate form of cultural expression.

As of 2017, news headlines continue to link drug trafficking and promiscuity with favela funk. Parties inside slums remain heavily regulated or not allowed at all by Rio's military police. Thus, the promise of a liberated favela funk has not been fulfilled with the passing of the 2009 statutory law. While the waves of mainstream popularity help give visibility to specific artists and songs, members of favela funk continue to fight for the movement's decriminalization inside favelas utilizing unique rhetorical strategies. Some of these strategies flourished after the promise of the 2009 statutory law was not fulfilled. Others emerged as a result of the movement's internal tensions, such as artists' relationships with cultural gatekeepers like mainstream media and production monopolies within favela funk. In order to uncover these strategies, this essay employs Ono and Sloop's (1995) vernacular discourse, a theoretical enterprise that concentrates on the critique of contextually specific "speech that resonates within local communities" (p. 20), and of which is usually marginalized in mainstream culture.

As favela funk continues to fight for cultural legitimation, its rhetorical practices are too reinvented. Scholars interested in the movement are slowly starting to reflect on the directions the favela funk is taking as new contextual issues arise. Facina and Passos (2015), for instance, have made an important contribution in examining troubles stemming from the application of the 2009 statutory law. Coutinho (2015) has studied how the rhetoric of the bill that became the 2009 law calls for recognition of favela funk as "cultural heritage" by its comparison with samba. Others like Lopes (2011) and Laignier (2012) have focused on the emergence of events such as favela funk circles, with limited focus on its rhetorical functions for the movement. All of these are fundamental for understanding current and changing issues favela funk faces. Bennett and Janssen (2016) pose that "popular music has become an object of memory and, in turn, a focus for contemporary renditions of history and cultural heritage" (p. 1). As such, members of favela funk use the cultural memory of samba to (re)invent rhetorical practices with the goal of reaching similar institutional legitimacy as the now-acclaimed Brazilian genre. I expand on the analysis of these rhetorical practices favela funk has reinvented in connection with samba's cultural memory.

In this essay, I examine three distinct, but related, expressions of favela funk's vernacular discourse in its quest for legitimation. Specifically, I start by investigating the oppositional and self-affirming rhetoric of a 2008 manifesto published by APAFunk (Association of Professionals and Friends of Funk), the most prominent political organization in the movement. I then examine a relatively recent development in the movement's vernacular, the favela funk circles, events in which artists and supporters protest internal and external issues of favela funk, while putting forth a resilient movement identity that is modeled after samba's cultural memory. Finally, I analyze the vernacular discourse of MC Carol, an Afro-Brazilian MC who embodies both cultural syncretism and pastiche by successfully transiting in both conventional and marginalized spaces while able to deliver a fresh oppositional message in mainstream culture. I then conclude that favela funk's crafted authenticity and the rhetorical expressions associated with it suggest that the movement's vernacular discourse is not a monolith, being a result of internal tensions and contextual changes. These expressions give favela funk ability to creatively use samba's cultural memory to reinvent itself while fighting for its survival.

Vernacular Discourse

Ono and Sloop's (1995) essay "The Critique of Vernacular Discourse" has become foundational in the study of critical rhetoric. Their essay incorporated and refined ideas such as McKerrow's fragmentation and McGee's polysemy with the intention to study texts that are not produced by the dominant culture. Specifically, Ono and Sloop (1995) have argued that even though uncovering the functioning of power relations has been a part of rhetorical criticism's goals, the so-called focus on "evil power," such perspective writes "out of history" other texts that empowered and shaped "local cultures first, then affect[ed], through the sheer number of local communities, cultures at large" (Ono & Sloop, 1995, p. 19). As noted by Calafell and Delgado (2004), "rather than conceptualizing separate critiques of domination and freedom [like McKerrow], [Ono and Sloop] ask that we recognize the ways in which these projects are inseparable or identical" (p. 5). Hence, Ono and Sloop (1995) had proposed a theoretical enterprise that concentrates on the critique of "speech that resonates within local communities" (p. 20), and that have been historically swept to the margins. It is through texts, they note, that those discourses become accessible. Even though Ono and Sloop have placed emphasis on verbal texts, they contended that vernacular discourses also have a cultural dimension located in music, art, dance, etc.

Ono and Sloop (1995) called attention to the fact that even though it is imperative to make vernacular discourse visible, it is not enough to merely "recuperate, locate, and catalogue" discourses that originated in marginalized communities (p. 21). Consequently, uncovering vernacular discourse is not a liberatory practice in itself. This approach disregards critics' intentions, biases, and purposes because criticism is performed non-reflectively, without acknowledging that the very process of recounting and translating vernacular is not a neutral one, removed from contexts, ideologies, and power relations. While the authors praise the task of exposing vernacular discourse, they highlight that a "more important goal is to construct a critical framework within which to discuss vernacular discourse" (Ono & Sloop, 1995, p. 21). Thus, scholars should give vernacular discourse the same critical suspicion given to mainstream texts. Ultimately, different communities have particular analytical needs based on power dynamics that pushed those vernacular discourses to the margins in the first place (Ono & Sloop). That is why critics need to study oppressed groups' discourses from the perspective of their own production. As Calafell and Delgado (2004) have put it, critics must meet the "text on its terms" (p. 18).

Vernacular discourse has two defining characteristics that are used as critical tools: cultural syncretism and pastiche (Ono & Sloop, 1995). Cultural syncretism refers to the ways in which marginalized folks engage in a "simultaneous process of cultural expression and affirmation of community" (Holling & Calafell, 2011, p. 19). Accordingly, this vernacular mode "constructs social relations and protest representations" of marginalized groups that circulate in the dominant culture (Ono & Sloop, 1995, p. 22). Though the idea of affirming while protesting is not novel to rhetoric, the culturally specific rhetoric of marginalized communities negates dominant culture in distinct, unique ways (Ono & Sloop, 1995). In short, rhetorical criticism that focuses on vernacular discourses places a greater emphasis on what is socially and culturally specific in a community.

In the process of critiquing dominant culture from the standpoint of marginalized communities, subjectivities that defy majority culture are created. Culture and protest are, then, intertwined elements of vernacular discourse's cultural syncretism. That is to say that marginalized communities' discourses do not operate only in counter-hegemonic ways; they are also affirmative, "articulating a sense of community that does not function solely as oppositional to dominant ideologies" (Ono & Sloop, 1995, p. 23). Furthermore, Ono and Sloop have contended that the affirmation of those subjectivities happen in various ways. For example, a Black American community would not build their vernacular solely in opposition to racism, but they also constitute their subjectivities "as affirmers" of civil rights (Ono & Sloop, 1995, p. 22).

Pastiche, another tool in Ono and Sloop's conceptualization of vernacular discourse, works "as a metaphorical description" of Calvin McGee's fragmentation of texts and contexts: a construction of a "unique discursive form out of cultural fragments" (Ono & Sloop, 1995, p. 23). Pastiche is theorized as an ever-changing practice that, while borrowing hegemonic elements from mainstream culture, is largely based on invention, reconstitution, and reorganization of discourses from specific sociocultural locations. Pastiche is not a simple mimicry of dominant cultural artifacts; instead, it borrows fragments from hegemonic discourse; at the same time it rearticulates them with peripheral discourses, creating something unique. For instance, favela funk music was at first fully formed by imported sonic elements from U.S. popular music; over time, artists from Rio began to add indigenous elements to the imported samplers, generating then a culturally specific but hybrid musical genre.

In order to understand marginalized communities' constructions of their vernacular discourse, the critic should start by locating and situating the text within socio-historical contexts that explain how and when the representations of a given community were produced (Ono & Sloop, 1995). The history and sociocultural contexts of favela funk, which I expose next, illuminate not only how their representations in mainstream culture came to be, but also how the rhetoric of the movement that defy and embrace such dominant depictions developed throughout the years.

Favela funk operates as vernacular discourse in diverse ways; from the beats and the lyrics to the clothes, the dancing, and the parties, the movement is constantly negotiating its unstable relationship with mainstream culture. A fundamental part of that negotiation is the recognition and affirmation of its marginality, but also its versatility and willingness to meddle with the dominant culture. Some of the movement's advancements toward acceptance in mainstream culture include the growing popularity of specific artists and the previously mentioned passing of the 2009 statutory law defining favela funk as legitimate folk culture. There is growing backlash against these advancements, and in turn, new vernacular modes of protest and affirmation within favela funk—which is ultimately this essay's object of analysis. Accordingly, as favela funk continues to fight for its decriminalization and cultural legitimation, how do members of the movement use samba's cultural memory to engage in cultural syncretism and pastiche? How have these practices worked to build a collective favela funk identity before and especially after the passing of the 2009 statutory law? How do these rhetorical expressions point to tensions within the movement? Finally, how do these expressions of vernacular discourse point to tensions historically present in the relationship between Rio de Janeiro and marginalized folks from the city's slums? Before diving into the issues outlined above, I provide a brief history of favela funk, from its emergence in the to the passing of a 2008 statutory law officially criminalizing parties in Rio's slums, or *bailes*.

Favela Funk's Continuous Marginalization

Favela funk is a musical movement born in the outskirts of Rio de Janeiro, Brazil. As a musical genre, favela funk has been consistently popular in

Brazil since the 1990s (Sá, 2007), reaching global markets in the mid-2000s (McNally, 2017). But its expressions go beyond music. From the movement's parties (*bailes*) and rich dialect, to its particular dance moves and fashion, favela funk is the embodiment of contemporary expressions of Rio de Janeiro's African diaspora: it is creative, resilient, and dynamic. In this section, I explore some of the most important contextual aspects in which favela funk's vernacular discourse emerged, as well as the movement's volatile trajectory of marginality and popularity in mainstream culture.

Rio's favela funk became a mass phenomenon in Brazil even though it developed on the fringes of the mainstream music industry (Sá, 2007). This contradiction means that, as a cultural product, favela funk has been accepted by ample sections of Brazilian society, including the middle class (Lopes, 2011). Notwithstanding, the movement still faces institutional discrimination and stigmatization, be it in mainstream media or through government sanctions (Facina, 2009). Lopes (2011) has argued that there was a process of professionalization of favela funk that has led to the development of a specific "chain of production and consumption, creating new opportunities specially to impoverished young people" (p. 102). This happened especially in the 1990s, when DJs and MCs from Rio's slums begun to produce the music, as opposed to importing samplers from the United States (Sá, 2007). As a result, favela funk is structured in ways that are similar to mainstream culture industry, in that few actors dominate the production and marketing process; however, the movement's aesthetics, styles, and even monopolies developed on the margins of Brazilian dominant culture.

Favela funk is a uniquely hybrid genre. Since its emergence, DJs and MCs combined different aesthetic forms whose elements were already the result of other hybrid musical practices, such as U.S.-based Miami bass, samba, and *Cadomblé* (an Afro-Brazilian religion) (Laignier, 2011). Nonetheless, as a cultural product, cultural elites have framed favela funk as one of the most detestable genres in Brazilian popular culture, according to Facina (2009), with its melodies and lyrics deemed "poor," its singers never in key, "ruining" too many pop and classic songs with their own versions. This criticism is not surprising given that music and other artistic expressions from marginalized groups tend to be labeled "inferior" in comparison to other already validated genres, such as Brazilian Popular Music (Laignier, 2011). Favela funk scholars have agreed that the aesthetic elements that compose the genre reflect its socio-historical emergence, so it would be hard to divorce the music from the conditions in which the social movement emerged (Facina, 2009; Laignier, 2011; Lopes, 2011). In addition, critics only validate cultural expressions from the African diaspora in Brazil once they have been appropriated by elites—and the samba is an example of this (Lopes, 2011). Favela funk artists noticed this tendency, which recently resulted in a strategic comparison between samba's past struggles and favela funk's current stigmatization (Lopes, 2011).

In the 1990s, after *bailes* were popular in clubs all over the city for almost two decades, mainstream media more consistently picked up on the movement's popularity, resulting in both praise and condemnation (Lopes, 2011). Lopes (2011) has proposed that in all of the reports glamourizing funk as the hottest beat in town, its marginalized origins were erased as much as possible. This suggests that favela funk's supposed drawback was more about who produced it and where it came from, rather than the genre itself (Lopes, 2011, p. 45). After several years of favela funk's concurrent popularity and marginalization, artists began to respond to this erasure by intentionally using samba's cultural memory to draw parallels with favela funk's struggles: like samba in its early days, favela funk was being both enjoyed by the middle and upper classes while its connections with the favelas and African diaspora in Brazil were overlooked. Lopes (2011) poses that the rhetorical move to create an "authentic" favela funk, though based on the cultural memory of samba, presents a fundamental difference with the now-acclaimed Brazilian genre. Favela funk's authenticity was not rhetorically created by the elite, like samba's; it was artists from the slums, usually without access to mainstream media or the favela funk industry monopoly, who reclaimed this historical connection with samba, favelas, and the African diaspora.

A few crucial events served to solidify mainstream culture's vilification of favela funk. With the rise of violence in Rio, especially drug and territory-related conflicts, the favelas were already under scrutiny in mainstream media in the early 1990s. The idea that violence, along with poor people of color, would (and should) remain within the limits of the city's slums changed in the early 1990s with the so-called arrastões[1] (Lopes, 2011). Those events were characterized by local media as mass robberies happening at the famous Ipanema beach, and were supposedly perpetrated by favela funk fans. Facina (2009) clarifies that the so-called arrastões were, in fact, clashes between groups from "beyond the tunnel"[2] (dark-skinned, favela youth), mainly from Vigário Geral, a favela where a police-dealer related mass slaughter had frightened the city in that same period. The fact that poor youth was intoning battle cries using the name of favelas and the word *bonde*[3] together made the media presume that there was an inevitable connection between the assumed criminals and favela funk. After those events, mainstream media seemed to make efforts to link all sorts of crimes to favela funk in general, but *bailes* in particular. Favela funk supporters from Rio's slums were gradually portrayed as if they were "the cause of several social ills," while their voices were systematically erased from media coverage that worked to outlaw the movement (Lopes, 2011, p. 41).

Despite heavy stigmatization throughout the 1990s, favela funk was part of an alternative music industry by the end of the decade. Improvised recording studios and radio stations were flourishing across the Greater Rio de Janeiro (Facina, 2009). If during the 1980s, favela funk parties were seeing solely as a form of entertainment, by the end of the 1990s, the movement had gathered a significant number of successful MCs, DJs and sound teams, dancers, radio and TV hosts, etc. (Lopes, 2011). Above all, favela funk became an aggressive shout for public visibility for the people living in Rio's poorer areas. Late in that decade, Rio's government was aggressively targeting successful *bailes* across the city with heavy regulations, making the legal organization of parties really difficult (Facina, 2009). As a result, many of them closed between the late 1900s and the early 2000s (Coutinho, 2015). As the 2000s approached, media coverage of the movement remained paradoxically immersed in approval and condemnation.

Favela funk started the 2000s facing a series of violent charges, from child prostitution to involvement with drug trafficking (Lopes, 2011). At that point, the *bailes* that used to happen in clubs throughout the city were pushed into Rio's slums (Facina, 2009). The symbolic connection between favela funk and crime was then solidified. The most significant media event associating the two was the murder of one of Rede Globo's[4] reporter inside the favela Vila Cruzeiro, in 2002. Lopes (2011) argues that there was little factual evidence suggesting that the murder had happened after the reporter attended a *baile* in the favela, but mainstream media discourse was unison in establishing that association. By the mid-2000s, local media once again accused a group of MCs of "crime propaganda" through the performance of *proibidões*[5] or "evil funk"—a fact that had already happened in the 1990s (Lopes, 2011). This time, however, media's campaign against those MCs lead to the arrest of several them (Facina, 2009; Lopes, 2011). But the highest point of criminalization came with a 2008 statutory law tightening the already harsh restrictions imposed on funk parties in 2000. This law resulted in the total prohibition of *bailes* inside slums (Coutinho, 2014; Lopes, 2011). The move happened in articulation with an extensive government policy termed "pacification": major slums in the city would be slowly occupied by the military police, which would in turn expel drug dealers while monitoring illegal (musical) activities (Facina, 2009). Together, mainstream media and state coagulated homogeneous discourses about Rio's slums and favela funk as expressions of "evil, danger, and barbarism," which brought great financial despair and social stigma to those involved with the movement (Lopes, 2011, p. 63).

Parallel to the movement's criminalization, the 2000s also marked a noticeable increase in favela funk's popularity. Imported samplers and romantic lyrics were replaced with the locally developed and hybrid beat, *tamborzão*,[6] and tunes that narrated the "neurotic reality of the favelas," be that gang and police violence, or casual sex and conquest (Facina, 2009). Women, who had been mostly in the margins of favela funk up until then, were no longer just dancers or supporters. They were in fact becoming successful MCs with performances about sex and relationships (Moreira, 2017). Mainstream media continued to emphasize the fact that favela funk was fun and creative, as long as it was detached from slums and "evil funk" (Lopes, 2011). As the analysis in the next section shows, favela funk's vernacular discourse has been responding to tumultuous contextual changes within and outside of the movement with creativity and reinvention.

Favela Funk's Vernacular Discourse

An analysis of favela funk's vernacular discourse, particularly in its quest for legitimation, is challenging for a few reasons. First, the movement is horizontal in that there are no clear leaders—at least no one who can speak for the whole movement. This could be due to the fact that favela funk is only partially politically organized. Second, even though music is what is most identified as favela funk's primary activities, the movement developed other vernacular strategies such as parties, fashion, a particular dialect, etc. In sum, favela funk's vernacular discourse is multifaceted. Third, the context in which favela funk is inserted changes constantly. Because the movement exists on the fringes of legality, when socioeconomic and political changes as often as they do in Brazil, public attitudes (including those of the government and mainstream media) toward the movement also change. For those reasons, examining a single rhetorical expression of favela funk from a singular point in time is challenging.

I address the above challenges by focusing mostly on the oppositional ways favela funk's vernacular fight against current attempts at criminalization, including the fissures that the same fight creates within the movement. I center the analysis on diverse expressions of oppositional vernacular in favela funk, having the 2009 statutory law as a point of reference for its significance in the movement's most recent history. Accordingly, I start with the 2008 APAFunk manifesto, which marks a fundamental step in the formal political organization of sections of favela funk while highlighting tensions within the movement. Next, I focus on the proliferation of favela funk circles, events that model samba circles and, in many respects, replaced *bailes* inside slums, working as both affirming and oppositional spaces for artists. Finally, I examine MC Carol's rhetoric as another recent development of the movement's oppositional rhetoric. I focus especially on her ability to embrace and reject dominant culture, while transiting in both mainstream and marginalized spaces. Each of these vernacular expressions represents contemporary political tendencies within favela funk, as well as the various ways the movement battles stigmatization and fights for its survival. Not all strands of favela funk are represented in the analysis, in part because I am limiting this essay to more explicit expressions of oppositional and self-affirming vernacular. Given that favela funk as a whole, and non-mainstream artists in particular, have a contentious relationship with mainstream culture, digital platforms are gradually becoming central media tools in the spread and promotion of the movement. Therefore, the texts I analyze next can be found in digital platforms.

Politicizing Favela Funk: The 2008 APAFunk Manifesto

Many public discussions about favela funk tend to homogenize the movement's identity (Lopes, 2011). Lopes (2011) has contended that even critical research that intends to "deconstruct prejudices that middles and upper classes have against funk" (p. 100) are centered on how the movement is represented, and not on its backstage and internal tensions. Thus, it is common for researchers to forget that favela funk is not homogeneous, and that many of the tensions within it stem from the fact that these artists are workers whose life either fully or partially depend on movement. With the closing of *bailes* in Rio's slums in 2008, along with the monopolization of the other few available spaces to perform, many artists were then out of work (Facina, 2009; Lopes, 2011). The politicization of part of favela funk happened in response to these contextual conditions, including the creation of APAFunk.

The 2008 APAFunk manifesto brought together a mix of MCs, DJs, scholars, and politicians that formulated together a five-paragraph text employing cultural syncretism to affirm the collective character of favela funk struggles, as well as to contest abusive practices, both from mainstream culture and from those few producers who control the movement's culture industry. The text was the first major political act from APAFunk, which later showed its political force when its proposed bill to recognize favela funk as folk culture was turned into a statutory law in 2009 (Laignier, 2012; Lopes, 2011). In the following paragraphs, I analyze the manifesto's vernacular, which in turn highlights some of favela funk's most conspicuous tensions.

The manifesto opens and closes emphasizing the origins of favela funk, as well as the movement's need for collective organization. Activists stress favela funk's origins at the end of the first paragraph, suggesting that "funk . . . is directly related to the lifestyles and experiences of youth from outskirts and slums" (APAFunk, 2008). As favela funk's popularity oscillates, this excerpt works as a reminder that no matter how much mainstream media compartmentalizes "favela" and "funk," the movement and its music are unequivocal creations of marginalized folks. Additionally, the last paragraph ends with calls for political organization:

> To politically demand the recognition of favela funk as an expression of culture will strengthen us collectively, so we can fight the stigmatization we suffer and the arbitrary power that, by the influence of money or the law, tries to silence our voices. (APAFunk, 2009)

In this sense, the general tone of the manifesto is oppositional to mainstream culture, but it also works to affirm the community's roots and future political goals.

Most of the manifesto, however, focuses on issues within favela funk, such as the monopoly over who produces and circulates the movement's music. In the second paragraph, activists suggest that "under the monopoly of few agents, the funk industry imposes a dynamic that suppresses diversity of musical creations, establishing a kind of censorship when it comes to the themes of songs" (APAFunk, 2009). The call for political organization, thus, is not only to protest government and media criminalization of favela funk. These activists wish to change the industry, which became monopolized precisely as a result of government sanctions and media smear campaigns (Lopes, 2011). Accordingly, even though favela funk developed on the fringes of culture industry, DJs and producers took advantage of the movement's restricted access to media and physical spaces for *bailes* to control its production and distribution, thus mimicking the lack of diversity present in mainstream culture industry. Asking for a more diversified production of favela funk works simultaneously to reaffirm the movement's commitment to hybridity (and pastiche), and to oppose mainstream culture's tendency to co-opt creative endeavors from marginalized groups.

Part of the criticism directed at favela funk that reaches dominant culture is that the content of songs is vulgar and apolitical. APAFunk, manifesto partly agrees with this critique, asserting that this trend in favela funk songs is another consequence of the industry's monopoly: "instead of social critique, the sameness of 'dirty funk,' with lyrics that have pornography as a single theme" (APAFunk, 2008). Though not mentioned in the manifesto,

women in favela funk tend to almost exclusively sing about sex and relationships, a trend that dominant culture both embraces and criticizes, ensuing
simultaneous public criticism and mainstream success for some (Lopes, 2011;
Moreira, 2017). It is then not surprising that female artists tend to be absent
from initiatives like APAFunk, who excludes them from the possible public legitimacy such endeavors might bring to the movement, that is, public funding of parties in which women could participate (Facina & Passos,
2015; Moreira, 2014). Even though the manifesto, along with the passing
of the 2009 law recognizing favela funk as an expression of folk culture, are
important political markers for the movement, the initiative might also alien-
ate some of its members.

    While MCs and scholars are slowly starting to evaluate the political
results of the 2009 statutory law for favela funk artists, the formation of
APAFunk generated other initiatives that have had greater impact on the
movement (Laignier, 2012). One such initiative is the creation of favela funk
circles. The next subsection analyzes the importance of such events as recent
developments in favela funk's vernacular discourse. They symbolize a novel
way artists found to support those who are outside of mainstream and favela
funk culture industry.

Favela Funk Circles as Spaces of Affirmation and Protest

Favela funk circles (*rodas de funk*) are public events in which DJs and MCs
perform live for relatively small audiences. These circles are political in nature
(Lopes, 2011). Scholars who research the movement have credited the previously mentioned APAFunk with kicking off the first events of this kind
(Laignier, 2012; Lopes, 2011). MCs and DJs who were successful in the
1990s host these events, which ultimately give visibility to artists who are
"outside of corporate media and have no contract with major favela funk
agents" (Laignier, 2012, p. 10). Yet, the spread and popularity of these events
have made them attractive for artists who transit in mainstream spaces as well.

    Favela funk borrows the long-established idea of music circles from
samba. This is one way activists strategically compare samba's past struggles
to favela funk's current stigmatization, perhaps as an attempt to realize the
promise of cultural legitimacy achieved by the former. Like traditional samba
circles, these events allow artists to share new tunes and old hits while fostering a positive, "joyful" sense of a socially mixed community (Laignier, 2012,
p. 4). But favela funk circles are also calculated occasions in which artists and
activists politically organize and protest practices that hurt funk artists more
specifically, and poor people of color in general—hence the association with
samba (Lopes, 2011).

The industry's exclusionary monopoly, along with the shrinking of spaces to perform after the shutdown of *bailes* in slums, makes favela funk circles an important contemporary development of the movement's vernacular discourse. While the contributions from other scholars are fundamental for the understanding of how favela funk circles were created, these analyses are not invested in the movement's use of cultural syncretism and pastiche for self-legitimation. Consequently, I illustrate these vernacular strategies with a YouTube video from a particular circle, the São Gonçalo *Roda de Funk*, from 2013. There is no particular reason I chose this video, other than it looks representative of the other visual recordings of circles, as well as scholars' accounts of such events. It is important to note that these recordings are absent from traditional corporate media. Henceforth, digital media becomes an important tool to find and disseminate favela funk content.

In an all-pink outfit, MC Marcelly is surrounded by 1990s male MCs and DJs, who are all sitting behind tables organized like a long rectangle. The female MC from one of Rio's largest slums, Complexo do Alemão, passionately reaffirms the connection between favela and funk before performing in the circle:

> You have no idea what this means to me, to have the respect of real MCs, of favela MCs, who perform over rifle shots [...] us, favela MCs, don't need radio, you feel me? We don't need radio or TV. It's quite the opposite. They need us ... do you think it's fair that there's no Cidinho [1990s MC] songs on the radio? [...] It's disrespectful, you feel me? But you know, I won't worry about that stuff. I'll start worrying when the favela, the community, stops enjoying our tunes [...] real funk came from the favela, and I'm proud of being from the favela! (Roda de Funk Original, 2013)

MC Marcelly's rant is at times self-affirming ("favela funk is one"), but the artist spends most of her time protesting the industry's treatment of older MCs and DJs, even though her song "Bigode Grosso" (Thick Mustache) was a major hit in mid-2013 (Marques, 2013). Her back and forth between self-affirmation and protest becomes evident when she references "real" MCs, those who come from favelas and perform under violent situations ("over riffle shots"), implying that there are those funk artists who are not from favelas, thus not "real" MCs. By doing that, MC Marcelly simultaneously articulates a sense of community with those present in the circle while battling the industry's exclusionary practices. In order to affirm that community, then, she chooses to oppose parts of it.

Favela funk circles seem to have a greater impact on favela funk's vernacular of survival and reinvention in comparison to initiatives that propose the movement's official acceptance, such as the passing of the 2009 statutory law. Unlike the implementation of the law, which generated very few state-sponsored events (Facina & Passos, 2015), favela funk circles are sponta-neously spreading while maintaining its open-mic, democratic environment. As I watched a few more episodes of the São Gonçalo circle, it became clear that those spaces are at the same time celebratory and oppositional. It is not unusual for one of the hosts, MC Alexandre, to give short speeches before performances lamenting the shutdown of large, popular *bailes* in Rio's slums, such as Pistão and Chatuba. These protests often end with the reaffirmation that favela MCs are welcome to perform in his circle. Laignier (2012) has proposed that favela funk circles are "one of the most fundamental elements of APAFunk's political discussion," calling these events "noticeable achieve-ments" for the association (p. 9). Lopes (2011) has emphasized, through a participant-observer account of the first circle ever organized, that these events are political in nature. Like many other aspects of a horizontal, lead-erless movement, the spread and subsequent iterations of such events are as multiple as favela funk itself.

MC Carol Bandida and the Vernacular of Popularity and Marginality

Favela funk exists between marginalization and mainstream popularity. Existing in this liminal space complicates the movement's vernacular dis-course because favela funk as a whole is multiple and contradictory. In fact, those characteristics made deciding which favela funk vernacular texts to ana-lyze extremely difficult. Thus, the decision to consider MC Carol Bandida's vernacular seems appropriate, given that the artist symbolizes favela funk's contradictions by transiting in mainstream and marginalized spaces.

MC Carol Bandida is an Afro-Brazilian woman who has achieved rea-sonable popularity while maintaining strong ties to her community and favela funk in general. MC Carol was born and raised in the slum Morro do Preventório (Sodré, 2015), a fact that gives her credibility within marginal-ized favela funk spaces. She received the nickname "Bandida," which loosely means "criminal," for playing with boys while growing up in the favela: "To avoid calling me a lesbian, they'd say: 'this girl is going to be a criminal!'" (Sodré, 2015). The MC also circulates in mainstream spaces: she was part of the reality TV show *Lucky Ladies,* on Fox Life Brasil (Pereira, 2015), and she was a guest on both São Paulo's Lollapollooza Music Festival (Pasin, 2016), as well as on the runaway of the São Paulo Fashion Week (MC Carol, 2017), Brazil's most important fashion event. It is unusual for a favela MC to occupy those spaces that, more than mainstream, are typically elitist—even more so if that artist is a large Black woman. Her presence also signals that favela cultures are sold as "cool" in elitist spaces from time to time, and favela funk is now possibly the most commodified aspect of marginalized cultures in Brazil (Canônico, 2017). However, this commodification usually includes what favela folks produce, and rarely the actual people who produced it (Lopes, 2011). Thus, MC Carol's presence is relevant because it is extraordinary.

MC Carol's vernacular discourse embodies many of the contradictions that generate tensions within favela funk and between the movement and dominant culture. Many of her songs are sexually explicit; others evoke social critique. For instance, in July 2017, she performed a medley of her songs at the previously mentioned São Gonçalo favela funk circle, opening the performance with the lyrics "What's going on, honey/what's going on, love/ I've barely started/And you already came all over yourself . . . You fucked me poorly/I moaned to fool you" (Roda de Funk Original, 2017). Based on APAFunk's previously analyzed manifesto, some of her music, like that of many other women in the movement, could be regarded as "apolitical," or part of the "sameness" of mainstream "pornographic" favela funk.

But like the movement, MC Carol's performances are diverse. In her 2016 album, out of nine tunes, three offer some sort of social commentary. What sets MC Carol's oppositional vernacular apart from the rest of the movement is its focus beyond being poor and living in Rio's favelas. In "Não Foi Cabral" (It Wasn't Cabral), for instance, the MC narrates an interaction with a teacher in history class in which she challenges the colonial narrative that Portuguese explorer Pedro Alvarez Cabral "discovered" Brazil, like it is usually taught in grade schools in the country (MC Carol, 2015). The song opens with the Brazilian national anthem and a few seconds later favela funk's *tamborzão* mixes with it. The lyrics reference the massacre of indigenous people by Portuguese colonizers ("Thirteen caravels/Brought a lot of death/One million Indians/Died of tuberculosis"), as well as the struggles and resistance of enslaved Africans ("If it wasn't for Dandara [female Afro-Brazilian warrior]/ I'd still be getting flogged"). The other two songs in the album reference black feminism and violence against women ("100% Feminist"), as well as the double standard poor people of color face in the Brazilian justice system, which protects political corruption while incarcerating and killing favela folks ("Plea Deal"). MC Carol's explicit references to issues that affect favela funk, but that are greater than the movement—namely racism, colonialism, sexism, and state violence—are an example of the different directions favela funk vernacular takes as context changes.

MC Carol is by no means the only favela funk artist who is this complex. Other artists also circulate within and outside of the movement, performing songs that could be considered political in favela funk's own complex ways (Moreira, 2017). In many respects, MC Carol's aforementioned songs and mainstream media presence represent the movement's engagement with pastiche and cultural syncretism: fragmented, simultaneously localized and mainstream, oppositional and self-affirming, as well as inventive and reconstructive. These strategic insider/outsider dynamics some artists embody contribute to favela funk's survival and prosperity.

Conclusion: Vernacular Discourse as Limiting and Liberatory

In May 2017, the "legislative idea" proposing that favela funk should be criminalized received over 20,000 supportive signatures (e-Cidadania, 2017). These were enough endorsements to call for a public hearing on the matter, according to the Brazilian Senate website. The author of the proposal suggests that favela funk is no more than a "recruitment tool for the organized crime on social media," while also calling the movement "fake culture" (e-Cidadania, 2017). Even though the chair of the Senate's Human Rights Commission demonstrated little interest in pursuing this call for criminalization, the news of such attempt mobilized artists, scholars, and supporters to speak out against such grotesque act of censorship (Anitta, 2017; Garonce, 2017; Porto & Castro, 2017). This reaction is not unreasonable, considering that favela funk is already not fully legal, a fact that even the 2009 statutory law could not change.

The passing of the 2009 statutory law marks an important political turn for favela funk, but that significance seems to be more symbolic than material. So far, the promise of a liberated favela funk has not yet been realized as suggested by the law. That promise becomes more unlikely to happen with the imminent bankruptcy of Rio's state government, as well as the recent rise of violence in the city and police brutality in Rio's slums (Ribeiro, 2017; Virgilio, 2017). If favela funk's presence in public discourse is largely impacted by context, the current scenario sure looks gloomy. Moreover, it is hard to imagine that a favorable law would address the movement's historical marginalization, especially while other systemic issues, such as racism and economic inequality, are also not seriously addressed.

Favela funk reinvents itself in the face of adversity. The most notable starting point for this rhetorical reinvention of favela funk is the use of samba's cultural memory to draw parallels between the two artistic expressions. Unlike samba, however, favela funk's constructed authenticity is yet to elevate the movement to samba's contemporary status. The development of vernacular expressions I examined in this essay, be they political organizations or favela funk circles, reinforces the movement's inclinations to readapt and recreate. That process is simultaneously complicated and propelled by tensions within the movement and between favela funk and dominant culture. In this essay, I have mostly highlighted the ways in which favela funk survives outside of mainstream media by utilizing self-affirming and oppositional rhetorical strategies. Artists and supporters encourage their communities by promoting political organizations and events in which those outside of culture industries are invited to participate. At the same time, they use these spaces to protest the condition that created the necessity for those events and organizations in the first place, namely government sanctions, media negative campaigns, and monopolized culture industries.

The paradox in the tensions outlined above is that they keep favela funk alive and reinventing itself. There would be no favela funk if not for the almost three-decade long marginalization the movement faces, and its consequent diversity and fragmentation. But at what cost does that come for those marginalized folks? Or yet, what are the limits of marginalized communities' vernacular discourse in inviting social change? Are the practices of pastiche and cultural syncretism enough to combat the movement's contemporary stigmatization? On the other hand, if those vernacular expressions are not validated and disseminated, what else is left for those communities? The closest favela funk gets to legitimation is through its visibility in corporate media, such as that of MC Carol, or through supposed institutional acceptance, such as in the 2009 statutory law. The former generates mixed results, in that the visibility in dominant culture has proven important for the movement's spread, acceptance, and support, but negative media coverage generates further cultural marginalization and government sanctions. The latter did not end the prohibition of *bailes*, and its implementation proved to be ineffective, as detailed by Passos and Facina (2015). These scholar-activists tracked a DJ's attempt at applying for a publicly funded grant for favela funk *bailes*. More than the frustration with the low funds offered by the grant and slow government bureaucracy, the artist recounts Rio's military police efforts to determine what type of songs would be allowed in his Chatuba party, when the event should start and end, among other provisions (Passos & Facina, 2015). Legal favela funk had become disciplined favela funk.

There is a growing conservative wave in Brazil right now in which even traditional forms of art are being persecuted (Phillips, 2017). This might be an indication of further, more ferocious institutional opposition to favela funk. It is likely that favela funk will continue to reinvent itself, despite the high financial and emotional cost artists, and others who depend on the movement to survive, face each time that needs to happen (Facina, 2009; Lopes, 2011). Scholars committed to the movement's importance for giving marginalized communities voice should monitor how these changes in context impact favela funk's vernacular discourse, which new practices arise, and what are their limitations. At the end of the day, favela funk will continue to be "a necessity," and not just a "trend" for its supporters while there is no racial and economic justice in Brazil.

Notes

1 A literal translation would be "trawlers." The term was actually created by the local media (Facina, 2009).
2 Rio's wealthy side, the South Zone, connects with the different parts of the cities through tunnels.
3 *Bonde* literally translates as "tram." It is a slang generally used in "funk-raps" to designate, among other things, territory.
4 Broadcasting company belonging to Brazil's largest media oligopoly.
5 The word stands for "forbidden" or those songs that are not played in mainstream media. These are usually raw descriptions of the violent realities in Rio's slums.
6 The beat is a combination of heavy bass lines with Brazilian sounds. There's contention over the origins of the beat, but many artists suggest it was created inside City of God.

References

ALERJ (2009, September 22). Lei N° 5543, de 22 de Setembro de 2009. Retrieved from: http://alerjln1.alerj.rj.gov.br/contlei.nsf/f25571cac4a61011032564fe0052c89c/78ae3b67ef30f23a8325763a00621702?OpenDocument
Anitta [Anitta] (2017, June 9). E não criminalizar uma das poucas formas que essa gente conseguiu pra ganhar a vida, amores... aí não [Tweet]. Retrieved from: https://twitter.com/Anitta/status/873316081498304512
Bennett, A., & Janssen, S. (2016). Popular music, cultural memory, and heritage. *Popular Music and Society, 39*(1), 1–7.
Calafell, B. M., & Delgado, F. P. (2004). Reading Latina/o images: Interrogating Americanos. *Critical Studies in Media Communication, 21*(1), 1–24.
Canônico, M. (2017, July 27). "Rouanet não deve apoiar porque é pobrezinho", diz criador do Rock in Rio. Folha *Ilustrada*. Retrieved from: http://www1.folha.uol.com.br/ilustrada/2017/07/1903363-lei-nao-deve-apoiar-porque-o-cara-e-pobrezinho-diz-criador-do-rock-in-rio.shtml
Claudinha, (2008, December 10). Manifesto "Movimento Funk é Cultura." *Associação de Profissionais e Amigos do Funk*. Retrieved from: http://apafunk.blogspot.com/2009/01/manifesto-movimento-funk-cultura.html
Coutinho, R. A. (2015). The acknowledgment of funk carioca as "patrimônio cultural": Daily life and social and political clashes around the Law 5543/2009. *Antíteses, 8*(15), 520–541.

e-Cidadania (2017). Criminalização do funk como crime de saúde pública a criança aos adolescentes e a família [sic]. *Senado Federal*. Retrieved from: https://www12. senado.leg.br/ecidadania/visualizacaoideia?id=65513

Facina, A. (2009). "Não me bate doutor": Funk e criminalização da pobreza. Proceedings from V ENECULT 2009. *Encontro de Estudos Multidisciplinares em Cultura*. Salvador: BA, Brazil.

Garonce, L. (2017, September 13). Em debate no DF, antropóloga questiona criminalização do funk: "Terá que censurar toda indústria criativa". *Gl*. Retrieved from: https:// g1.globo.com/distrito-federal/noticia/em-debate-no-df-antropologa-questiona-criminalizacao-do-funk-tera-que-censurar-toda-industria-criativa.ghtml

Holling, M., & Calafell, B. M. (2011). Tracing the emergence of Latina/overnaculars in studies of Latin@ communication. In M. Holling & B. M. Calafell (Eds.), *Latina/ o discourse in vernacular spaces: Somos de una Voz?* (pp. 17–29). Lanham, MD: Lexington Press.

Laignier, P. (2011). Towards a political economy of funk carioca: Notes on postmodern theory and its developments in contemporary popular music. *Ciberlegenda, 2*(24), 61–76.

Laignier, P. (2012). Rodas de funk: Remixando música e política com alegria. Proceedings from XXXV Congresso Brasileiro de Ciências da Comunicação. *Intercom – Sociedade Brasileira de Estudos Interdisciplinares da Comunicação*. Fortaleza: CE, Brazil.

Lopes, A. C. (2011). *Funk-se quem quiser: No batidão negro da cidade carioca*. Rio de Janeiro, RJ: Bom Texto.

Marques, C. (2013, October 18). Do cabelo ao bigode: MC Marcelly muda visual em tarde mulherzinha. *Globo.com*. Retrieved from: http://ego.globo.com/famosos/noticia/ 2013/10/do-cabelo-ao-bigode-mc-marcelly-muda-visual-em-tarde-mulherzinha. html

MC Carol [McCarol BandidaVEVO] (2015, July 11). MC Carol – Não foi Cabral (audio). [YouTube]. Retrieved from: https://www.youtube.com/watch?v=Hfkkeo-Vmc8

MC Carol [Mc Carol Oficial] (2016, July 15). Mc Carol – Delação premiada (prod. Leo Justi). [YouTube]. Retrieved from: https://www.youtube.com/watch?v=ZfZLPX LGwUs

MC Carol [Mc Carol Oficial] (2016, October 7). MC Carol & Karol Conka – 100% Feminista (prod. Leo Justi & Tropkillaz). [YouTube]. Retrieved from: https://www. youtube.com/watch?v=W05v0B59K5s

MC Carol [mc_caroloficial] (2017, August 30). #SPFW #LabFantasma #Avua. [Tweet]. Retrieved from: https://twitter.com/mc_caroloficial/status/902734765022994432

McNally, J. (2017). Favela chic: Diplo, *funk carioca*, and the ethics and aesthetics of the global remix. *Popular Music and Society, 40*(4), 434–452.

Moreira, R. (2014). *Bitches unleashed: Women in Rio's funk movement, performances of heterosexual femininity, and possibilities of resistance*. Thesis (PhD). University of Denver.

Moreira, R. (2017). "Now that I'm a whore, nobody is holding me back": Women in Rio de Janeiro's favela funk and feminist possibilities. *Women Studies in Communication*, 40(2), 172–189.

Ono, K., & Sloop, J. (1995). The critique of vernacular discourse. *Communication Monographs*, 62, 19–46.

Pasin, L. (2016, March 16). MC Carol relembra participação no Lollapalooza: "Choro ao ver vídeos". *EGO*. Retrieved from: http://ego.globo.com/lollapalooza/2016/noticia/2016/03/mc-carol-relembra-participacao-no-lollapalooza-choro-ao-ver-videos.html

Passos, P., & Facina, A. (2015). "Baile Modelo!": Reflexões sobre práticas funkeiras em contexto de pacificação. Proceedings from the VI Seminário Internacional de Políticas Culturais. *Fundação Casa de Rui Barbosa*. Rio de Janeiro: RJ, Brazil.

Pereira, M. (2015, May 25). Funkeiras cantam, gritam e armam barracos em novo reality show. *UOL*. Retrieved from: http://noticiasdatv.uol.com.br/noticia/televisao/funkeiras-cantam-gritam-e-armam-barracos-em-novo-reality-show-7993

Phillips, D. (2017, September 12). Brazilian queer art exhibition cancelled after campaign by rightwing protesters. *The Guardian*. Retrieved from: https://www.theguardian.com/world/2017/sep/12/brazil-queer-art-show-cancelled-protest?CMP=share_btn_tw

Porto, A. C., & Castro, J. (2017, July 27). O funk estigmatizado e criminalizado: inconcebível num Estado Democrático de Direito. *Justificando*. Retrieved from: http://www.justificando.com/2017/07/27/o-funk-estigmatizado-e-criminalizado-inconcebivel-num-estado-democratico-de-direito/

Ribeiro, G. (2017, April 16). Falência do Rio: Como sair da crise? *O Dia*. Retrieved from: http://odia.ig.com.br/rio-de-janeiro/2017-04-16/falencia-do-rio-como-sair-da-crise.html

Roda de Funk Original (2013, January 22). MC Marcelly: Papo reto: Ao vivo na nossa roda de funk. [YouTube]. Retrieved from: https://www.youtube.com/watch?v=wURPmTKusQI

Roda de Funk Original (2017, July 24). MC Carol Ao vivo no palco da Roda de Funk (vídeo especial) classificação 18 anos. [YouTube]. Retrieved from: https://www.youtube.com/watch?v=9kUvI0mmWBI

Sá, S. P. (2007). Funk carioca: Música electronica popular brasileira? Proceedings from XVI Compós. *Associação Nacional dos Programas de Pós-Graduação em Comuminação*, Curitiba: PR, Brazil.

Sodré, L. (2015, July 6). MC Carol: a 'bandida de Niterói' que tomou de assalto uma legião de fãs. *O Globo*. Retrieved from: http://oglobo.globo.com/rio/bairros/mc-carol-bandida-de-niteroi-que-tomou-de-assalto-uma-legiao-de-fas-16660833#ixzz4A4d1hBmK

Virgilio, P. (2017, July 29). Dados do ISP confirmam aumento da violência no Rio no primeiro semestre de 2017. *EBC*. Retrieved from: http://agenciabrasil.ebc.com.br/geral/noticia/2017-07/dados-do-isp-confirmam-aumento-da-violencia-no-rio-no-primeiro-semestre-de

Contributors

Ahmet Atay (Ph.D., Southern Illinois University- Carbondale) is Associate Professor of Communication at the College of Wooster. His research revolves around cultural studies, media studies, critical intercultural communication, and critical pedagogy. In particular, he focuses on diasporic experiences and cultural identity formations of diasporic individuals; political and social complexities of city life, such as immigrant and queer experiences; the usage of new media technologies in different settings; and the notion of home. He is the author of *Globalization's Impact on Identity Formation: Queer Diasporic Males in Cyberspace* (2015) and the co-editor of 11 books, including *Queer Communication Pedagogy*. His scholarship appeared in number of journals and edited books.

Bernadette Marie Calafell (Ph.D., University of North Carolina) is Chair and Professor in the Department of Critical Race and Ethnic Studies at Gonzaga University. She is author of *Latina/o Communication Studies Theorizing Performance* and *Monstrosity, Performance, and Race in Contemporary Culture*, co-editor with Michelle Holling of *Latina/o Discourse in Vernacular Spaces: Somos de Una Voz?*, and co-editor with Shinsuke Eguchi of *Queer Intercultural Communication: The Intersectional Belongings in and Across Difference*. Bernadette is also the Editor-Elect of the *Journal of International and Intercultural Communication* and Film Review Editor of *QED: A Journal in GLBTQ Worldmaking*.

Yea-Wen Chen (Ph.D., University of New Mexico) is Associate Professor in the School of Communication at San Diego State University. Her research examines how communication—including silence—about cultural identities impacts diversity, inclusion, and social justice across contexts such as identity-based nonprofit organizations. She is the winner of numerous top paper awards at regional, national, and international communication conferences. Dr. Chen has published over 40 works, including peer-reviewed articles in *Communication Monographs, Journal of International and Intercultural Communication,* and *Departures in Critical Qualitative Research.* Also, she has co-edited *Our Voices: Essays in Culture, Ethnicity, and Communication* (6th Edition, Oxford University Press, 2015). Aligned with her scholarship, she serves as a Professor of Equity on her campus leading and facilitating seminars on implicit bias and microaggressions to promote equity and inclusion

Shinsuke Eguchi (Ph.D., Howard University, 2011) is Associate Professor in the Department of Communication and Journalism at the University of New Mexico. Their research interests focus on global and transcultural studies, queer of color critique, intersectionality and racialized gender politics, Asian/Pacific/American studies, and performance studies. Their mostly recent work has appeared for publication in *Women Studies in Communication, Cultural Studies↔Critical Methodologies, China Media Research, Departures in Critical Qualitative Research, Critical Studies in Media Communication, Journal of Homosexuality,* and *QED: A Journal in GLBTQ Worldmaking.* With Bernadette Marie Calafell, they are also a co-editor of *Queer Intercultural Communication: The Intersectional Politics of Belonging in and across Differences* (2020).

Peter Ehrenhaus (Ph.D., University of Minnesota) is Professor Emeritus of Communication, Pacific Lutheran University. His research has concerned cultural memory as a site of struggle in matters of cultural trauma, with particular focus on the legacies of America's Vietnam War and the nation's history of white-on-black race violence, especially regarding race lynching. His work has been published in journals including *Argumentation and Advocacy, Communication Monographs, Critical Studies in Media Communication, Journal of Communication, Journal of International and Intercultural Communication, Quarterly Journal of Speech, Text and Performance Quarterly,* and *Western Journal of Communication,* as well as in various edited collections.

Alberto González (Ph.D., The Ohio State University) is Distinguished University Professor in the School of Media and Communication at Bowling Green State University. He is a co-editor of *The Rhetorical Legacy of Wangari*

Maathai: Planting the Future (2018) and *Our Voices: Essays in Culture, Ethnicity, and Communication, 6th Edition* (2016).

Kathryn Hobson (Ph.D., University of Denver, 2013) is an assistant professor in the School of Communication at James Madison University. She is a white, queer-femme, mixed-class, chronically-ill, scholar-teacher-mentor. Her research focuses on coalition building, intersectional identity performance, and social change. She primarily teaches courses in the school's Cultural Communication concentration, like Intercultural Communication, Ethnographic Approaches to Communication, and Critical Sexuality, Culture, and Communication. She has adopted "Safe Zone" office hours for folks of difference to gather and build community, build mentoring relationships, and co-create spaces of empowered learning.

Eun Young Lee (Ph.D., Bowling Green State University) is Assistant Professor in the Department of Communication at Central Washington University. Her scholarship lies in intersections between Rhetorical Studies and Critical Intercultural Communication. Her research interests include the rhetoricity of place and space, cultural representations on media and in popular culture, politics in globalization, and critical pedagogy. Her publications can be found in *Communication Studies, Women's Studies in Communication,* and the variety of academic books. Her recent scholarship on critical pedagogy titled "Feminist rhetorical strategies to 'make it real' in Communication courses: A Korean woman's embodiment of critical pedagogy" appears in *Working in the margins: Domestic and international minority women in higher education* (Peter Lang, 2020). Her co-authored piece, "Airport (in)security," is published in *The personal is political: Body politics in a Trump world* (Brill, 2020). She is the recipient of the Outstanding Dissertation Award (International and Intercultural Communication Division of the National Communication Association, 2016) for her doctoral dissertation titled *The rhetorical landscape of Itaewon: Negotiating new transcultural identities in South Korea.*

Mariko Izumi (Ph.D., University of Minnesota-Twin Cities) is Professor of Communication at the Columbus State University in Columbus, GA. Her research explores the intersection of ethics and politics, especially the ways in which a nation remembers its wartime past, how such memories travel across generations as well as national borders, and how such communicative processes shape the discursive formation of humanitarian agendas in international politics.

Spencer Margulies, B.A. (James Madison University, 2019) is pursuing a M.A. degree in Communication at the University of South Florida. Their research is situated at the intersection of Critical Intercultural Studies, Queer Studies, Latinx Studies, Autoethnography, and Performance Studies. Currently, their thesis looks at Latinx embodiments in the every day, specifically how living in the Borderlands coupled with being a nepantlera, informs, and sometimes governs processes of im/migration and identity formation (i.e. queerness, transness).

Raquel Moreira (Ph.D., University of Denver) is Associate Professor of Communication at Graceland University. Her research focuses on the political possibilities of transgressive performances of femininity by marginalized people of color in Brazil. Part of Moreira's ongoing research has been published in *Queer Studies in Media & Popular Culture* and in *Women's Studies in Communication*. Her essay in *WSiC*, '"Now that I'm a whore nobody is holding me back!': Women in favela funk and embodied politics," received the 2017 Feminist Scholar of the Year Award from the Organization for Research on Women and Communication. Additionally, Moreira's teaching interests include race, gender and sexuality, critical intercultural communication, and media.

A. Susan Owen (Ph.D., University of Iowa) is Professor Emerita of Communication Studies and African American Studies, University of Puget Sound. Her research has focused upon critical media studies, including film, television and photography. More specifically, she has focused upon female characterization in action adventure, war, science fiction and apocalypse. She also studies representations of race violence spanning the 20th century. Her more recent work focuses upon representations of traumatic memory in film. She is co-author of *Bad Girls: Cultural Politics and Media Representations of Transgressive Women* and *Parallels: The Soldier's Knowledge and the Oral History of Contemporary Warfare*. Her scholarship has been published in *Critical Studies in Media Communication, Journal of Homosexuality, Journal of Popular Film and Television, Quarterly Journal of Speech, Rhetoric and Public Affairs, Text and Performance Quarterly*, and *Western Journal of Communication*, among other venues.

Chunyu Zhang (Ph.D., Ohio University) is Assistant Professor of School of Journalism and Communication at Wuhan University, China. Her research areas include rhetorical criticism, public memory, media studies, gender, and communication development. Her works have appeared in various journals including *American Journalism, Women's Studies in Communication*, and *China Media Research*.

Index

activists 23, 96, 105, 108, 153, 156,
    173–174
African Americans 13, 16, 23, 25, 99,
    102–103
Albania 7, 69–70, 75, 86, 90–91
albums 139, 143–144, 148, 177
American citizenship 125, 128
American communities 13
American football 115, 117, 119, 122,
    124–25, 128–129
American monomyth 103, 105, 108–111
    Danny's story 96–97, 100, 103–109
    See also queerness; Stonewall Riots
American nationalism 115, 117,
    119, 122
anti-communism 75–76
anti-lynching 27
anti-queerness 117, 121, 127–128
art 51, 62, 73, 76, 84, 91, 136, 165, 179
artifacts 77, 79, 84–85, 88
artists 8, 152, 164, 167, 169,
    172, 174–80
    and supporters 8, 179
Asian Women's Fund (AWF) 151–152
Asia-Pacific War 150–153, 156
Atay, Ahmet 4, 7–8, 120, 135–136,
    138–140, 142, 144, 146–148
audience 20–23, 70, 97, 104–105, 107,
    109, 154, 174
Austria-Hungary 137

bailes 167–170, 172–173, 175, 179
Bandida, MC Carol 165, 176–179
BBHC (Buffalo Bill Historical
    Center) 71
Best, Steven 149
Biesecker, Barbara 155–156
bisexual 125, 128
Black gay 117, 122, 124, 128
Black male body 117–119, 124–126
Black masculinity 117–118
Black players 116, 118–119, 129
Black trans-woman 104
borders 38, 42, 91
    national 8, 151
    shared 39
Brazil 8, 167–169, 171, 176–177, 179
bronze statues 53, 59, 153, 157
brown bodies 97, 112

Cairo Conference 57
Calafell, Bernadette Marie 7, 48–49, 95,
    97, 99, 110, 117–118, 165–166
Cammisano, Vito 115, 126–127
Canadian Football League (CFL) 116
capitalism 119, 121–122, 125–126,
    128–129
Chen Shui-bian 54, 57, 61
Chen, Yea-Wen 2, 8, 54, 56, 58, 60,
    62, 64, 66

Chiang Kai-shek Memorial
    Hall. *See* CKSMH
Chiang Kai-shek Memorial
    Park. *See* CKSMP
Chiang Kai-shek 6, 53–58, 66–67
China 37, 56–57, 59, 66–67
cisgender 96, 100, 103, 105–106, 108–
    110, 115, 122
cisheteronormativity 117, 129
cisheteropatriarchal 117
cisheterosexism 118
cisnormativity 106
Civil Rights Movement 99
CKSMH (Chiang Kai-shek Memorial
    Hall) 6, 53–55, 58–67
    depoliticizing and neutralizing 62–64
    public memory 55–60, 63–65
    renaming and restoring 60–62
CKSMP (Chiang Kai-shek Memorial
    Park) 54, 58, 60
class 97, 104–106, 120, 123, 148
collective memory 54, 60, 66, 71, 91,
    102–103, 147, 149–150, 152–153
    re-theorization of 157
colonial past 4, 135, 137, 151
colonialism 150, 177
commemoration 5, 13, 150, 153–
    154, 158
communism 73, 76–77, 81, 88–91
    House of Leaves (HL) 80–89
    Site of Witness and Memory
        (SWM) 71–80
communist past 7, 69–70, 72, 80–81,
    84–85, 89–90
communist regime 70, 72–73, 76–78,
    81–82, 90
contestations 2, 5, 15, 54–55
controversies 54–56, 60, 62–63, 97,
    109, 151
Coreanos 6, 34, 37–40, 44–48
corporate media 174–175, 179
Cosmopolitan Movement 156
cosmopolitan 13, 40, 45, 112
counter-memory 69–70, 72–73, 76,
    78, 89–90
counter-monuments 152, 154–155, 157
COVID-19 pandemic 136, 144

Creolization 49–50
crimes 17, 20, 23, 88–89, 91, 105, 108–
    109, 119, 153, 169–170
criminalization 163, 170–171, 178
cultural experiences 4, 35, 136, 148
cultural expressions 163, 166, 168
cultural identities 2, 6, 34–35, 43, 46–
    48, 139, 148
cultural memory 2–8, 93, 97–98, 100,
    102, 164–165, 167, 169, 178
    sensemaking 5–6
cultural syncretism 36, 165–67, 172,
    175, 178–179
Cyprus 137–140, 142, 144–147

DDR Museum 70, 90
Deleuze, Gilles 157–158
democracy 54, 59–62, 67, 69, 77
Democratic Progressive Party. *See* DPP
diaspora 35, 46, 50–51, 139, 146–148
diasporic communities 2, 135, 139,
    141, 146
diners 41–44, 46–47
discourses 7–9, 63, 97, 103, 106, 147,
    151, 153, 156, 165–166
displaced memorials
    comfort women 150–158
    new and old trauma 156–159
    people's responses 149–151
    political nature 151–156
diversity 107, 119, 173
DJs 168, 172–175, 179
dominant culture 165–168, 172–174,
    177, 179
Dorsey, Dorothy 16
Dorsey, George 18
Dorsey, Mae 16, 18, 22
DPP (Democratic Progressive
    Party) 54, 57, 60
drag queens 99–100, 103, 105, 107–109

Eguchi, Shinsuke 7, 115–116, 118, 120,
    122, 124, 126, 128
Ehrenhaus, Peter 6, 13–14, 16, 18, 20,
    22, 24, 26, 28

Emmerich, Roland 96–97, 99, 104–109, 111
Enck-Wanzer 42, 49
ESPN 115–116, 121
ethnic groups 57, 63–64
ethnicity 4, 50, 120, 147

F-4 visa 37
family albums 139–140, 143
family 8, 20, 22–23, 27, 76–79, 107–108, 110, 122–123, 141–142, 144–145
favela funk
	affirmation and protest 174–176
	artists 163, 169, 174, 177
	circles 8, 164, 172, 174–176, 178
	continuous marginalization 167–171, 176–178
	cultural legitimation, its rhetorical practices 163–165
	2008 APAFunk Manifesto 172–174
	vernacular discourse 165–167, 171–172, 178–180
femininity 97, 99, 103, 105–108, 112, 118
feminist 4, 13, 177
First African Baptist Church 26
Foucault, Michel 69, 91
freedom 61, 73, 77, 157, 165

gay 95–97, 105, 107, 115–116, 119, 121–123, 125–128, 147
	rights movements 98, 101
gender 28, 50, 101, 103–5, 108–110, 112, 120–123, 148
genre 15, 51, 168–169
Georgia Association of Black Elected Officials 23
Georgia Bureaus of Investigation 15
Georgia WAND 17
Gjoci, Nina 7, 69
globalization 8, 36, 40, 43–44, 147, 151
González, Alberto 1–3, 6, 33
Griffin-Gracy 103, 111, 118

Hester, Barney 16, 18–19, 24
heteronormativity 97, 102, 111, 118, 126, 128–129
heterosexism 117, 124
heterosexuality 115–118
HL. *See* House of Leaves
Hobson, Kathryn 7, 97, 95, 108
homoerotic inter-racialism 117, 121, 125, 127, 129
homonationalism 117, 121–22, 124, 126–127, 129
homonormativity 97, 108, 111, 126
homophobia 7, 103, 117–118, 124, 128
homosexuality 108–109, 119, 122, 124
homosexuals 98, 121, 125
House of Leaves 70–71, 80–81, 84–85, 88–89
hyper-heterosexual 115, 119

identity politics 6, 35, 47–48, 93
ideologies 4, 110, 150, 154, 165
immigrant 135, 144, 147
immigration 4, 9, 34, 37, 148
intercultural communication 2–3, 9, 111, 120, 146
	queer 117, 120–21
Izumi, Mariko 149–150, 152, 154, 156, 158, 160

Japan 56, 151–53, 155
justice 15, 20, 22–23, 27, 29, 60, 103, 108, 152, 155

KMT 53–54, 56–57, 59–61
Korea 34–38, 41, 44–48, 51, 152, 154
Koreamericans 6, 33–49
	in Itaewon 36–39
	restaurant owners 39–43
Korean identity 6, 33–35, 43, 46–48
	diaspora and (a sense of) home 35–36
	food functions 43–46
Koreans 34–35, 37–38, 40–41, 43–48, 152

Lee Teng-hui 54
Lee, Eun Young 3, 6, 33, 35, 37
LGBT 108, 113, 116
LGBTQ+ community 96, 98, 101
liminal space 14–15, 17, 20, 26–27, 98,
    136–137, 176
lynching 13, 15–16, 20, 22–23, 125
    conspiracy narratives 16–17
    reenactments 15–16, 18–26
lyrics 163, 167–168, 173, 177

Malcolm, Dorothy 16, 18–19, 21–23
manifesto 8, 164, 173–174, 177
Margulies, Spencer B. 7
material rhetoric 6, 33, 48, 98, 101–2
media 2–3, 5, 76, 80, 122, 124, 126,
    138, 148, 169, 173, 179–180
MFMC (Moore's Ford Memorial
    Committee) 17, 21
migration 3–4, 37, 51, 66, 138
Moore's Ford Lynching Reenactment 6,
    13–14, 17, 27
Moore's Ford Memorial
    Committee. See MFMC
Moreira, Raquel 163–164, 166, 168,
    170, 172, 174, 176, 178
museums 7, 33, 69–78, 80–82, 84–86,
    88–89, 91, 152
music 117, 165, 168, 171, 173, 177

National Chengchi University
    (NCCU) 53
National Taiwan Democracy Memorial
    Hall 54, 60–61
nation-state 34, 42, 66, 118, 121–
    22, 151
NFL 115–119, 121, 124, 127–129
    Black masculinity 117–119
    players 115, 119, 127
    2014's draft 122, 126, 128
Nicohls, James 100
1946 lynching
    Moore's Ford Lynching
        Reenactment 6, 13–14, 17, 27
    ABC's Dancing with Stars Season 20,
        123–124

Obama, Barack 116, 121
Owen, Susan 6, 14, 16, 18, 20, 22,
    24, 26, 28

patriarchal masculinity 118–119, 126,
    128–129
patriarchy 103, 126, 128–129
Paul, Bobbie 18, 21–22, 27
people of color 98–99, 110, 119, 121
People's Republic of China (PRC) 56
perpetrators 15–17, 19–20, 25–26, 72,
    81–83, 85, 89
photography 9, 147
photographs, Turkish Cypriots in UK,
    diasporic families 137–141
    of homeland 141–144
    idea of home 136–137
    reconnection with past 143–146
photos 25, 28, 74–77, 84, 86–87, 137,
    139–43, 145–47
PIM (Plains Indian Museum) 66, 71, 91
police 98–99, 101, 105, 107, 109
    brutality 171, 178
political organizations 8, 164, 173,
    178–179
politics 35, 38, 51, 56, 60, 63, 66,
    71, 97–98
popular music 164, 167
power 2–3, 35, 38, 43, 50–51, 54, 59,
    62, 66, 100, 117–119, 157–58
prisons 74–75, 78–79, 91
privileges 99, 124–125, 143
production 25, 46, 50, 166, 168, 173
propaganda 76, 79–80, 87
property 19, 76, 118, 124, 142
protests 49, 54, 97–98, 152, 166–167,
    174–176, 179
public discourse 3, 54, 72, 178
public memory 6–9, 15, 50, 55–56, 58,
    61–64, 66, 69–72, 81–82, 89–90,
    101–103, 110–111

queer 2, 97, 99, 101–102, 108–109, 111,
    117, 120, 125, 128
    fantasy 7, 115–116, 119, 121, 123,
        125, 127–129

queerness 2, 116–17, 119–23, 128–129
  homoerotic inter-racialism 125–127
  homonationalism 122–125
  performative rhetoric of 7, 116, 120–121, 125, 127–128

race 4, 6, 28, 35, 50, 103–105, 119–120, 123–124, 148
  violence 13–15
racism 7, 103, 108, 117, 124, 128, 166, 177–178
radio 86, 170, 175
recollections 98–99, 101–102, 145, 153
Reenactment Day 21–26
remembrance 9, 13–15, 80, 155
resistance 49, 69, 77, 89, 117, 153, 177
restaurants 3, 6, 34–35, 37–44, 46–48
rhetoric 36, 42–43, 45, 47, 49–51, 85, 90, 122–123, 156, 164, 166–167
Rio's slums 163, 167–70, 172, 176, 178
  See also bailes
riots 95–96, 98–102, 104, 108–109
RMCA (Royal Museum for Central Africa) 9
ROC (Republic of China) 56–57

Sam, Michael 7, 115–17, 121–129
  big gay kiss event 121–125, 128–129
samba 8, 163–64, 168–69, 174, 178
  cultural memory 8, 163–165, 167–169, 172, 174, 178
same-sex interracial coupling 126
same-sex marriage 122
same-sex partners 127
same-sex 119, 122
Seoul 3, 6, 33–35, 38–40, 44, 49–50, 153
sexism 7, 112, 128, 177
sexuality 4, 115, 120–21, 123, 128
Shkoder 7, 70, 72–73, 75–76, 78, 89–90
  See also SWM
Site of Witness and Memory. *See* SWM
society 5–6, 47, 62, 125, 158
South Korea 6, 33–34, 36–39, 47, 50–51, 151–153

spectators 14, 17, 19, 21, 24–26, 28, 39
SSS (State Security Service) 81–83, 86–89
statutory law 163–164, 167, 170–172, 174, 178–179
Stonewall Riots 7, 96, 98, 100–102, 107–108, 112
  cultural memory and material rhetoric 101–102
  public memory, definition 101
storytelling 4–5, 7, 102, 144
Sullivan, Ariel Young 22–23
surveillance 71, 80, 82–85, 88–89, 117, 119

Taiwan 2, 6, 53–61, 63–64, 66–67
technologies 38, 86–88, 119, 122, 124, 129
torture 73–75, 78, 80, 88
totalitarian regimes 84, 90
transgender women 99
transnational 8, 36, 39–40, 46, 48, 156–158
traumas 14–15, 156–157
TRNC (Turkish Republic of Northern Cyprus) 138

United States 8, 16, 56, 69, 90, 149–151, 154–156, 168

Vatos 6, 34–35, 38–40, 45–48, 51
vernacular discourse 8, 164–167, 178–179
victims 8, 19–21, 25, 70–71, 73, 75–78, 80, 88–89, 150, 152–157
videos 38, 79, 86, 111, 175
violence 13, 18–19, 21, 3107, 155, 169, 177–178

White 118–119, 122, 125, 127, 148
  gays 97, 125
  perpetrators 16, 21
  supremacy 103, 118

whiteness 49, 110, 117–122, 124–126,
    128–129
witness 7, 14, 17, 23, 27, 46, 72–
    73, 78, 80
women 16, 25, 145, 150, 154, 171,
    174, 177

Young, James 149–50, 152

Zhang, Chunyu 54, 56, 58, 60, 62, 64,
    66

www.ingramcontent.com/pod-product-compliance
Lightning Source LLC
Chambersburg PA
CBHW050652280326
41932CB00015B/2878